Sentimental Readers

Sentimental Readers

The Rise, Fall, and Revival of a Disparaged Rhetoric

Faye Halpern

UNIVERSITY OF IOWA PRESS
IOWA CITY

University of Iowa Press, Iowa City 52242

www.uiowapress.org
Printed in the United States of America
Design by Sara T. Sauers

The University of Iowa Press is a member of Green Press Initiative and is committed to preserving natural resources.

Printed on acid-free paper

Library of Congress Cataloging-in-Publication Data
Halpern, Faye.
Sentimental readers: the rise, fall, and revival of a disparaged rhetoric / Faye Halpern.
pages cm
Includes bibliographical references and index.
ISBN: 978-1-60938-186-8; 1-60938-186-6 (pbk.)
ISBN: 978-1-60938-210-0; 1-60938-210-2 (ebook)
1. Sentimentalism in literature. 2. Narration (Rhetoric) I. Title.
PN56.S475H35 2013
809'.93353—dc23 2013007535

for Jeremy, Toby, and Norah

Contents

Acknowledgments

Portions of chapters 1 and 2 appeared in *Nineteenth-Century Prose* 27:2 (2000), 47–61, in an article entitled "Why We Should Trust Harriet Beecher Stowe." A version of chapter 5 was originally published in *College English* 70:6 (2008), 551–77 (copyright 2008 by the National Council of Teachers of English): "In Defense of Reading Badly: The Politics of Identification in 'Benito Cereno,' *Uncle Tom's Cabin*, and Our Classrooms." A version of chapter 6 appeared in *Narrative* 19:1 (2011), 51–71: "Unmasking Criticism: The Problem with Being a Good Reader of Sentimental Rhetoric." The three journals have generously agreed to let me reprint the material here.

Introduction

The How of Sentimentality

In *Alternative Alcott,* a collection of lesser-known works by Louisa May Alcott, editor Elaine Showalter excises the marriage that occupies the last part of *Work: A Story of Experience.* In the original version, published in 1873, the protagonist, Christie Devon, marries a good Quaker man after having taken a series of more and less satisfying jobs. Christie's husband dies soon after their marriage, leaving her free to pursue one last career as a public speaker and activist on behalf of working women. By snipping out the marriage, Showalter makes sure that Christie's professional life takes precedence over her domestic one. Although Showalter presumably wanted to make *Work* into a more congenial feminist allegory for modern readers, she seems also to have wanted to prevent a certain generic label from being applied. Showalter concludes her introduction with the hope that "Alcott can now be re-evaluated in terms of her full accomplishments as a novelist and realist" (xliii). As I read the implication, Showalter intends to popularize the view that Alcott is *not* a sentimentalist. Elsewhere Showalter's introduction reveals that she associates sentimentality with social conservatism and benighted gender relations, a common enough view that has nevertheless been contested by many other feminist literary critics,[1] most famously Jane Tompkins. But Showalter's editing practice reveals that she also links sentimentality to certain plot elements and themes.

No project concerning the sentimental women authors of nineteenth-century America can avoid trying to pin down the slippery term "sentimental." My work on the sentimental fiction of mid-nineteenth-century America began in graduate school by trying to separate what sentimentality was from how it made me feel. Like Showalter, I associated sentimentality with certain kinds of plots and themes. I divided up the universe of sentimental novels into plots of ascent (the girl learns to be a good woman and is rewarded by a worthy husband) and descent (the girl whose loss of virtue or inability to cultivate selflessness ends in her death) and noticed themes like the celebration of domesticity and, as Joanne Dobson helped me see, human connection.

But plots and themes cannot get at what is most distinctive about sentimentality. Let me demonstrate this by way of a counterexample, a novel that features a beautiful girl let loose in the world with no one to protect her. This delicate girl falls in love with a man not worthy of her and, not realizing this, allows herself to be seduced. Her lost virtue costs her any pity that she might have received from neighbors and relatives. Spurned by both her lover and her family, our heroine drowns herself. At the end of the novel, her mother declares her forgiveness of her daughter in a tearful scene of conversion. I have just related the plot of Stephen Crane's novella *Maggie: A Girl of the Streets* (1893). No one has ever accused it of being a sentimental novel (it is, of course, often classified as "realist"). This is not simply because it was written at the end of the century by a man or even because it concerns dialect-speaking slum dwellers (after all, many sentimental novels feature impoverished characters who speak nonstandard English, Harriet Beecher Stowe's Uncle Tom being one of them). To explore why this novel is not just unsentimental but antisentimental, I turn to its final scene. Crane depicts how a neighbor, "a woman in a black gown" (67), rushes in to comfort Maggie's mother, Mary, after the neighborhood has learned that Maggie died. "'Ah, poor Mary,' [the woman in black] cried, and tenderly embraced the moaning one. 'Ah, what ter'ble affliction is dis,' continued she. Her vocabulary was derived from mission churches" (67). The scene continues with the neighbor pleading with Maggie's mother, who is referred to as the "the mourner."

> "Yeh'll forgive her, Mary!" pleaded the woman in black. The mourner essayed to speak but her voice gave way. She shook her great shoulders frantically, in an agony of grief. Hot tears seemed to scald her quivering face. Finally her voice came and arose like a scream of pain.
>
> "Oh, yes. I'll fergive her! I'll fergive her!" (69)

On the surface, this seems like a typical sentimental scene. As in a sentimental novel, weeping signals that a conversion is taking place: the death of the heroine propels the transformation of the person in need of saving. But the resemblance stops there. The woman in black's initial words of sympathy do not come from the heart. Instead her words, the narrator tells us, are derivative. Crane thus deflates the possible nobility of her sentiment. His narrator's affectless revelation of the characters' clichés reveals that their words do not express their true selves. In fact, characters' "selves" seem wholly derivative: scraps picked out from the ragbag of culture.[2] Maggie's mother's words are tainted by this same derivativeness. She performs for her neighbor, taking on the scripted role of the penitent ("essayed to speak" is a moment of burlesque, but the words also suggest to the reader how Mary would describe herself at this moment if she had the vocabulary). Right before her final lines of forgiveness, Mary and her neighbors hold an impromptu call-and-response service. The woman in black leads off:

> "[Y]eh'll forgive yer bad girl? She's gone where her sins will be judged."
>
> "She's gone where her sins will be judged!" cried the other women, like a choir at a funeral.
>
> "Deh Lord gives and deh Lord takes away," said the woman in black, raising her eyes to the sunbeams.
>
> "Deh Lord gives and deh Lord takes away," responded the others.
>
> "Yeh'll forgive her, Mary!" pleaded the woman in black. (68–69)

The repetition of these conventional sentiments makes these women seem mindless, parroting the pieties of the day. This scene gives a physical embodiment to the absurdity that has shadowed the entire novel:

the way these lower-class characters cling to bourgeois morality. Maggie, they insist, is a girl who has sinned and thus given up any claim to their sympathy, never supposing for a second that their rejection of this poor girl is a much bigger sin than Maggie's loss of "purity."

We can judge Maggie's mother's words of forgiveness in two ways. We can completely reject them: Mary is just playing her part in a prescripted scene of maternal piety. For this reading, we might bring forth as evidence the way Crane has portrayed Mary up to this point. We have known for most of the novel that Mary is, to use the parlance of the book, a slattern. The final chapter opens with further information that she is also a pig: "In a room a woman [Mary] sat at a table eating like a fat monk in a picture" (67).[3] Knowing what we know about the mother makes her unsympathetic, and perhaps nothing makes her more unsympathetic than her gross physicality. She has too much flesh and too specific fluids: "quivering" and scalding tears. She is a physically distasteful woman whose gluttony symbolizes her selfishness and whose physical repulsiveness mirrors her moral turpitude. Yet she claims that she has been changed. We know that this is a lie, all the more pathetic for being so transparent. Mary is not feeling any pain and does not forgive her daughter. She feels morally superior to Maggie and quite confidently feels that her daughter will be judged. Mary cannot identify with her. And this inability to sympathize with her daughter means that we lose sympathy with Mary. This scene enacts a hierarchy: everyone is positioned either above or below everyone else. Mary thinks that she is above Maggie, but the reader knows that she is really below her; knowing more than Mary does, the reader is thus positioned above *her*.

Yet this reading, though it seems plausible, does not wholly capture the feel of the scene: it seems to many readers that Mary does feel pain and does forgive her daughter (this would be my reading, in fact). Though we might think that this clears the way for a sentimental reading, in fact it makes this scene even less sentimental. We still cannot take Mary's words at face value; but instead of rejecting them, we find that they are true although not in the way that Maggie's mother wants them to be. Maggie's mother says that she forgives her daughter, but we understand that she is not in a position to forgive her. Maggie's mother has sinned much more than Maggie has. Furthermore, we cannot forget the words themselves, their scripted quality, the way they slot into that impromptu, empty religious service. Mary lacks knowledge about herself and her world, which we, in contrast, possess.

Crane seems well aware that this scene has all the elements needed to make it sentimental. Rather than allow it to happen, he indicts sentimentality with his mentions of "mission churches," scripted poses, and clichéd language. Yet these associations, though damning (and quite familiar to the modern reader), are not devastating: what is devastating to sentimentality is the way in which the scene positions the reader in relation to the characters. The scene—the whole novel, in fact—enacts a chain of judgment. No character escapes judgment (even Maggie), whereas in the sentimental novel most of them do, except the villains. The characters in Crane's novella, even the heroine, are deluded about themselves and the world around them. Identification and intimacy are replaced by judgment and distance from the characters but not from the imagined author, who, we have a strong sense, shares our indictment. Thus the scene cannibalizes sentimentality: it steals its ingredients, arranges them into something utterly unsentimental, and has us ingest the result.[4]

At this point, many people might argue that they read sentimental conversion scenes the same way: for example, many modern readers read Little Eva's conversion of Topsy in Stowe's *Uncle Tom's Cabin* as ironically as they read this conversion scene in *Maggie*. They find themselves looking down on the characters and their platitudinous remarks. But there is a crucial difference here: these readers cannot claim that they are reading the scene as Stowe wants them to read it. Stowe gives readers no clues that we are meant to doubt Little Eva's words. In contrast, Crane does everything he can to make us feel that we are reading properly when we read against his characters' perceptions and beliefs. Even if we feel uncomfortable with the position of easy superiority over his pathetic or disgusting characters that Crane has given us, we have to acknowledge that we are reading with the grain in having the reactions we do. Certainly, sentimental novels do have favorite plots and themes, but it is a premise of this book that we should see sentimentality as less a *what* than a *how*: how does a sentimental text direct its audience to read? The observation that modern readers, especially professional literary critics, might find it hard to read that way directly inspires the last two chapters of this book.

Sentimental novels have struck different readers quite differently, so how do we get at the excessive, apt, moving, laughable, galvanizing, infuriating "how" of sentimentality? Rather than employing the term "sentimentality," I use the term "sentimental rhetoric" throughout this book. Viewing sentimentality as a kind of rhetoric allows us to think of it as a set of textual strategies—including a way of structuring a particular relationship between text and reader—that the popular mid-century women writers developed to persuade readers of their worldview. "Sentimental rhetoric" also suggests new contexts for the sentimental authors. First is "rhetoric" as in nineteenth-century American rhetoric and oratory, a flourishing academic discipline and practical set of skills deemed necessary for every educated man. There is also "rhetoric" as in the modern and flourishing discipline of Rhetoric and Composition (or "Rhet/Comp" as people more often refer to it), which, among other things, investigates the way in which students can be taught how to read critically. Neither of these contexts has been readily apparent to literary scholars interested in these sentimental women authors, for different reasons.

The initially popular "scribbling women," as Nathaniel Hawthorne contemptuously and memorably called them, suffered a long period of critical neglect.[5] They were rescued, as I discuss in more detail in chapter 3, starting in the late 1960s, with the development of the "separate spheres" paradigm, which held that American women's nineteenth-century writing (and lives) could be understood and appreciated in the context of women's confinement to a private, domestic sphere. The form that this literary rescue took and its legacy—even after critics began dismantling the paradigm—discouraged scholars from seeing these women writers as enmeshed in the public, male world of rhetoric and oratory. As for the second, ignored context for the sentimental authors, Rhet/Comp has been moving further and further away from literary studies in the last few decades. The once-close siblings now appear eager to enumerate each other's defects. Yet in this book I hope to make the case for rapprochement, intellectually if not institutionally, by showing how a "literary" study of sentimental rhetoric has implications for reading pedagogy.

This book charts the rise, fall, and revival of sentimental rhetoric. For most of the nineteenth century, women, even privileged white women like Stowe, were barred from attending universities and discouraged from speaking in public. Yet they were exposed to the ideals and problems animating the discipline of rhetoric and oratory and responded to them in their novels: they stage scene after scene of oral performance, although their favored orators persuade less through their words than through their voice and presence. The sentimentalists thus addressed the problem of "disingenuous eloquence," which beset the professional male orators and rhetoricians: the fear that a skillful orator could persuade an audience of an untruth. The sentimental women authors were, in fact, able to solve it. The first two chapters describe the rise of sentimental rhetoric by describing how the sentimental authors triumphed over the professional male rhetoricians. Yet this solution—the creation of a text that denies its own textuality—begins to cause problems in the late nineteenth century as a more diverse group, including Stowe's own silver-tongued, scandal-ridden brother, Henry Ward Beecher, began to wield sentimental rhetoric. Starting in the later nineteenth century, sentimental rhetoric ceases to have the persuasive power that it had in the mid-century, when *Uncle Tom's Cabin* galvanized the nation.

I might have left the book there: a story of the rise and fall of nineteenth-century sentimental rhetoric, confined to one century. Yet I did not want to let sentimental rhetoric seem like a historical artifact, which has ceased to resonate for a modern audience. I wanted to revive sentimental rhetoric. This same urge, I imagine, drove the original feminist rescuers of these novels, who also wanted to show that sentimental writing is more than a historical curiosity. For these earlier rescuers, sentimental novels could allow their contemporary readers not only to reimagine what they thought they knew about gender relations in the nineteenth century but to reimagine (and revise) the gender relations that structured their own experience.

I pursue a different and less explored way to make these novels resonate with contemporary readers. In fact, sentimental rhetoric already *does* affect us, but not in a way that is easy for professional literary critics to write about. In my own case at least (and I suspect I am not alone), reading sentimental novels—and now please forgive my literary jargon—used to drive me crazy. As I recount in more detail at the beginning of chapter 5, I originally had a strong, contemptuous reaction to them, the emotional companion to the sense that I had moved past or really existed *above* (was smarter and more sophisticated than) the original audience for these sentimental novels. Yet when I investigated my reaction I found that this emotional reaction was more complicated than simple contempt, that sentimental rhetoric *qua* rhetoric was not something that I had actually gotten past—and, further, that sentimental rhetoric had something to teach me. I do not mean that I learned to love sentimental writing; nor do I now devote myself to teaching my students to write like Harriet Beecher Stowe. Instead I realized that sentimental rhetoric can illuminate how our own account of what we do as literary critics and how we teach critical reading to our students does not always match what we actually do. An examination of sentimental rhetoric can lead the way to a more self-aware practice.

The last third of the book makes explicit a move that many of us make implicitly in our scholarship, which often shows up in our subtly resonant conclusion: the claim that our research into the past, especially research that scrutinizes obscure or critically marginalized texts, can guide us to a better future. By making this claim explicit, this study considers how the "lessons" of sentimental rhetoric can offer a way out of some contemporary critical and pedagogical impasses. How can we train students to become critical readers by reevaluating the denigrated role that "identification" has in our students' reading practices? Why does so much criticism of the "scribbling women," even celebratory accounts, take the form of an unmasking, with the critics demonstrating that they can identify the real—rather than the evident—aims of the sentimental text?

"Audience" provides the conceptual bridge between the nineteenth- and twenty-first-century contexts for these women authors. Using theories of audience developed by Walter Ong and Peter J. Rabinowitz, I explore how different audiences read and evaluate sentimental rhetoric differently. This may seem like an obvious point, but it produces analyses that differ from previous criticism, which has often characterized sentimentality as either essentially excessive or essentially liberatory. The last two chapters, in particular, consider how modern audiences have *constructed* sentimental rhetoric. By attending to these different audiences, we can add nuance and a sense of chronology to the history of sentimental literature in America.

The first chapter lays out a vexing problem that faced the professional male orator in nineteenth-century America: disingenuous eloquence. Nineteenth-century New England rhetoricians were not the first to contend with this problem, but the solution they tried to develop was distinctive, keyed to what they prescriptively described as the temperate characteristics of the young nation. In fact, the solution lies out of reach of these men charged with *training* men to be eloquent, yet they do not give up easily. Edward Tyrrel Channing mounts ingenious but vain attempts at solving the problem through recourse to character, taste, and the natural. Each attempt founders on Channing's unwillingness to assure his audience that a match will exist between the orator's inside (his passionate conviction) and his outside (his modulated delivery). The untrained man might be more persuasive and deserving of the trust that a diverse audience is willing to invest in him; but, as Channing asks with a moue of distaste, "[S]hall the frantic man come to our assemblies?" (*Lectures* 58).

Chapter 2 discusses how Stowe succeeds where Channing fails. Stowe's *The Minister's Wooing* can be read as a contest between different kinds of orators. Unlike Channing, Stowe elevates the unlearned; she guarantees the speaker's veracity by her *ignorance* of the formal arts of rhetoric, by her inability to use words effectively—or at all. Words, then voice, then tears—this is the ascending hierarchy of certainty that the sentimental novel establishes, a solution to the problem of disingenuous eloquence that results in texts (like *Uncle Tom's Cabin* and *The Minister's Wooing*) that deny their own textuality and want to be seen as oratorical productions rather than written ones. The solution to the problem of disingenuous eloquence is a paradoxical one, and later audiences will find it hard to swallow.

Chapters 3 and 4 offer a new explanation for why the persuasive power of sentimental rhetoric in America declines toward the end of the nineteenth century. The latter part of the nineteenth century sees the emergence of a new kind of reader, whom Louisa May Alcott and Henry Ward Beecher have inadvertently helped call into being in the process of trying to democratize sentimental oratory, to wrest it from its home in the body of the true woman. (They ultimately fail in doing this, which allows us to revisit the "separate spheres" argument and see that it does still have some merit.) Alcott's *Work* as well as Beecher's *Norwood* and *Yale Lectures on Preaching* link persuasive speech to methods laid down by the nineteenth-century French actor and elocutionist François Delsarte, who insisted that inner emotional states follow from external gestures and facial expressions. His anti–Method Acting methods aroused suspicion about whether the sentimental orator could now be faking her heartfelt appeals. She requires a reader who can believe her outpourings to be artless and spontaneous, something that a modern reader finds difficult to do. Beecher and Alcott might have it right; emotions might, in fact, follow from external gestures as June Howard and Robyn Warhol affirm. Yet I suggest that this correctness does not matter: modern readers have a hard time overturning their belief that emotions proceed from the inside out.

Chapter 5 marks a turning point in the book. Here and in the final chapter, I switch from considering sentimental rhetoric in its nineteenth-century context to considering it in ours. Chapter 5 takes up a "lesson" of sentimental rhetoric: its reliance on the process of identification in order to forge bonds between readers and the oppressed that they are reading about. I compare Herman Melville's and Stowe's differing opinions about the role of identification in combating racial injustice and use that discussion to defend identification as a reading practice, offering a way to take advantage of our students' tendency to identify with literary characters (a habit that their professors normally try to stomp out). In "Benito Cereno," Melville does not allow the reader to identify with any of the characters, having so successfully shown the danger of identification through his depiction of the genial, racist, and almost fatally misinformed Amasa Delano. So opposed is Melville to identification that he prevents the reader from actually figuring out whether his own novella comes out against slavery. Unlike Melville, Stowe embraces identification in *Uncle Tom's Cabin* and kills off Augustine St. Clare, who resembles a kind of ideal Melvillean reader and whose ironic worldview prevents him from freeing his slaves. Sentimental texts connect identification—and definitive interpretation—to political action, and this claim might not be so far-fetched. We must reexamine the extent to which we reject identification as a reading practice in fledgling English majors. Stowe allows us to rethink this position and notice the extent to which we literary professionals ourselves identify when we read, just differently from the way our students do.

The final chapter takes up an issue that the previous chapters have considered only glancingly: many modern readers' (especially modern literary critics') discomfort with sentimental rhetoric. Why does so much contemporary feminist criticism of sentimentality take the form of an unmasking? Most feminist critics demonstrate that sentimental appeals, despite their claims to the contrary, are hardly artless. The feminist critic thus gets to sound like a professional, but in the process she loses the ability to experience the emotional power of sentimental rhetoric. Thus we have the bind in which sentimental rhetoric puts the critic: deny the possibility of a rhetoric free of artifice and lose the ability to recognize the power of sentimentality or acknowledge this power and cease to sound like a critic. Using Rabinowitz's theory of audience, this chapter explains why contemporary feminist critics have such a hard time becoming part of Stowe's authorial and narrative audience. Yet this chapter also notes that many of us did once (or still do) cry at sentimental texts, until our own critical training made us forget or disavow this unschooled reaction. In earlier chapters, this book demonstrates how sentimental rhetoric changes as a result of the negotiation between an authorial audience and an actual one, whose beliefs change over time. The final chapter further nuances the idea of audience by showing that we do not always require the passage of time to introduce us to new actual audiences: literary critics already contain different actual audiences within themselves.

Sentimental Readers shows that focusing on the *how* of sentimentality allows us to get at the *now* of sentimentality, the help that it can provide in seeing contemporary reading and teaching practices anew. Sentimental rhetoric strong-arms readers: it elicits a powerful emotional reaction from us, although not always the one it wants. Our emotional reactions are not incidental to our understanding of sentimentality; instead they are crucial to it. They allow us to articulate our own predilections and practices as readers rather than take them for granted. My early efforts to separate what sentimentality *was* from what it *did* to me moved the reader outside the equation. This book is an attempt to correct that omission.

I would like to thank Bob Scholes for his encouragement and support from first to last. Thanks as well to Philip Gould, Mari Jo Buhle, Nicolle Jordan, and Sean Latham, early readers of this work. Jim Phelan introduced me to the work of Peter J. Rabinowitz and offered invaluable advice on how to develop what would become the final chapter of this book. I would also like to thank my colleagues Stefania Forlini and Michael Ullyot for offering their own comments on sections of this work and Ian Sampson for performing some emergency surgery on the title. The English Department at the University of Calgary has given me both time and financial support for my research. Final thanks go to Elisabeth Chretien, my editor at the University of Iowa Press, as well as the two anonymous readers of the manuscript.

Sentimental Readers

1

Edward Tyrrel Channing and the Matter of Disingenuous Eloquence

THIS CHAPTER EXAMINES A PROBLEM THAT BESET THE PROFESSIONAL male orators and rhetoricians of nineteenth-century America. It explains why this problem would remain insoluble for them despite their great exertions to solve it. It is likely that most contemporary readers will not have a great deal of sympathy for the professional conundrum that faced a New England elitist like Edward Tyrrel Channing, the third Boylston Professor of Rhetoric and Oratory at Harvard. But his problem and the impossibility of its solution form the context according to which we can make sense of sentimental rhetoric, which promises to give the disenfranchised the lion's share of rhetorical power. Sentimental rhetoric wants to be viewed as both spontaneous and timeless. By analyzing, here and in the next chapter, how sentimental rhetoric developed in conversation with professional male rhetoric and oratory, I am thus involved in a paradoxical gesture: on one hand, denying sentimental rhetoric's favorite story about itself; on the other, explaining why the story it chose makes perfect sense. Such paradoxes punctuate this book, the result of describing a rhetoric that throws off paradoxes for the contemporary reader the way a knife held to a whetstone throws off sparks.

The problem that these two groups sought to solve has to do with orators and the nature of persuasive speech, both of which fascinated nineteenth-century Americans.[1] The problem is brought about by the specter of disingenuous eloquence. The critic Janet Gabler-Hover describes the problem as the possibility, feared by many in the nineteenth century, that "persuasive language, artfully invented, could be so potent as to sway a vulnerable audience to believe falsehood rather than the truth" (41). Both the professional rhetoricians and the sentimental authors want to answer the question of disingenuous eloquence in the negative. But the male rhetoricians have certain constraints placed on them that the sentimental authors do not: they need to defend their profession, the training of future orators and rhetoricians. This forces them into a tight corner. The professional rhetoricians can solve the problem of disingenuous eloquence, but their solution is really no solution at all: it makes oratory safe only for a small, elite section of the populace.

To trace this failed solution, which will propel the sentimentalists' successful one, I show here that the problem of disingenuous eloquence has dogged orators since classical times, as can be seen in a conversation between the wily Socrates and the hapless rhapsode Ion. I also describe how this classical problem manifested itself in nineteenth-century America. I focus on the work of one professional rhetorician and orator in particular, the aforementioned Edward Tyrrel Channing, the less famous brother of the transcendentalist reformer William Ellery Channing. E. T. Channing by all accounts was a less than riveting orator. Gabler-Hover calls him "representative of and perhaps at least partially responsible for the view of rhetoric during his time" (43). Thus to trace his multifarious attempts to solve the problem of disingenuous eloquence is to suggest the defensive nature of professional male rhetoric and oratory in the nineteenth century and to understand the leaky rhetorical world that sentimental rhetoric managed to repair.

E. T. Channing's appointment as the third Boylston Professor of Rhetoric and Oratory at Harvard almost did not happen. He was only twenty-eight in 1819, the year the position came open. Before that he had trained as a lawyer, though he had hardly practiced law. Instead he edited a literary magazine, the struggling *North American Review*. When his candidacy for the Harvard position was announced, his detractors pointed to his lack of experience; one of these, under the pen name

Alumnus, marveled that the corporation could think of electing anyone other than an "able, practical orator" (qtd. in R. Reid 245). Channing had spoken just once in public before his appointment, a Fourth of July oration honoring James Monroe's visit to Boston. Channing's appeal, his detractors claimed, lay only in his connections.

Channing did receive the appointment that year and kept it through 1851. Though his career was by most accounts a success (he was the teacher of quite a few famous New England writers and reformers, including Thomas Wentworth Higginson, James Russell Lowell, Ralph Waldo Emerson, and Henry David Thoreau), his detractors were prescient about his lack of skill as an orator. No one ever accused him of having been a particularly compelling one. Andrew Peabody, an ex-student, wrote in his reminiscences that "[h]e had, as a speaker, no grace, nor any great diversity of modulation" (88) and that "his gestures were awkward, seeming to denote his discomfort at being obliged to speak" (88). They did not reveal his "mood of thought or feeling to which he gave expression" (88). Channing was far from electrifying; neither was he transparent. Yet we shall see how these limitations were exactly what his theories about rhetoric and oratory required. Channing had a healthy fear of electrifying orators: how did the audience know that what the orators were persuading it of was true?[2]

The handful of contemporary scholars who have written about Channing have also noted his antipathy to the electrifying orator, which he handily enacted in his own delivery. Adam Potkay, for example, sees Channing as part of a trend in the early part of the nineteenth century away from the classical ideal of the irresistible orator-politician. Elizabeth Larsen asks us to mark Channing's commitment to literacy rather than orality: by such commitments Channing forecloses the idea of an orator whose audience of "immediately reactive human beings" (Larsen 169) lies in the palm of his hand. Both Potkay and Larsen see Channing as a seminal figure in the increasing nineteenth-century association of rhetoric with belletrism and literariness. Yet they do not spend their time probing why Channing and others might have turned away from the classical ideal of the electrifying orator. I would like to build on their work by suggesting why he might have gone in these less than electrifying directions. Channing's turn away from the irresistible orator in favor of the contemplative man reading and composing alone in his study is an attempt, however futile, to solve the problem of disingenuous eloquence.[3]

Divine Inspiration versus Self-Possession in Socrates

The problem of disingenuous eloquence, or how to guarantee that an audience will not be persuaded of something untrue, has a distinguished history. I begin my story of how this problem affects nineteenth-century professional orators in general as well as one stiff Brahmin in particular by retelling Plato's story of Socrates and Ion. This story would have been familiar to nineteenth-century professional American orators because they still looked to the Greeks to provide them with the principles of persuasive discourse.[4] John Quincy Adams's *Lectures on Rhetoric and Oratory*, for example, a printed version of the series of lectures he gave to Harvard juniors and seniors between 1806 and 1809, might today get him expunged from Harvard for plagiarism, so heavily does he rely on the writings of Greek rhetoricians.[5] Nineteenth-century American rhetoricians inherited the problem that Plato outlines. In the story of Socrates and Ion, we find an audience at the complete mercy of a speaker.

The dialogue involves the seemingly friendly interrogation of the rhapsode Ion by Socrates. No one can recite or comment upon Homer so well as this performer; he is the winner of many competitions. Ion claims that his skill comes from understanding Homer better than anyone else: "I, of all men, have the finest things to say on Homer" (Plato 216). It is this understanding, Ion claims, that allows him to be such a good rhapsode. This is what allows him to electrify an audience.

Socrates begins by taking Ion at his word that he is a Homeric expert. He tries to assess what exactly this expertise reflects and finds, surprisingly, that it reflects no real knowledge. For if it did, Ion would have equal skill in reciting other poets who speak of the same things: namely, wars and crops and gods. But Ion can recite and comment only on Homer. Socrates concludes that Ion has been divinely inspired. His famous metaphor about the magnetic iron rings follows:

> As I just now said, this gift you have of speaking well on Homer is not an art; it is a power divine, impelling you like the

> power in the stone Euripides called the magnet.... This stone does not simply attract the iron rings, just by themselves; it also imparts to the rings a force enabling them to do the same thing as the stone itself, that is, to attract another ring, so that sometimes a chain is formed. (Plato 219–20)

The gods inspire the poet, who inspires the rhapsode, who inspires the audience. This is poetry as a divinely inspired phenomenon, without reason: "[F]or a poet is . . . never able to compose until he has become inspired, and is beside himself, and reason is no longer in him" (Plato 220). It is poetry as contagion, with the implication that everyone below the gods is powerless against it. Ion remarks, "As I look down at them from the stage above, I see them, every time, weeping, casting terrible glances, stricken with amazement at the deeds recounted" (Plato 221). The audience too has been infected.

To further his point about the distinction between real knowledge and what a rhapsode knows, Socrates quizzes Ion about whether he speaks equally knowledgeably on all points of Homer. When Ion, the fool, says yes, Socrates shows the impossibility of Ion's speaking more knowledgeably about a horse race in Homer than a charioteer could. Socrates shows that Ion knows nothing about any art (*technē*, or art in the sense of a craft, like divination or cookery). Socrates concludes that Ion is to be thought of as "divine, and not an artist, in praising Homer" (Plato 228). Not realizing that Socrates has shown his skill to be nonexistent, his art to be irrational, Ion is thrilled.

So Socrates uncovers a problem in the relations between speaker and audience that will continue to resound into the nineteenth century: a speaker who can completely disarm an audience by speaking, who bypasses reason—both in himself and in his audience—and appeals directly to the emotions. Though Socrates does not address this specifically, one ramification of this state of affairs is the unteachability of the rhapsode: if rhapsodes are only divinely inspired then there is no point in trying to train them. Socrates has shown that the rhapsode does not possess a body of knowledge the way a doctor or a cook does. Orators have no real knowledge yet still sway their audiences, a problem that nineteenth-century professional rhetoricians and orators addressed.

Another problem bedeviled them. A speaker who appeals to an

audience's emotions has a great advantage: without reason to control themselves, the members of an audience are defenseless against him.[6] We can see the potential problem: what if the speaker cares only about furthering his own interests? This, it turns out, is exactly the case with Ion. Ion is controlled by inspiration only some of the time; at other times, he is animated by self-interest. Then comes an odd moment in the dialogue, a turnaround. Until now Ion claimed always to be carried away by his discourse: "[W]henever I recite a tale of pity, my eyes are filled with tears" (Plato 221). Now he says: "[I]f I set them weeping, I myself shall laugh when I get my money, but if they laugh, it is I who have to weep at losing it" (Plato 221). Far from being swept out of himself, Ion reveals that he has maintained his wits about him. It is less a case of divine possession than of emotional manipulation.

Socrates never follows up on this comment. To do so would be to undermine his point about divine inspiration. But at least at certain moments Ion is not divinely inspired; sometimes he is in his right mind, plotting how to further his own ends. And it is this possibility, the speaker who can inspire his audience without being inspired himself, that scared these American rhetoricians and orators most of all. How do you arm an audience completely at the mercy of an unscrupulous yet riveting man whose unscrupulousness they cannot detect?

Socrates, through Plato, bequeaths to later rhetoricians a lingering idea of persuasive discourse as contagion, as diametrically opposed to rational thought and hence able to bypass the understanding. Nineteenth-century American rhetoricians feared that an orator might persuade the audience of something untrue. What also lingered, slightly transformed, into their day is a distinction between the rhapsode's speech and the speech of an honest craftsman. This distinction leads to the eighteenth- and nineteenth-century aspersions cast on rhetoric: rhetoric became associated with empty discourse and showmanship, the two qualities that mark Ion.[7]

We can see why Socrates's understanding of persuasive speech as divinely inspired might be appealing to later rhetoricians: because the rhapsode is in thrall to a higher power, his own self-interest cannot possibly intrude. They must also argue, however, that the orator has agency and is not simply possessed by his orations. These professionals want a justification for training orators, yet training is exactly what introduces the possibility of calculation. So the possibility that Ion introduces with his offhand remark is a real one in the nineteenth century—one that these professionals, unlike Socrates, must try to forestall (even though in the end they will not be able to). They must find ways to guard against the possibility of insincerity without taking recourse to divine inspiration.[8]

Seeing how Plato's dialogue resonates for nineteenth-century American rhetoric and oratory means that we must abandon its historical specificity, its crystallization of a particular and partially lost worldview. "Rhapsode" becomes "speaker," and inspiration loses its close connection to the breath of the gods. These nineteenth-century American men were talking about orators not rhapsodes. They did not understand the rhetorical world in terms of divine inspiration and divine possession but through a completely different vocabulary (eloquence and persuasion and taste) introduced by the British rhetoricians George Campbell, Hugh Blair, and Richard Whately.[9]

Eighteenth- and nineteenth-century rhetoricians understood these terms much more systematically than we do. For example, they believed that "persuasion" was distinct from "conviction." Conviction results from engaging the understanding; persuasion from touching not just the rational part of the brain but also the imagination and the will. "The rational process, Locke held, must be reinforced by an emotional appeal that ultimately becomes the principal determinant of action" (Golden and Corbett 9–10). John Locke was not alone in believing that only persuasion will result in action. Early nineteenth-century American rhetoricians subscribed not just to classical principles but to the New Rhetoric, the legacy of the three rhetoricians named above.[10] Unlike classical rhetoricians, the proponents of the New Rhetoric self-consciously incorporated theories of human nature. Campbell, in particular, took up the new "science of man." He concurred with the commonsense philosophers when he looked into the matter: the human brain is divided into faculties. For Campbell, these faculties rather resemble the Great Chain of Being, but with Eloquence, not God, at the endpoint:

> In general it may be asserted, that each preceding species, in the order above exhibited, is preparatory to the subsequent; that

> each subsequent species is founded on the preceding; and that thus they ascend in a regular progression. Knowledge, the object of the intellect, furnisheth materials for the fancy; the fancy culls, compounds, and, by her mimic art, disposes these materials so as to affect the passions; the passions are the natural spurs to volition or action, and so need only to be right directed. (146)

Without engaging the passions, the orator cannot hope to incite people to action. This sentiment makes it across the Atlantic, as we can see in the 1794 Harvard Commencement Address "An Oration on Eloquence" of Joseph Perkins, a veritable treasure trove of rhetorical commonplaces: "After fairly convincing the understanding, [the orator] may, without the imputation of disingenuousness, proceed to address the fancy and the passions. In this way he will more effectually transfuse into his hearers his own sentiments, and make every spring in the human machine co-operate in the production of the desired effect" (22). (Or, as Henry Ward Beecher pithily put it eighty years later: "[T]ruth is the arrow, but man is the bow that sends it home" [*Oratory* 9].) Perkins's "without the imputation of disingenuousness" suggests a flicker of doubt; this flicker becomes a steady flame in the nineteenth century.

For nineteenth-century American rhetoricians, the necessity of engaging the passions is at once acknowledged and increasingly viewed as a problem. Campbell's chain is well tempered, but it cannot quite lock up specters of demagoguery and violent mass movements, at least not for those on whom the memory of the Revolution weighs, with its potential legacy of violence and radical change. Channing reacts to this possible legacy by denying it: he spends his first oration, the only one he ever gave in public, declawing the Revolution. The revolutionaries, it turns out, were driven less by passion than by reason. This is his first of many attempts to vitiate what he cannot reject, the dependence of eloquence on passion.

The Problem of Passion

Channing's first and only performance speaking before the general public, given before his appointment as Boylston Professor, was a Fourth of July oration given in 1817, on the occasion of President James Monroe's visit to Boston, as noted above. Channing celebrates the Revolution, but in a characteristically temperate way: the freedom that the revolutionaries sought "was a steady, generous moral freedom, which, without repressing enthusiasm and fervour, appealed more to men's sober convictions and to their consciences; inspiring the purest hopes, and the coolest heroism" (*An Oration* 10). His revolutionaries remain tepid, warmed by reason rather than fired with passion. Even in his earliest speech, we can see how delicately Channing navigates his way through the thicket of the passions. He inherits Campbell's assumption about the necessity of engaging the passions as well as the understanding, but it frightens him. He devotes the bulk of his lectures on rhetoric to downplaying it.

By the time of Channing's second speaking performance, upon his inauguration to the Boylston professorship, eloquence's link with political liberty has become an explicit problem.[11] In this oration, Channing compares ancient eloquence with contemporary eloquence. He begins by describing how the ancient orator held his audiences spellbound; he possessed a power unheard of in Channing's day. Yet what might have seemed a cause for lament quickly becomes a cause for celebration. Channing associates the ancient and electrifying orator with violent mass movements—a case of passion run amok, to the vast detriment of the state. Channing insists both that this kind of orator does not exist in his own peaceful and enlightened times and (contradictorily) that contemporary audiences would reject him if he did.

In this inaugural address, entitled "The Orator and His Times," Channing's description of the difference between ancient and contemporary eloquence has the wistful feel of prescription. No longer do orators speak to an "inflammable population" (*Lectures* 5); the people of this new republic are "too wary, conscientious, or wilful to be easily and suddenly operated upon" (*Lectures* 19). Channing compares ancient republics, with their wars and domestic disorder, to his own society, where "you see everywhere a disposition to place the security of nations and of every individual on the broad foundation of laws and institutions, and to make it the interest of the highest as well as humblest citizen to respect and trust in them" (*Lectures* 15). Channing's oration has the same feel as that famous question by the defense: "So when did you stop beating your wife, Mr. Jones?" Channing structures his sentences so that the presence of "wary, conscientious" citizens becomes fact, not yearning, in this inverted jeremiad. The nostalgia is not for a time past but for a time present that Channing tries to will into existence.

Channing gives the audience a reason to stop longing for a return of the orator to preeminence: orators necessarily reflect their times, which is the thesis of this oration. The preeminent orator reflects a time of instability and a population too easily swayed by eloquence. For the present populace, "[t]he subject is more thought of than the orator, and what he says must come from the subject rather than from his art" (*Lectures* 17). Today's orator is "but one of the multitude, deliberating with them upon common interests" (*Lectures* 17).

There is a reason why Channing represents the orator in thrall to his listeners. What characterizes the contemporary audience is its receptiveness to truth: "[Eloquence] has only to secure a lodgement for truth in the mind, and by and by the truth will quietly prevail" (*Lectures* 19). However incredible this statement seems to us today, it guards against the possibility that the orator could convince the audience of something that is untrue. This chain of logic has a corollary. It guards against revolution: because "a love of social order and temperate government" (*Lectures* 6–7) reflects the true state of affairs in Channing's own time, no audience could be convinced of the need for an uprising. Yet the more Channing insists on the audience's capacities, the more the question arises of what need they have for trained orators in the first place. By extension, what need is there for a Boylston Professor of Rhetoric and Oratory? Why is special training necessary to fit someone to take a place alongside the common man? The answer lies in the orator's ability to point out certain truths that even a discerning populace might avoid if left on its own. Channing's fellow citizens are "so intelligent and thoughtful, that they cannot wholly escape the power of just sentiments, however unwelcome they may be" (*Lectures* 19). So the orator is necessary as a kind of heeded Cassandra; the truths he points out will quietly prevail. The orator's superior understanding of the world around him seems to set him apart.

Yet here is the rub: Channing knows that a superior understanding is not enough. Orators must engage an audience's heart as well as its head. But it was the contagious passion of the ancient orators—echoes of Socrates's magnetic chain—which led to the turmoil of those early war-obsessed republics. Passion can be excited regardless of the truth of the issue at hand. So Channing must insist that the passion of today is different. As evidenced in "[o]ur religion" (*Lectures* 22), impassioned eloquence "has spared no language, or beauty, or imagery that could delight and refine our taste, and make our conception of its truths distinct and glowing" (*Lectures* 22). Passion is different today because it does not exist apart from truth: it is just truth's necessary coating. Passion makes the medicine go down.

The assertion of the inextricability of passion and truth is an ingenious solution to the ancient problem of disingenuous eloquence, but it is also a tenuous one. It is the most delicate of balances: the more one emphasizes reason, the more the balance tips toward the obsolescence of the orator; the more one emphasizes passion and the electrifying orator, the more the possibility of demagoguery and disingenuous eloquence arises.[12] Yet other people disagree with Channing's turn from the irresistible orator. Here is how an old student of his put it in the *North American Review* in 1850: "eloquence and political liberty go hand in hand, flourish under similar favoring influences, and dying together, are buried in the same grave" (qtd. in Baskerville 13). Channing diverges from his contemporaries in his rejection of such a homily. For Channing, eloquence pulls against political liberty: the more eloquent the orator, the more liberty is threatened. What a bind for someone entrusted with training men to be eloquent. Channing must find a way to drain eloquence of its potential danger and tries to do so by relying on character.

The Recourse to Character

Quintilian famously wrote that the perfect orator must be above all a good man (6). Later rhetoricians have used variations on this assertion to solve the problem of uncertainty that their theories generate. How do listeners know that they are being persuaded of the truth? Because the orator, being a good man, would not lie. As for nineteenth-century rhetoricians, the mid-twentieth-century speech critic Barnet Baskerville has commented, "[n]or did many of them flinch from defending the necessary concomitant of this position—that it is impossible to be eloquent in defence of the wrong or untrue" (15). Channing does not fall into this extreme camp. Or, rather, Baskerville's formulation leaves out a step that Channing would take in his defense of the unpersuasiveness of disingenuous eloquence. How can the audience be sure that it is not being persuaded of an untruth? Channing adds the concept of character to Quintilian's dictum. Character acts as the guard against falsehood. The audience could not be persuaded of an untruth because before that happened the disingenuous orator would have revealed himself as someone not to be trusted. Channing writes: "I would mention the importance of character to all successful eloquence. It is his virtues, his consistency, his unquestioned sincerity that must get the orator attention and confidence now. He must not rely too much upon the zeal or even the soundness with which he treats a question under immediate discussion" (*Lectures* 23).

Character guarantees that the audience cannot be persuaded of an untruth. It exists apart from either what the orator says or how he says it. The logic goes like this: enthusiasm is dangerously seductive even yoked to truth, so there must be some way to make sure that only the proper kind of person will use it. The proper person is the man with a good character. Notice that the variation on Quintilian's dictum mentioned above, the impossibility of false persuasion, has lost its inviolability. The audience *can* be persuaded of an untruth, but only if the orator has a bad character, as Channing believes some of the ancient orators did.[13]

Now a crucial question arises: how does the audience assess the character of the orator? This becomes a troubling question because, as Channing formulates it, the audience cannot look to the speech itself. It has to do with a feeling that the orator generates: "His hearers must believe that his life is steadily influenced by the sentiments he is trying to impress on them,—that he is willing to abide by principle at any hazard" (*Lectures* 23). Character translates into sincerity: the orator must believe in what he says and live his life accordingly.

In offering this solution, Channing has only restated the problem. His hearers "must believe" that the orator lives an unhypocritical life. But how does the orator *make* them believe it; and even if he does so, why should they trust that belief? Character would solve the problem of disingenuous eloquence only if the audience could be certain that the appearance of good character meant the actual presence of good character (substituting "truth" for "character" merely restates the problem of disingenuous eloquence). A recourse to character creates a *mise en abyme.*

How does the audience read an orator? Is he a nonentity, merely a conduit for the truth? Channing wishes that this were so, at the same time as he acknowledges that it is not. Channing does stress the orator's role as a transparent medium, which allows the truth of the issue in question to shine forth. But the orator is not simply a window. He is more like a magnifying glass. It is that added element that allows the truth to move from the merely understood to the acted upon that distinguishes the orator. Channing calls it passion or enthusiasm or zeal. An orator needs this quality in order to persuade his audience, but it is also passion that makes the persuasion potentially dangerous. Passion bypasses the higher faculties so that they cannot act as brakes. Passion, by itself, would run roughshod over our will.

Passion is a curious quality in rhetorical theory: it resides originally in the orator, in the fervor of his own commitment to what he is talking about, but it moves to each member of the audience, infecting them with the same sense of rightness. Once infected, the audience members have no defense against it. They need to have assured themselves before they were swept away that the orator is a good man. Audiences must be vaccinated against disingenuous eloquence because once they have become infected they cannot be cured. Witness the hapless citizen of ancient times: "To the orator, he was a being formed of imagination and passion,—the powerful slave of those who kindled and flattered him" (*Lectures* 4). In contrast, the American citizen is free, and this freedom comes from discernment and self-control.[14] So Channing seems to trust that the audience will be able to ferret out the disingenuous orator. Yet in his simultaneous effort to demonstrate that the rhetor is not irrational and the rhetoric is not empty of truth he undermines this hard-won idea.

The Recourse to Philosophy

Channing knows that many people are suspicious of rhetoric. He himself is. He quotes Richard Whately to demonstrate the ill repute in which rhetoric has been held. Whately regretted that he even had to use the word "rhetoric" in his *Elements of Rhetoric*; "[it] suggests to most minds an associated idea of empty declamation or dishonest artifice" (qtd. in Channing, *Lectures* 28). Yet Channing will not let this suspicion get the best of him and his job: he claims that rhetoric leads neither to showmanship nor to sophistry.

Channing drains the orator of particularizing characteristics in order to remove any suspicion that he could be acting in his own self-interest. The good orator is exhausted by his oratory: that is, no excess of personality comes into conflict with the truth that he has been commissioned to reveal. Character means that the orator has given it his all; he has kept no part of himself aloof from what he is saying (ignoring, for the moment, that Channing provides the audience with no way of knowing that).

If this makes orators curiously alike, with no excess of personality to distinguish them, in a later lecture, "General View of Rhetoric," Channing also drains different modes of persuasive discourse of their singularity. "It [rhetoric] does not ask whether a man is to be a speaker or writer,—a poet, philosopher, or debater; but simply,—is it his wish to be put in the right way of communicating his mind with power to others, by words spoken or written" (*Lectures* 31). It is merely a convenience that rhetoric is taught by studying rhetoric and oratory; the orator could as easily learn the principles that will aid him by studying poetry or philosophy.

Channing categorizes the world of discourse in a strange way. In the Lockean tradition, poetry and philosophy occupy polar extremes. Philosophy records an external truth, to which anyone (potentially) has access. That is, anyone with the proper training could have written it. The language of philosophy is a shared one: as much as possible, philosophical language needs to become a transparent medium. In "An Essay concerning Human Understanding," Locke explains that as to

> the mistakes in men's disputes and notions, how great a part is owing to words, and their uncertain or mistaken significations. . . . I am apt to imagine, that, were the imperfections of language, as the instrument of knowledge, more thoroughly weighed, a great many of the controversies that make such a noise in the world, would of themselves cease. (396)

The philosopher is unimportant; what is important is his subject, truth.

Poetry, in contrast, is not true, because it does not refer to a real outside world even if it seems to. Yet poetry can defend itself against its potential falsity because it does not have a role in civic life: poetry is a "luxury" according to Channing (*Lectures* 30). Even Locke concedes that figurative language might find an excuse for itself in the "pleasure and delight" it affords (411). In poetry, unlike philosophy, the author is extremely important: no one else could have written what the poet has; Channing himself refers to the poet's "peculiar genius" (*Lectures* 30). Philosophy does not depend on the particular philosopher in the same way that poetry depends on the particular poet.

Channing, as I have suggested, does occasionally pay lip service to the distinction between poetry and philosophy: "[I]n the poetic art, images rightly exceed the truth" (*Lectures* 53). Yet in the end he chooses to assert that what these two discourses have in common is more important: they want to persuade. Both poetry and philosophy—like rhetoric—concern themselves with the question of how to "be put in the right way of communicating . . . with power to others" (*Lectures* 31). Why might he make this claim of similarity? Another way to state the charge against rhetoric—and Channing knows this very well—is to show that rhetoric is poetry masquerading as philosophy. Here is what Locke has to say on the subject: "But yet, if we would speak of things as they are we must allow, that all the art of rhetoric, besides order and clearness, all the artificial and figurative application of words eloquence hath invented, are for nothing else but to insinuate wrong ideas, move the passions, and thereby mislead the judgment; and so, indeed, are perfect cheats" (411). Rhetoric does not just ignore the truth; it does something much worse. It pretends to be the truth when it is not. It denies its own status as poetry and pretends to be philosophy. Channing must defend against this view by showing that poetry and philosophy are in fact the same.

This conflation guards against another charge leveled against rhetoric: it is a disingenuous art because it is an irrational one. This charge, as we have seen, has its roots in the classical tradition. Steven Knapp has interpreted the "Ion" dialogue in ways that bear on what Channing tries to do for the orator. Knapp sees Socrates as making a distinction between Ion and a genuine craftsperson. In a genuine art or *technē*, "the content is fixed" (Knapp 56) so "the agents who practice a genuine art are mutually comparable and, for the same reason, replaceable. If what counts is the content of the art itself—if that is what governs speech about the art—then it cannot matter very much who does the talking" (Knapp 56). The rhapsode, in contrast, finds himself in the reverse position: irreplaceable but "devoid of any rationally accessible content" (Knapp 56). Ion rivets his audience but has no real knowledge, no hold on the truth. Either the subject matters or the practitioner does; either the orator is preeminent or he is ignored. Both cannot be true. Yet this will not do for Channing, who does want it both ways.

Channing insists that the philosopher and poet (and orator) are in any important sense the same. In his case, the merging of distinct discourses does not take characteristics from both but erases the irrational from poetry. Channing ends up finding nothing in poetry (including the things about it that make oratory suspect too: its potential untruth, its lack of external reference, its overvaluing of a particular practitioner) that would make it different from philosophy.[15] The poet, who is a figure of utter passivity (inspired, like the rhapsode), has become the philosopher, who uncovers the truth through his own efforts: "I will only add that rhetoric is no more invented by man, and no more pretends to make eloquence or eloquent men, than induction was invented by Bacon, and, with the help of a teacher, pretends to make philosophers" (Channing, *Lectures* 42). What makes the poet different is merely a trompe l'oeil.

For Channing, it is also an optical illusion that persuasion and conviction are distinct from one another. Channing insists that there really is no difference: "[P]ersuasion has its proper topics and method, not less than the coolest addresses to the understanding, and is, for the most part, a brief and informal kind of reasoning" (*Lectures* 38). Not at all "heated and reckless," persuasion is merely "reason herself kindled and inspired" (*Lectures* 38). Persuasion has everything to do with proving and convincing; it just does not seem like it because "feeling makes perception so rapid that steps and processes are not recognized" (*Lectures* 38–39).

What does Channing's conflation of poetry and philosophy do for the orator? Channing wants rhetoric to resemble a *technē* rather than something irrational and emotional like poetry. The practitioner of a *technē* is replaceable and the knowledge of it is potentially universal (it is external to the practitioner, anyone has access to it). This assures us both that rhetoric can be taught and, even better, that any man could learn it, two of Channing's dearly held beliefs. Yet rhetoric's indiscriminateness, while solving some problems, opens up others. Even dissolute orators, presumably, could learn to be persuasive. Channing might have solved the problem of passive orators (orators are not simply inspired and thus can be taught), but the problem of potentially insincere ones remains.

Channing sets himself to solve this problem too. The orator must not "look upon it [persuasive address] as a weak point in men, that they are impressible and yielding, and so ready to be moulded to the purposes of another; . . . he *ought* to feel that, with poets and minstrels and prophets, he is permitted to approach with sovereign control the sacred and generous fountains of the heart" (*Lectures* 35; emphasis added). Notice how Quintilian's description ("the perfect orator cannot but be virtuous") has turned into an explicit prescription ("men ought not to use persuasion for their own ends"). Channing must defend rhetoric, the art of effective communication (*Lectures* 31), from the incursion of bad orators, who might use it to further their own selfish ends. He cannot forestall their entry, but he can problematically claim that oratory has some quality that makes sure the bad orator will not go unrecognized.

This was the same problem on which Channing's "The Orator and His Times" foundered. It is the problem on which all his lectures founder. In the earlier lecture, Channing tried to rescue rhetoric through recourse to "character." The orator of good character was sincere, and somehow the audience would be able to detect this sincerity. Character was internal to the orator but could be communicated to the audience; this internal quality somehow would show up on the surface, enabling the audience to detect it. That was the plan. The problem with character in his earlier lecture came from Channing's failure to make it give an account of itself to the audience. Channing's "General View of Rhetoric" exacerbates the problem: in draining the orator of particularity, Channing seems to drain him of character itself. He has assured his readers that American audiences do not lack discernment, but what exactly is there to be discerned? Everything in the end depends on the orator's character and the audience's ability to assess it.

The Recourse to Taste

Channing needs a way to make character visible and finds it in "General View of Rhetoric" by connecting character to the concept of taste: good orators—in the sense of both effectiveness and moral worth—have good taste. The cultivation of taste became an educational imperative at the elite schools in the nineteenth century. It was one of the central tenets of the rhetorics of both Hugh Blair and Lord Kames (Henry Home) and their ideas about belles lettres. Today we think of taste as what sets people apart. People like different things, although we might also acknowledge that tastes are shared by a group, often defined in terms of class (as when an old-money home is referred to as "tasteful").[16] But for Blair and Kames and Channing, taste was related neither to individuality nor to class formation. Taste, instead, makes everyone the same.

Blair and Kames are followers of Thomas Reid,[17] who states in his essay "Of Judgment": "The virtues, the graces, the muses, have a beauty that is intrinsic. It lies not in the feelings of the spectator, but in the real excellence of the object. If we do not perceive their beauty, it is owing to the defect or to the perversion of our faculties" (394). We must train our faculties to register the quality of objects, which exists apart from any idiosyncratic contemplator of them. Correct taste exists, and everyone could potentially acquire it. A cultivated taste would not set a person apart (as we believe today, with varying levels of cynicism), either as an individual or as a member of the elite.

Reid notes that "[m]en's judgments are often perverted by their affections and passions" (414). He believes that each individual's faculties can gradually become corrupted. Reid offers a pedagogy of removal rather than one of cultivation. Today we have a sense that speech training makes people more of what they are, that it emphasizes certain traits (Speak up! Be funnier! Be clearer! Be better organized!). But for Reid and also for Channing, the opposite was true. Channing quite literally took up Reid's pedagogy of removal. Channing's former student Andrew Peabody described how Channing went about criticizing his students' themes: "If there was a single word that did not contribute to the meaning of the sentence, it was marked for excision. Exaggerations of all kinds were toned down. The student was shown how to say precisely what he meant, and nothing more. . . . There were errors and deformities of style that were so dealt with that it was hardly possible that Mr. Channing's pupil should be guilty of them more than once" (87).

Channing uses such a pedagogy to lead him out of his theoretical problem about reading the character of an orator. For Channing, the cultivation of taste acts as a safeguard against false oratory. It protects against excess and anomaly:

> The faculty of taste, also, must be introduced as the great moderating or tempering power, that wars against excess, against false

> associations of images and the unbecoming intrusion of startling but disturbing ideas, and which, in these ways and by positive suggestion of true and apposite beauty, keeps down all unnatural vivacity and gives proper brightness to the genuine. (*Lectures* 31)

The cultivation of taste brings the student in line with others who have good taste. It is a lack of taste that leads to singularity. Oratory should not seem too startling, too new. It is a congenial belief for Channing the Federalist, a defender of the status quo. Of course, he would bristle at the suggestion that this belief reflects his personal predilections rather than universal truths. Channing believes that the qualities an orator evinces have a value that extends beyond the particular eye of the beholder. This value is be reckoned in the same way by every member of the audience, assuming that they all have cultivated taste. Because cultivated taste leads to particular associations, a particular degree of vivacity, good orators will resemble each other. An orator with taste will always appear a certain way. In this fashion, the audience can finally recognize the orator and judge him trustworthy.

But how shall this tasteful orator appear? He should be "natural." *The Columbian Orator*, the book that set Frederick Douglass on his path to eloquence, counsels the would-be orator that "[t]he more natural pronunciation is, the more moving it will be; since the perfection of art consists in its nearest resemblance to nature" (Bingham 3). For Channing and his nineteenth-century colleagues, "natural" has a very different association than it does today. Although "natural" sometimes could mean innate, the state that someone would be in if left untaught, at other times almost the opposite holds: "natural" is a state reached only with training. "Nature" is thus the term that shows most clearly the bind of the professional rhetorician: to offer the audience a way to discern whether the orator is calculating what he can gain from the audience while at the same time to defend the necessity of oratorical training. The idea of the highly trained natural orator is the last-ditch attempt for the professional rhetorician to escape this bind. In "Elocution: A Study," Channing defends elocution from those who say that the orator should not be trained but instead should "trust to nature" (*Lectures* 51).

The Recourse to the Natural

In the classical system, *elocutio* (best translated as "style" in the classical context) was the third office of rhetoric. It guided the speaker in punctuation and syntax, what words to choose, and what tropes to employ. Not until the eighteenth century did elocution begin to take on the meaning that we now associate with it, involving the training of the voice and body of an orator. Thomas Sheridan, an eighteenth-century Irish actor, was one of the pioneers of this discipline. He and his even more zealous colleagues were also responsible for the suspicion that elocution fell under: its reputation as a meretricious art, productive of artificiality if not outright charlatanism.

Sheridan juxtaposes elocution (the language of the passions and fancy as expressed in tones and gestures) to words. Foreshadowing Ferdinand de Saussure, Sheridan claims that words are linked to ideas only through custom; he refers to writing as "the dead letter" (*A Course of Lectures* [1762] xii). In contrast, Sheridan touts elocution, which relies on "the living voice" (xiii). Elocution is the "language of nature" (xiii), untainted by artifice. To prove this, Sheridan claims that animals have a language of their own, expressed only in tones. People, too, are capable of a language that eschews words:

> [W]henever the force of these passions is extreme, words give place to inarticulate sounds: sighs, murmurings, in love; sobs, groans, and cries in grief; half choaked [*sic*] sounds in rage; and shrieks in terrour [*sic*], are then the only language heard. And the experience of mankind may be appealed to, whether these have not more power in exciting sympathy, than any thing [*sic*] that can be done by mere words. (102)

Sheridan does not put elocution on the same footing as words. For him, words often come up lacking; instead he opts for the efficacy of a natural system of signs, which shows no danger of being misunderstood.

As with Channing, for Sheridan the natural does not always mean the readily accessible. Though a person "spontaneously breaks out in the exactest expressions" (*A Course of Lectures* (1762) 105) when it comes to expressing animal passions, it is a different story with the nobler passions: "the organs . . . and faculties of his mind, necessary to his rational life, are only in embryo; and it depends wholly upon the assistance of others, together with his own care, to give them birth, and bring them to maturity" (106). Thus training in elocution proves necessary. A lack of training will only take someone so far; elocution must be codified and internalized.

Sheridan never produced a fully developed system to guide would-be orators in elocution. Perhaps this is what saves him from the full onslaught of skepticism that met some of his elocutionary colleagues like Gilbert Austin, the sense that they were producing showmen rather than ripened orators. Austin's *Chironomia*, published in 1806, provides scripts—diagrams for how the body should be positioned, with an elaborate system of symbols denoting pauses and emphases—for achieving proper elocution. America's own *Columbian Orator* (1797) was part of this tradition when it counseled in its section "Of Gesture" that "[the head] should always accompany the other actions of the body, and turn on the same side with them; except when aversion to any thing [*sic*] is expressed; which is done by stretching out the right hand, and turning the head to the left" (Bingham 11). Harvard had its own Gilbert Austin, an assistant to Channing named Jonathan Barber, who was in charge of teaching elocution. Peabody describes the device that Barber invented to facilitate his teaching:

> His great glory was the invention, unique, I suppose, of a hollow sphere, six feet in diameter, made of some six or eight bamboo rods, which were its meridians, and were crossed by an equator, by at least two great circles besides, and by an adequate number of small circles corresponding to parallels of latitude. In this sphere the student stood to declaim, and the circles by their various altitudes and intersections determined the gestures appropriate to each specific mood of feeling, or form of mental action. (90)

The students, alas, were not pleased with either Barber or his contraption and one day decided to suspend it on a "*barber's* pole opposite the college yard" (Peabody 91; emphasis in the original).

Even when it comes to the less extreme techniques of Sheridan, many twenty-first-century readers cannot, I suspect, help but read them as unwitting advice in chicanery. Yet this seems like a modern reaction. Richard Whately could advocate Sheridan ("one of the best writers on the subject" [265]) and his "natural" method while still making scathing remarks about other kinds of elocutionary training: "Probably not a single instance could be found of any one [*sic*] who attained, by the study of any system of instruction . . . a really good Delivery; but there are many,—probably nearly as many as have fully tried the experiment,—who have by this means been totally spoiled" (374–75).

Like so many of his lectures, Channing's "Elocution: A Study" is structured as a defense: in this case a defense against a view of oratory that would remove the necessity for rhetorical training (which includes training in elocution). In this lecture, Channing defends elocution from the charge summed up in the maxim "trust to nature" (*Lectures* 51). He counters the view that elocutionary training is unnecessary because "[w]e have by our constitution an apparatus for sounds and bodily movements, universally significant of mental states and action" (*Lectures* 46); all the orator needs is "ardor, sincerity, and devotion to his purpose" (*Lectures* 57). In this view, rhetorical training merely dampens our natural capacities.

Channing disagrees with the mandate to trust to nature, but not in the way that we might expect. He does not dispute the assumption that men are born with a natural capacity for eloquence. Witness the natural eloquence of the child: "No actor, no pantomime of elder growth is to be compared with him." The child is "one visible mental expression" (*Lectures* 48): his visage expresses his inward feelings. Even better, he inevitably sways his audience. The child has not had his natural capacity dampened. Channing, like Thomas Reid, thinks that a bad delivery has to do with various perversions of this capacity. As adults, we invariably "clog it" (*Lectures* 46). To this extent, he agrees with those who want to "trust to nature" (*Lectures* 51).

Here is how they disagree: Channing's opponents assume that it is rhetorical training that clogs the capacities; Channing argues that it is a *lack* of attention to rhetoric that clogs it. From Channing's point of view, *rhetorical* training in fact unplugs it. Channing's opponents assume that rhetorical training creates something out of nothing, changes the orator into something different from what he would be if left on his own. For Channing, the "art [of rhetoric] is drawn directly from all that we have learned of the perfect in man's nature, and is intended to develope [*sic*] and train what he already possesses" (*Lectures* 49). For Channing, rhetorical training is the art of unclogging; it is an art that strips away idiosyncrasy and with it, he hopes, the possibility of deceit. As with "taste," delivery is objective and universal; a proper sort exists apart from the individual, who can nonetheless gain access to it with training. Art and nature, like passion and reason, like persuasion and conviction, are not very different after all.

Channing even manages to show that the "natural" and taught orator are one and the same. The natural orator is hardly untaught: "The very prodigies of genius . . . if they had the power to reveal the mystery of their growth, would probably show us a far more thorough course of education, a more strict though, perhaps, unconscious obedience to principles, than the most dependent of their brethren have ever been subjected to" (*Lectures* 49). Again, note how similar this reasoning is to that found in his earlier point about persuasion and conviction: feeling merely makes the workings of the understanding very rapid. The natural orator is different only in degree: he is a quicker study than the plodding student. He can fool people the way feeling fools them into thinking that it is opposed to reason (it *is* reason, only sped up).[18]

The problem with elocutionary training, then, is a problem only with a particular kind of training that makes the orator appear self-conscious, as if acting by rote. The proper training would make the orator *appear* natural. Channing suggests that lack of proper training makes an orator evince an artificial manner: "It is a consciousness of weakness or unpreparedness that betrays a conscious manner" (*Lectures* 55). Once someone has learned something very well, he appears natural.

By the end of the lecture, naturalness has changed from its earlier meaning as expressed by the child—a kind of absolute transparency. Naturalness in a child seemed to be characterized by a match between what his body expressed (voice, expression, gestures) and his inner thoughts and feelings. Channing observes: "How intelligible is every gesture, look and attitude which waits upon his imperfect speech or interprets his silence" (*Lectures* 47–48). Thus we would think that elocutionary training should merely remove all defects. Yet here is Channing's twist: the path to elocutionary mastery as an adult does not lie in unlearning all our perversions. The goal is not to return to the state that we were in as children. We are different now: "The more a habit is formed of revolving thoughts and ascertaining difficult truth, the less eager are we to make instant proclamation of feelings and ideas" (*Lectures* 53). He goes on in this vein, implying that a child's eloquence is no longer appropriate. We need to learn a new kind of eloquent speaking.

At the end of this lecture, Channing dismisses the adult version of the untrained, natural orator:

> The question may be asked, whether a common man, the least educated in any respect, ever fails to hit instinctively the true, thrilling tone, whenever he is deeply moved. Does his rage, his remorse, his agony of grief, need a teacher of vocal inflections? No,—but shall the frantic man come to our assemblies? Will the raw, naked passion, true as it is in expressing itself, appeal fitly to cultivated minds, preparing themselves by deliberation not less than by sympathy for just judgment and action? (*Lectures* 58)

Channing associates the uneducated with the unmodulated; in this, of course, he is not alone.[19] Even granting Channing's assumption, we would be hard pressed to think of his distaste for raw emotion as anything but a personal aversion (even if derived from his class position). Nothing about the ill-educated man would make him a bad speaker in principle. In fact, Channing's elitist position here contradicts his earlier point about the importance of the orator's intelligibility to his audience. The unmodulated, uneducated man is most like a child in his transparency. And we should also recognize how closely both the child and the uneducated man come to meeting Channing's requirements for identifying "character": with regard to either of these figures, the audience could be sure that what the orator is showing is what he is feeling. Yet Channing bans such unmodulated men from being orators.

This is a moment when the irreconcilability of Channing's imperatives becomes visible. If the uneducated, transparent man could be a good orator, there would be no need for Boylston Professors. Rhetorical training makes the elocution of the orator something other than transparent. Channing would claim that he is not just expressing an opinion; he is in fact recognizing an objective truth. We might be more suspicious: Channing seems less to be recording objective truths than to be embedding his snobbery in his "description" of rhetoric.

Channing does not realize what he has done: he has shown that rhetorical training instills in the orator a set of arbitrary signs (certain gestures, certain vocal inflections) that persuade the audience of the orator's inability to lie. Appearing natural is not the same as being natural; the orator develops a set of gestures and movements that are learned, that persuade the audience that he is on the level. This puts in doubt Channing's claim that the properly trained orator has access to true principles (*Lectures* 51). Channing wants to shore up the belief in the existence of a set of signs that will not lie, not realizing that the battle has already been lost as soon as we acknowledge that these are signs, not the thing itself.

Channing's commitment to a modulated delivery undermines his argument. In the strange climax to his lecture, he states: "Thus the most sincere passion needs the restraint of taste, and the moderation, the serenity of self-possession. Just as some men, who feel deeply what they want to say, speak as if they were unmoved,—others, equally sincere, fail from over-doing" (*Lectures* 59). Thus Channing unwittingly rescinds what he has said earlier. "Naturalness" now seems to manifest itself in a mismatch between outward demeanor and inward feeling.

Channing could very well argue that he is not responsible for the form that an orator's elocution should take: he is merely recording what he knows of "the perfect in man's nature," which is what determines proper elocution. Yet here again two of Channing's imperatives come into conflict. On one hand, Channing wants the orator to hew to universal, objective standards which, as he has argued, the orator needs the proper training to meet. On the other hand, Channing needs the audience members—who have not presumably had the same kind of rhetorical training—to be able to read the orator, to be able to tell if the orator is persuading them of an untruth.

Before this telling lecture on elocution, the audience members *could* tell about the orator's veracity in two ways. They might experience a visceral reaction, a heart's tremor, a gush of tears—the responses that Channing understands orators in classical times to have evoked (though this kind of confirmation terrifies him). This was acceptable because the classical orator was necessarily a good man (*pace* Ion). Or there was Channing's earlier solution, offered in a time when the orator's goodness could not be assumed: the audience could read the orator because he was transparent (the outer exactly corresponded to the inner; passionate gestures equaled passionate conviction). Notice that both these ways use the body to guarantee the truth of the utterance: either the visceral or the ocular empowers the audience to gauge the character of the orator. With his lecture on "Elocution," Channing moves into new, nonsomatic territory. Now the audience members can read the orator only if a certain rhetorical training has prepared them to know that certain signs correspond with certain inner states. Channing raises the suspicion that only arbitrariness unites certain signs to certain meanings. Now the orator's appearance does not match what he feels. To check for sincerity the audience needs to check that the orator's passionate conviction is not reflected in a passionate voice or gestures. The problem arises in Channing's bait and switch of signs: in a child, he looks for elocutionary zeal; in an adult, he looks for elocutionary moderation. The more the set of signs by which the audience can read an orator changes, the more the audience suspects that the set of signs is not a product of universal principles. The proper tone of voice, the proper gestures, the proper emotional register might all be arbitrary; they might reflect the times or the penchants or the class of the rhetorician, perhaps those of Edward Tyrrel Channing.

Furthermore, the audience can no longer feel or see that the orator means what he says. This is now a matter of intellectual training rather than somatic sensitivity. It is unfortunate for Channing that the way an audience can *tell* about an orator and the way the audience can be fired up to act both dangerously have to do with passion and persuasion (as opposed to reason and conviction)—things having to do with the body. Removing the dangerous possibility of one (passion) prevents carrying out the other (persuasion). Channing's lecture on elocution prevents the audience members from being revolutionaries but in so doing leaves them open to be dupes. Of course, everything would be fine if orators spoke only to other elites highly trained in rhetoric, which was in fact the case with these particular lectures. We have the sense, strongly here, that Channing's system only works when he preaches to the converted.

First and foremost, Channing wants to prevent an audience from being persuaded of an untruth. His theory of rhetoric and oratory can be seen as an endless searching after confirmation that this will not happen. In his first lecture, Channing took recourse to character, which opened up its own problem: how can an audience know what kind of character the orator has? Channing sought to solve this problem by suggesting that the orator will reveal certain visible signs that act as a guarantee to his good intentions. In "General View of Rhetoric," Channing's views on rhetoric assure us that a good orator will inevitably manifest a certain set of natural signs. His logic goes like this: he assures us that persuasive discourse does not depend on the potentially dangerous idiosyncrasies of a particular orator. An effective orator is one of cultivated taste, which assures us that an orator draws his words and manner from universal truths which could be revealed to anyone who has overcome perversions of taste and can see things clearly and in their right relations. To be assured that an orator is on the level, all the audience must do is make certain that the orator acts "naturally," that is, in correspondence with these universal truths. Yet in this last lecture on elocution, "natural" turns out not to be what we might have thought. It does not lie in an orator's unselfconscious acting out of what he inwardly feels (as Channing thinks children act). Channing specifies a set of signs that an orator should manifest (restraint, moderation) that seem to be exactly the opposite of what the orator really feels (passionate conviction). Channing opens up the possibility that these signs might be unreadable to an untrained audience, which has only gut reactions or ocular proof to rely on.

Gabler-Hover has noted to what a great extent Channing and his contemporaries trusted the audience "to compel honesty" from the orator (44). We see this trust in his first lecture, where he cautions the contemporary orator against trying to dupe his listeners. If the direction of control remained this way, such wonderful things would follow: no unscrupulous orator could come to prominence (because no audience would allow an unscrupulous orator); if an audience were persuaded of the truth then what was said must have been true. This would be a system where everyone was on one level. Here is Channing's utopia: that what works is also true. To get a sense of what this formulation means, contrast certain pragmatic understandings of "what works is true." For the pragmatist, a truth cannot be separated from its efficacy. For Channing, a discourse would be true even if it persuaded no one—but, wonderfully, it persuades everyone. Channing wants to have it both ways. Yet for his system to work, the level of both the audience and orator can only be reached by Harvard graduates (and perhaps also by those who attend Princeton). Channing ends by abandoning the mass audience. His contempt for the unmodulated and their easy sway turns him away from the untrained. As Harriet Beecher Stowe's narrator says of a character in *The Minister's Wooing*, "[H]e followed trains of thought suited only to the desk of the . . . lecture-room" (91).

Channing himself remains highly modulated even in times of rhetorical extremity. His lectures demonstrate his system of rhetoric; they are performative. They are marked by a total lack of personal information. No anecdotes dot his elucidation of principles; no unbecoming bursts of feeling interrupt the flow of his thoughts. Channing is a man without much personality in these lectures, and this is as it should be. The orator should not be characterized by singularity; he speaks what is universally true in a manner that is not particular to himself.

Richard H. Dana's short biographical sketch of Channing paints (somewhat unwittingly) the picture of a cultured if not snobbish man, a Brahmin of the bluest tint, who fits in well with the rarefied atmosphere of Harvard (which is referred to as "Cambridge" in the following):

> If it be said . . . that Cambridge has been less distinguished for boldness, idiosyncracies [*sic*] and vigor . . . we may reply that if true, or so far as it be true, this is not to be attributed to the department of rhetoric and belles-lettres, but rather to the classes of society from which the Cambridge students are chiefly drawn, and to the uniform set and drift of opinion in matters literary, political, and religious, which has so long marked the highly cultivated, but small and rather removed society of which the university and neighboring city have been the centre. (xiv)

The problem comes in with Channing's own class preferences. He does not become terribly excited in these lectures; they are neoclassical, filled with the balanced phrases and hypotactic structures of reasoned consideration and restrained by a calm and even punctuation. Channing would not stoop to the direct addresses or exclamation points that punctuate the sentimental novels. His orations conform to principles of good taste, not to popular taste. They do not manifest enthusiasm or zeal, at least in their rawer forms. If Channing nevertheless felt these emotions (who knows?), then he conforms exactly to his principle that "some men, who feel deeply what they want to say, speak as if they were unmoved." The passions of audience members would be touched by Channing only if their tastes had been similarly cultivated. Channing retreats both in his theory and in his practice from a position that seemed at least intuitively obvious: that an orator's passion would manifest itself in passionate expression.

Channing wants to defend the necessity of rhetorical training, and this urge prevents him from excluding unscrupulous orators. As soon as he clears the way for any man to be an orator, any man can be an orator. The untrained masses have no weapon against the disingenuous orator because they have no way of detecting him. Channing's own institutional position undermines his attempt to guard against disingenuous eloquence.

The discourse of professional rhetoricians and orators is an unstable one, despite the high regard in which the nineteenth-century populace held oratory. As Baskerville says about the nineteenth century: "[t]he orator, unquestionably, was king" (26). King he might be, but his rule was under siege. The system of professional male rhetoric and oratory is a discourse in crisis, a system riddled with self-contradictions and ad hoc repairs. An article from *Atlantic Monthly*, published in 1860 and bewailing the choking presence of too many commemorative statues and too many orators (related phenomena in the eyes of the author), evokes the instability that I am suggesting: "Even when we get one orator safely under-ground, there are ten to pronounce his eulogy, and twenty to do it over again when the meeting is held about the inevitable statue. I go to listen; we all go: we are under a spell" ("A Plea for Freedom" 745). This humorous acknowledgment of the simultaneous push and pull of oratory was written by James Russell Lowell, one of Channing's students. This kind of dual consciousness as well as the compulsive defense of oratory in every nineteenth-century oration about oratory that I have read—oratory as more than ornamental and other than meretricious—might be taken as evidence that the time was ripe for a rival to the professional male orator. This rival would take advantage of the orator's immense potential to rivet and sway an audience but would be neither professional nor male.

2

Why We Should Trust Harriet Beecher Stowe

EDWARD TYRREL CHANNING FACED THE BIND THAT ALL professional male rhetoricians and orators faced in nineteenth-century America. He could endorse the natural orator and make rhetorical training unnecessary. Or he could defend rhetorical training and ensure that most members of the audience would have no way of telling whether they were being duped. He opts for the latter, making eloquence trustworthy only for an elite sliver of the populace. He cannot resolve the conflict between rhetorical training and disingenuous eloquence. The sentimental authors could. They were not professors of rhetoric and oratory; their allegiances were not divided. They had no reason to reject the option that Channing turned away from, the anointing of the untrained and transparent orator.

Why have scholars not explored the connection between the sentimental women writers and the professional rhetoricians and orators? The separate spheres paradigm, which governed the rescue of the "scribbling women" starting in the late 1960s, surely contributes to this lacuna. According to this paradigm, women writers lived their lives in the domestic sphere and wrote their works within a distinct female tradition.[1] In fact, ample evidence indicates that these sentimental authors did not want others to think of them as professional authors, an identity that male authors were beginning to claim in the antebellum period.[2] "My baby is fisting my paper at a great rate as you can see by my chirography" (qtd. in Hedrick, "'Peaceable Fruits'" 312), Stowe once wrote in a letter. Female duties and authorship would coexist for Stowe, especially because her acknowledged shortcomings as an author had their origins in her own good mothering—as did the inspiration for her most famous work, *Uncle Tom's Cabin*.[3] These nineteenth-century sentimental authors wrote, they themselves asserted, out of moral or economic necessity, while maintaining their own separate sphere. This argument is also supported by other facts: like the other "scribbling women," Stowe did not go to a university (no universities would accept women); she did not become a preacher (there were no women preachers); she did not become a professor of rhetoric. Her life and her writing, the rescue critics would claim, belong to a different, female tradition.

Later critics have dismantled the separate spheres paradigm, however, as discussed more fully at the beginning of chapter 3. In this spirit, we can tell a different, less hermetic story of Stowe's life and writing. Stowe was very much exposed to the masculine subject of nineteenth-century American rhetorical theory, both religious and civil. She was the daughter of the famous Congregationalist minister Lyman Beecher, who encouraged his sons (who all also became ministers, including Henry Ward Beecher, one of the most famous ministers of the nineteenth century) in the development of polemical skill. Stowe was an avid witness of, if not a participant in, their theological debates (Hedrick, *Harriet Beecher Stowe* 21). Rhetorical performance was not just a feature of the dinner table: it formed the cornerstone of membership in her father's church, which required parishioners to attest to their conversion and to be examined on it.[4] Stowe was supremely aware of the rhetorical styles of different Protestant evangelical ministers, men like Jonathan Edwards and his younger colleague Samuel Hopkins and later her own father, a collection of ministers who spent over a century fomenting religious revivals and individual conversions in New England. She was also aware of the rhetorical possibilities that this tradition left for women.[5] (She herself participated in the revival that swept through her sister Catharine's Hartford Female Seminary in 1826.) Joan Hedrick characterizes her, in fact, as a kind of radical lay preacher, comforting and converting people out of her own painful experiences ("'Peaceable Fruits'"). But her rhetorical training was not just religious: Stowe acquired more secular knowledge of rhetorical theory at the Litchfield Female Academy under the tutelage of her favorite teacher, John Brace, whose textbooks included Hugh Blair's *Lectures*.[6] She went on to teach rhetoric and composition for a few years at the Hartford Female Seminary.

Although Stowe certainly did not espouse the particular rhetorical theories of the professional orators and rhetoricians of the time, she knew them. In fact she did not just know them, she grappled with them. I think it is fair to say that she solved the conflict between rhetorical training and disingenuous eloquence that the professionals could not. Stowe's power lay in the unofficial, noninstitutional ways in which she could persuade people. Unlike Channing's, Stowe's view of rhetoric would not founder on a need to champion rhetorical training as a prerequisite for persuasive speech. For the sentimental author, women almost always turn out to be more eloquent than men, and the most eloquent characters of all are slaves and children. As many critics have pointed out, this valorization could be simply the logical response of writers whose own interests lay in raising up the disenfranchised. Even so, these sentimental authors put forth as their most powerful orators people who were much less trained and privileged than they were.

I want to suggest some other characteristics of sentimentality's most eloquent orators that might make the authors' self-interest seem less important than their engagement with nineteenth-century professional rhetoric. Slaves, women, and children made up a class in the nineteenth century: those whose reason had not been developed.[7] While this view seems only an insult to a contemporary audience, it does contain possibilities for championing those thought to fall under its judgment. The sentimentalists would embrace the idea that these are people whose heads have not superseded their hearts. As Stowe's narrator from *The Minister's Wooing* puts it, "women are always turning from the abstract to the individual, and feeling where the philosopher only thinks" (25). Channing's trained orators have only a narrow appeal: their modulated tones, their stiff delivery, their seeming lack of passion cannot fire the masses. Sentimental heroes and heroines have no problem evincing their passion; in fact, in the view of Stowe and her colleagues, they have no choice.[8]

One very odd thing about many of the most persuasive sentimental heroes and heroines—Maria Susanna Cummins's Emily Graham and Gerty; Louisa May Alcott's Beth; Stowe's Tom, Little Eva, and Mary Scudder, to name just a few—is how little they actually speak. For the sentimental heroine, it is as if "her inspired silence had been a voice" (Stowe, *Minister's Wooing* 149). Sentimental characters are most persuasive in moments of speechlessness, in the pain of bereavement or the throes of illness or the finality of death. This characteristic allows them not only to be persuasive but to deserve the trust that their hearers will invest in them: they are transparent in their suffering. Stowe solves the problem of disingenuous eloquence that Channing could not solve for the life of him. Stowe offers a vision of the authentic orator that is the mirror image of Channing's potentially dissimulating one. In contrast to Channing's celebration of erudition, she substitutes the idea of woodenness; in contrast to the modulated orator, she offers us the orator *in extremis*. Sentimental novels always move, in their order of preference, from text to speech, from the "high style" to the conversational, and from the conversational to the embodied.[9]

The Winning Orator

I want to argue that Stowe's *The Minister's Wooing* is her rhetorical manifesto. Its plot, seen most readily as a tale about the legacy of Puritanism, ends with a new, less rigid Christian evangelical practice. But in this novel, set in the late eighteenth century, religious practice cannot be separated from rhetorical practice. The various proselytizers that the novel presents are also orators, who are more or less eloquent, more or less transparent, and more or less trustworthy. In this novel, we can see Stowe bringing to life different models of persuasive speech and then ranking them. In other words, this novel stages a contest between different kinds of orators.

In reading the novel this way, I hope to build on the approach that Hedrick takes in "'Peaceable Fruits'" (which rehearses material that she uses in her masterful biography of Stowe). Hedrick's article brings together the two approaches that critics have tended to take when examining *The Minister's Wooing*. On one hand, critics like Sandra Duguid, Lawrence Buell ("Rival Romantic Interpretations"), and more recently

Kimberly VanEsveld Adams have persuasively read the novel as a meditation on orthodox Calvinism; these articles foreground developments in the world of professional male theological debates and, in the case of Duguid and Adams, see James Marvyn as the focal point of the novel. On the other hand, critics like Susan K. Harris ("Female Imaginary") focus on the feminist subtext of the novel but do not see its meditation on Calvinism as particularly significant.[10] Hedrick manages to do both: to show how Stowe's meditation on Calvinism is also a meditation on the kinds of social power that white women were capable of wielding, not just during the time of the novel but in Stowe's own time. Yet—not surprisingly considering the direction that feminist thinking has taken since the 1980s when Hedrick's and Harris's articles were written—I find their suggestion that Stowe's novel can offer us a utopian feminist space, free from hierarchy, less convincing. Even if we grant that Mary Scudder produces a lovely space of female intimacy, this space is achieved only through the most hierarchical of methods: Stowe's comparison and ranking of the different kinds of rhetorical possibilities that her characters embody. Her novel is an implicit attack against the kind of elitist eloquence that men like Channing settled upon. Stowe might be railing against the hierarchy of rhetorical values that Channing puts forth, but she is not railing against the act of hierarchizing: she is out to win this rhetorical contest.

Each character in this novel embodies a different type of persuasion. It has long been noted that sentimental novels employ "types" rather than fleshed-out characters. These types remind us of the stock characters of melodrama, such as the evil villain and the pure maiden. In "Sentimental Power," Jane Tompkins refers to an earlier meaning of "types" and reads sentimental novels typologically, noting the Christ-figures, for example, or the way that incidents reoccur in the course of the novel. Yet these novels also proffer their characters as types of orators, good and bad, and this explanation might subsume the typological one: it is important to represent an author's favorite characters as Christ because Christ was the most persuasive orator around.

To enter the world of *The Minister's Wooing* is to enter into a contest between types of persuasion. The novel is built around a conventional marriage plot: a girl must choose between two suitors. In this case, Mary Scudder must choose between the venerable Dr. Hopkins, a character based on a real historical figure, the younger colleague of the famous Calvinist minister of Northampton, Jonathan Edwards; and James Marvyn, mischievous cousin and sailor, a man with a knack for plain-speaking. Mary's choice seems determined when James is apparently killed in a shipwreck; she agrees to marry Dr. Hopkins out of duty and respect. But James comes back, and Dr. Hopkins ultimately releases Mary from her pledge. She and James marry. The novel also features a subplot involving none other than Aaron Burr, who was, in fact, the grandson of Jonathan Edwards. Burr appears here in the guise of a rake who almost seduces a friend of Mary's, Madame Frontignac, and, conforming to what we know about him historically, comes to no good end.

But there is something odd about this plot: most sentimental novels trace the progress of the heroine on her journey toward becoming a good woman. Usually the heroine starts out flawed—not docile enough, not devout enough—and through a variety of calming and pious influences finally becomes worthy of a decent man (and worthy to raise children, because children, it was believed, were first and foremost influenced by their mothers). But Mary Scudder is perfect from the start: our very first vision of her compares her to "pictures of the girlhood of the Virgin" (19).[11] She has already achieved a more than sufficient level of piety and docility. In this novel, the burden of development shifts to the *male* characters: the question becomes which man will show himself worthy to receive the reward of Mary.

What criteria does the book use in order to choose between Dr. Hopkins and James? Youth and beauty are two areas where James triumphs (but Aaron Burr has them too, and he is the worst choice of all). What really distinguishes them are their different ways of speaking and, in turn, of representing the world. Dr. Hopkins is marked by his adherence to a "system" (72). It is both logical and abstruse. Though he is a revered minister and people dutifully go to his sermons, no one can understand what he is saying:

> His pulpit talents, too, were unattractive. His early training had been all logical, not in the least aesthetic; for, like the ministry of his country generally, he had been trained always to think more of what he should say than of how he should say it. Consequently, his style, though not without a certain massive

> greatness, which always comes from largeness of nature, had none of those attractions by which the common masses are beguiled into thinking. (87)

Hopkins says what he has to say logically and abstractly. He thus joins a cohort of Puritan ministers, including Jonathan Edwards. Though Edwards is now remembered for his hell-and-brimstone rhetoric, at the time he, like Hopkins, was noted for his intellectual rigor, the abstract systematizing evinced in his later works (his *Freedom of the Will* briefly caused one of Stowe's brothers to lose his faith, as Adams has noted). This description could also be applied to Edward Tyrrel Channing, who spends a great part of his lectures subsuming the aesthetic into the logical.

The passage cited above is a representative description of the sermons of Dr. Hopkins: it does not actually recount what he said. The novel gives us only indirect references to his sermons rather than eyewitness accounts, as when James gives this description of one: "Your good Dr. Hopkins spent a whole half-day, the other Sunday, trying to tell us about the beauty of holiness and he cut, and pared, and peeled, and sliced, and told us what it wasn't, and what was *like* it, and wasn't; and then he built up an exact definition, and fortified and bricked it up all round" (71; emphasis in the original).

Both this passage and the earlier one dwell on how Dr. Hopkins says what he says; the novel never allows readers the chance to read a whole sermon for themselves. Stowe will not fall into the same error as Dr. Hopkins: she will not attend to what Hopkins says but only to how he says it. Here the "how" of Dr. Hopkins has been filtered through James's perceptions and idioms. The way James says what he has to say is in marked contrast to the way Hopkins does. James uses a homely metaphor, the godly and the culinary all mixed up. It partakes of Stowe's own favorite blend of the heavenly and the housewifely.

For Stowe, elocution trumps content; the *how* of what people say matters more than the *what*. Of course, there is no how without a what: Stowe's emphasis does not free her from the need actually to say something, but it does lead her to consider her audience at every turn. In contrast, Channing's view of elocution leads him to abandon the mass audience. Both Channing and Stowe dream of having it both ways: of persuading an audience and revealing the truth at the same time. Yet they proceed from different directions. Channing must contend that what is true is also persuasive; for Stowe, what is persuasive is also true. Channing is always in danger of losing his audience; Stowe is always in danger of saying a lie.

We can highlight the differences in their views even more if we think of them in reference to predestination, a doctrine that *The Minister's Wooing* wants to reform. The novel shows that Dr. Hopkins's unbending belief in strict predestination, where only a very tiny number of people will be saved, and faith and good works count for naught, needs to be changed. The change in theology, it is suggested, will allow more people into heaven because character will be allowed to affect redemption. These religious formulations have a relationship to rhetorical principles. Strict predestination supposes that how someone seems does not matter at all; what matters is how someone is. And only God can tell how someone is. Of course, if someone really is predestined, that person will seem predestined too (or at least will not seem not predestined), but this is rather a backdoor way of aligning the two. This formulation corresponds roughly to Channing's eventual unwitting profile of the proper orator: his outward appearance might not look like his inner state (at least not to the uneducated). In addition, not everyone who seems predestined is predestined, just as not everyone who speaks the truth will persuade his audience. Strict predestination supposes that a huge split between seeming and being might exist. In this account, neither the state of a person's soul nor the truth of a discourse can be influenced by the person.[12]

Stowe differs in both her views on predestination and her rhetorical principles. Once someone moves away from strict predestination, outward manifestations—expressions of faith, good works—can be taken as proof of salvation because they lead to it (they are not just incidental). We can depend on an impression of a person in forecasting the state of her soul; analogously, the picture that an orator presents determines how persuasive the person will be. Thus how a speaker speaks comes to be of the utmost importance; her outward manifestation outweighs what she actually says. And the most persuasive speaker will not speak at all. The issue of seeming has ceased to be of any importance because seeming equals being: a person's outward manifestation equals the state of her soul. Elocution supersedes content.[13]

Stowe's characterization of Dr. Hopkins correlates to an older view of oratory characterized by reason. In *The Minister's Wooing,* this kind of oratory, as well as Dr. Hopkins's brand of ministering, is clearly past its prime (Dr. Hopkins himself is a little too old for Mary). It is only a "certain massive greatness" that redeems his sermons, which comes from his "largeness of nature." What redeems his orations is character. Stowe, like Channing, places great emphasis on the quality. For Channing, character authenticates the truth of an oration. But it also trails it. The orator's good character might be necessary for an effective oration, but it exists apart from it. For Stowe, as we shall see, character *is* content. In the absence of words, who the orator is conveys what she wants to say.

"Much of [Dr. Hopkins's] preaching about men is as like live men as Chinese pictures of trees and rocks and gardens,—no nearer the reality than that" (72). This is James speaking again, another candidate in the contest of oratory that this book sponsors. He stands opposed to Dr. Hopkins not just because he is also interested in the saintly Mary Scudder but because he has doubts about Dr. Hopkins's ministering, the mismatch between Hopkins's words and how things really are. As a consequence, James has never joined the church. It is not that James does not believe in God but that "all this invisible world of religion is unreal to me" (72). James goes on: "I must have real things,—real people; abstractions are nothing to me" (72).

James has a reality problem, and it is instructive that he would associate Dr. Hopkins's preaching with the East. In this novel, the East exists as a fantasy: a magical place not just of limitless plunder (as in other sentimental novels, the hero garners his wealth there) but of a fantastical style of representation. When Stowe wants to express the gap between Hopkins's representation of people and actual live people, Stowe does not refer simply to the gap between pictures of trees and rocks and gardens and actual trees and rocks and gardens, the way Plato would. Instead Stowe compares "Chinese pictures" of trees and rocks and gardens to actual trees and rocks and gardens. "Chinese" is an important adjective, not just because of its imperialist connotations but because an adjective is there at all. With it, Stowe suggests that certain pictures would in fact exactly correspond to real life. A *Chinese* picture does not represent the way things actually are, but, Stowe implies, another kind of picture really could. Some pictures would take on the immediacy that we grant only to living things. Stowe suggests that some representations transcend representation and not only become exactly accurate but even attain life.

Other elements indicate that Stowe actually does imagine that pictures can provide a viewer with an accurate experience of the thing itself and perhaps even become it. In one instance in the novel, a life and a picture are equivalent. Here the narrator describes the life of James's mother: "Life was a picture painted in low, cool tones, but in perfect keeping; and though another and brighter style might have pleased better, she did not quarrel with this" (106). Whereas an author like George Eliot might compare a character to a painting in order to imply the character's artificiality,[14] Stowe's use of such a trope holds no such implication.

For contemporary readers, pictures lack life even though they can mimic it; for Stowe, pictures have an overwhelming immediacy. Here is Stowe discussing her plans with her publisher for *Uncle Tom's Cabin* (a quotation discussed again in chapter 4): "My vocation is simply that of a *painter*, and my object will be to hold up in the most lifelike and graphic manner possible Slavery, its reverses, changes, and the negro character, which I have had ample opportunities for studying. There is no arguing with *pictures*, and everybody is impressed by them, whether they mean to be or not" ("Letter to Gamaliel Bailey," emphasis in original).

Stowe is not talking about future paintings but about future words. What does it mean to aspire to make words into pictures? It implies a distrust of words, for one thing. Both written accounts and paintings might be representations after the fact (Stowe does not think that a picture really is the thing itself), but pictures can make the thing live again in a way that words cannot. The difference lies in a picture's being seen and immediately recognized (as opposed to words, which are also seen, but initially only as squiggles on a page). Pictures, as Stowe understands them, do not rely on the understanding. They bypass the faculties that allow someone to be distanced from the object of contemplation; they go right to the heart, with no detours through the head. Pictures can persuade a reader in a way that words cannot. It is as though a picture can bring to life the thing that it is representing because it has no intellectual pretensions. It should come as no surprise that Stowe likes people who similarly bypass the head and whose words paint pictures.

This brings us to James. What kind of speaker is James? He is not an intellectual. Unlike Hopkins, James is very concerned about reaching everyone, and his syntax and vocabulary reflect this: he is plain-speaking. At the end of the novel, James is examined successfully and is admitted into the church. Miss Prissy, the village seamstress, recounts his examination in a letter to her sister:

> At first the Doctor seemed a little anxious, 'cause he didn't talk in the regular way; for you know Jim always did have his own way of talking, and never could say things in other people's words; and sometimes he makes folks laugh, when he himself don't know what they laugh at, because he hits the nail on the head in some strange way they aren't expecting. If I was to have died, I couldn't help laughing at some things he said; and yet I don't think I ever felt more solemnized. He sat up there in a sort of grand, straightforward, noble way, and told all the way the Lord had been leading of him . . . till the Doctor's spectacles got all blinded with tears, and he couldn't see the notes he made to examine him by; and we all cried. (565)

This would seem to be the ideal orator, a man who speaks in the voice of the people. Like other great nineteenth-century orators, James manages to bring his audience to tears. Even the cerebral Dr. Hopkins clouds up. Yet I think the novel hesitates to anoint James as the perfect orator even though he would seem to fulfill the criteria for it: full of feeling, able to evoke feeling, on the same level as his audience. (And he receives an added boost because critics have identified James as being modeled on Stowe's beloved brother, Henry Ward Beecher.) The clue to his deficiency comes in Prissy's many references to how he makes her laugh.

It is James's verbal incompetence that makes him competent as an orator. James "hits the nail on the head in some strange way they aren't expecting" and is then surprised by the laughter. He does not realize that he is being funny and cannot judge his own effect. James has the necessary ability not to seem smarter than his audience because he is not. In his case, the problem of disingenuous eloquence is solved because he seems to be exactly what he is. The problem arises when we consider that his power as an orator—his verbal ingenuousness—places him squarely in the ranks of Stowe's "low" characters, the comic ones, who often turn out to be awfully persuasive speakers.[15]

James knows not what he speaks; the same quality is found in Prissy herself, as we can see by her letter. The letter invites the reader at once to believe in the absolute sincerity of what she says and to feel superior to her quaint ways of putting things. I do not think that Stowe envisions her audience as millions of Prissys—we are meant to laugh at Prissy, feel a little distanced from her. We are a bit more cosmopolitan, more dignified.[16] Stowe does not envision her audience as made up of comic characters. James's verbal ingenuousness, though it suits him to be the ideal orator in a certain way, the antidote to Dr. Hopkins's intellectual sermons, goes too far. Stowe wants no separation between orator and audience: no sense of hierarchy must come between audience and speaker. Dr. Hopkins makes the audience feel inferior, and James makes the audience feel the opposite. James makes us laugh because we realize that he has a funny way with words. As in the case of Dr. Hopkins's sermons and Chinese pictures, James, though he is a natural and utterly unselfconscious, actually speaks in a stylized way. His words call attention to themselves as words. He makes you think—what a funny way with words he has!—rather than simply experience the truth of what he is trying to get across.

Dr. Hopkins and James occupy two different sides of the oratorical fence. But they both fail, although Stowe obviously would take James over Dr. Hopkins in a heartbeat. The readers get stuck on the words they are using: Dr. Hopkins because he is stiff, and James because he is funny. We become distracted; they make us think about how terribly difficult it is for mere words (tricky little things, as Stowe's slaves are always finding) to get across the truth. First place in this contest of oratory remains open. It is being held for an orator who has figured out not how to use words to paint pictures but how to persuade her audience without resorting to words whatsoever, how to make a picture of herself.

Before leaving this discussion of James, I want to point out how close he comes to winning first place. The novel does seem to set him up to lead us into the future. It ends with him in the forefront, successful and philanthropic and eloquent. But he is still male, and this characteristic has plagued him throughout the novel. James is a strange character in this book: he is the only character who develops, beginning as a willful child and maturing into a pious, conventional adult. In a way, he is the sentimental heroine whose trajectory most sentimental novels rely on to give them a plot. Yet his maleness disables him in two ways: it sends him offstage for most of the novel because he needs to go to the East to make his fortune and necessitates turning him into a comic character. This is a book that defuses tension between the sexes through a kind of quaint humor:[17] "Spite of all the treatises that have lately appeared, to demonstrate that there are no particular inherent diversities between men and women, we hold to the opinion that one thorough season of house-cleaning is sufficient to prove the existence of awful and mysterious difference between the sexes" (493–94).

Men never become particularly threatening in this novel because they lack basic survival skills. Even the otherwise awe-inspiring Dr. Hopkins needs to be shaken out and dusted off whenever company comes.

In general, the sentimentalists further their own position in the battle of the sexes not by showing women to be the equals of men but by rendering men, especially good men, ridiculous. Women get to be better than men because good men are silly. Poor Simeon Halliday in *Uncle Tom's Cabin* is banished to the corner of the kitchen to engage in the "anti-patriarchal operation of shaving" (122) while his wife, Rachel, exerts her gentle, comprehensive rule. Good men are often laughable, which allows women's competence to shine all the more brightly in comparison.

Who would make the consummate orator? We might think it would be someone who, unlike Dr. Hopkins, thinks mightily about how he should say what he means to say and someone who, unlike James, is always in control of his utterances. The best orators, we might think today, are those who have mastered language and are capable of sophisticated rhetorical maneuvers. Aaron Burr would seem to be our man. Yet he is the villain of the novel because he is a seducer, a close relative of Susanna Rowson's Montraville and Hannah W. Foster's Major Sanford, villains of two early American seduction novels. Like them, he is an epistolary character, revealing his nefarious aims in letters. But things have changed in the intervening half-century. Burr, unlike his luckier progenitors, never actually succeeds in seducing anyone; Madame Frontignac, his target, is converted to the true path by Mary's irresistible powers of persuasion. In the early novels, the villains were bad because they ruined women. Their silver-tonguedness merely allowed them to accomplish their deflowerings. For Burr, unlucky in love, it is precisely his way with words that makes him a villain.

Burr is handsome and charming, "peculiarly graceful in form and moulding" (211), with a "beautifully-formed head" (211) and an "indescribable air of high breeding which marks the polished man of the world" (211). He possesses the "quickest perceptions and keenest delicacy of fibre" (213). Burr is the only character who seems particularly smart in this novel. He is also the only character who is able to form judgments of the other characters rather than existing in a kind of benevolent but oblivious haze. Here is an example of how he relates to people: "The Doctor was soon wide awake, talking with fervent animation on the topic of disinterested benevolence,—Burr the mean while [*sic*] studying him with the quiet interest of an observer of natural history, who sees a new species developing before him" (260).

Burr is a naturalist, examining the "simple-minded" Dr. Hopkins (259) while Hopkins goes animatedly on, unaware. In other words, unlike the other characters, Burr is quite conscious of his audience in order to appear to them in a way that would fulfill their desires, which he has previously figured out. This acuity is a terrible thing for Stowe, who associates persuasion with naturalness and not with craft (unlike Channing, who paradoxically insists that educated men need to study oratory in order to be true to nature). Burr resembles Plato's Ion at the moment when he peruses his audience for the signs of a reaction that will translate into his own gain. As noted in chapter 1, Ion remarks that "if I set them weeping, I myself shall laugh when I get my money, but if they laugh, it is I who have to weep at losing it" (Plato 221). Like Ion, Burr is not subsumed by the truth of his oration; like Ion, he always keeps his wits about him, searching after the main chance.

Stowe does not want the contrast to escape us between the doctor's topic, "disinterested benevolence," and Burr's overriding interestedness—"not [to] care a *sou* for truth on any subject not practically connected with his own schemes in life" (260; emphasis in the original). Aaron Burr is the only character who consciously maintains a distance between himself and others, the only one who sets himself apart from the common herd. He is also the only one who manipulates what he says. He not only accedes to the distance that words put between audience and speaker and the refuge that it provides for those who want to explore some of the shadier consequences of representation but embraces them. He values craft over transparency. I am describing at once what someone needs to be both a sentimental villain and (as discussed in more depth below and in the final chapter) an artist like Nathaniel Hawthorne.

Burr is also the kind of modulated, highly trained orator whom Channing valorizes (although Burr went to Princeton, not Harvard). Burr has learned the principles of oratory just like one of Channing's students; he uses them to gull his audience and gain his own ends. He *seems* like a trustworthy fellow and comes very, very close to spoiling two embodiments of virtuous womanhood in the novel, not to mention subsequently indulging in conspiracy and murder. So finally Burr is also the corrupt orator, the kind whom both Channing and Stowe most fear and fortify their theories against, though Channing fails to keep out such a man. Stowe reveals this failure.

Stowe wants to deny what is to us undeniable: the depth that people possess, the distance that can exist between seeming and being. She tries to close up this potential gap, to present a world of transparent orators. The sentimentalists' ideal orator is not an adept at language—far from it. The doctor and even James need to spend time working on the *how* of what they say, in order to make their delivery transparent, to remove from Dr. Hopkins the barrier of his erudition and from James the barrier of his comedy. The orator must develop a styleless style.

One way to avoid the slipperiness of words, their nasty habit of opening up spaces between seeming and being, is to avoid words altogether. Stowe's most favored characters, her winning orators, hardly speak at all. Rachel Halliday, Simeon's wife and Stowe's ideal character as many critics note, manages all the people around her with a "gentle 'Hadn't thee better?'" (*Uncle Tom's Cabin* 121). "Rachel moved gently, and quietly about, making biscuits, cutting up chicken, and diffusing a sort of sunny radiance over the whole proceeding generally" (*Uncle Tom's Cabin* 127). Her control emanates from her very presence.

In *The Minister's Wooing*, Mary Scudder manages to influence everyone around her, and like Rachel she does so with an incredible economy of speech. "With Mary it [the phrase "the strivings of the spirit"] was a living form,—as were all her words; for in nothing was the Puritan education more marked than in the earnest *reality* and truthfulness which it gave to language" (224; emphasis in the original). What does it mean for language to be a "living form" and to have "reality"? We get a hint if we turn to another reference in this novel to language as a living form, which occurs in another description of Mary. Mary is reading to her Catholic friend, Madame de Frontignac, who is in imminent danger of having an adulterous relationship with Aaron Burr. As Mary reads a prayer to the madame, Mary's face is "solemnly transparent, as of an angel" (396): "The greatest moral effects are like those of music,—not wrought out by sharp-sided intellectual propositions, but melted in by a divine fusion, by words that have mysterious, indefinite fulness of meaning, made living by sweet voices, which seem to be the out-throbbings of angelic hearts" (396).

Madame de Frontignac is led, at this instant, to the divine path. Unlike the description of James's moment of oratorical persuasiveness, this one depends for its effectiveness not on the way the speaker has put her words together but instead on innate qualities of the orator—a sweet voice, an angelic heart. Readers, we have found a winner.

Critics have commented on sentimentality's sodden quality, the copious amount of tears that drench these novels. In addition, note how often characters grow pale and wan, rosy glows suffuse cheeks, hearts throb. These kinds of descriptions alert readers that they are reading a sentimental novel, and we think it is because these kinds of descriptions show such a lack of imagination that only a scribbling woman could write them. That is not correct. These kinds of descriptions do not show a lack of imagination; they demonstrate a solution to a problem that the sentimentalists took very seriously: disingenuous eloquence. These phrases are always used (such clichés!), which implies that the language does not matter: it is the feeling behind it, the person behind it, who does.[18] The sentimental always moves toward the physical. "The Body Does Not Lie" could be its motto, with the implicit "But Words Do" as its corollary.[19]

We should note also how much the passage about Mary cited above resembles Thomas Sheridan's description of the inarticulate sounds that people make in times of extremity. He said that these sounds have "not more power in exciting sympathy, than any thing [*sic*] that can be done by mere words" (102). This belief, which Stowe and her colleagues share, might account for the copious numbers of heroes and heroines *in extremis* in these novels. Bodies hardly ever lie, but bodies undergoing the stress of overwhelming grief or the onslaught of illness are absolutely trustworthy.

To say that the sentimentalists provide a somatic solution to the problem of disingenuous eloquence is not to say that they find a refuge in gross corporeality. Here is a description of another character in *The Minister's Wooing,* Mrs. Jones, "a broad, buxom, hearty soul" (49): "[T]hey [her type] are as necessary to make up a world as cabbages to make up a garden; the great healthy principles of cheerfulness and animal life seem to exist in them in the gross; they are wedges and ingots of solid, contented vitality" (50).

Mrs. Jones varies from Mary in the matter of her sensitivity: she has none. "Those keen distinctions as to motives, those awful warnings . . . which made poor Deacon Twitchel weep, she listened to with great, round, satisfied eyes" (50). Her solidity puts into relief the sentimental heroine's thin and susceptible body.[20] Mrs. Jones's body is all wrong; it insulates her from the shocks of the world rather than leaving her exposed to them. Mrs. Jones is solid, and her body makes her impassive, whereas the frail, transparent body of the sentimental heroine registers her every emotion. She could not hide anything if she tried.[21]

Stowe's narrator in this novel observes: "The All-Father treats us as the mother does her 'infant crying in the dark'; He does not reason with our fears, or demonstrate their fallacy, but draws us silently to His bosom, and we are at peace" (425–26). It does not seem surprising that God in these sentimental novels might be rendered female, the All-*Father* in name only. God is just like Mary Scudder, and they share more than a certain gender marking. They are both quiet, offering physical succor rather than comforting words. The sentimental is motivated by the problem of disingenuous eloquence. The refuge from the problems of disingenuous eloquence found in the surprisingly articulate bodies of women is really only the oratorical idea of "character" taken to an extreme. The orator needs to be absolutely transparent to her audience, and she finds that words get in the way. The sentimental is after transparency. The surface of the body presents a picture that cannot be argued with because it does not engage the understanding. God is the silent nurturing mother, whose kindness you can see and feel, and the devil is the male who has a way with words.

Stowe does not think that anyone could become an orator, or at least a perfect one; rhetoric cannot be learned as a set of principles. Because persuasiveness depends on character—and this is still character defined the way that Channing defines it, sincerity as a kind of transparency—the best a person can do is to try to develop a perfect one (the seeds of which seem to be largely a matter of genetic inheritance). But if someone *is* blessed with a frail body and a thin skin, the way she knows that she has attained the height of development is the moment when she starts persuading other people that they need to develop their own characters. Sentimental eloquence has one end: the propagation of sentimental eloquence. This eloquence can be used to advance great social reforms—the humanizing of religion or the abolition of slavery. Unlike Channing's characterization of rhetoric as a means to an end, however, the accomplishments that the sentimentalists desire for society fall into place in the process of instituting a new kind of persuasiveness. What a wonderful world would ensue if we were all perfectly transparent to each other.

Sentimental persuasion takes on Channing's fears and his initial solution: the fear of disingenuous eloquence and the solution of the transparent orator as embodied in the child. Stowe's heroes and heroines—her winning orators—either are children or seem childlike in their unselfconsciousness and transparency. Their own bodies are the guarantors of their truthfulness. It is not so much that their bodies register their every thought. Even this formulation is misleading in that it supposes an inside that then appears on the outside, confirming our sense of their discreteness. It does not seem to me that these sentimental orators have thoughts, really; they only feel. They do not consider, they emanate. Their eloquence becomes detached from their volition. An utter passivity guarantees that the orator is not making things up; no excess of personality can sway the orator toward her own self-interest because she has no personality whatsoever. No wonder many people find sentimental characters flat.

Sentimental Immediacy

Stowe wrote *The Minister's Wooing* in 1859, seven years after she wrote *Uncle Tom's Cabin;* it has never been identified as having changed the course of history. It has nowhere near *Uncle Tom's Cabin*'s epic scope, with innumerable subplots whose geography encompasses a good chunk of the nation. *The Minister's Wooing* has just one and takes place in one small New England village (for a long time, the novel was labeled "local color").[22] This book involves slavery, but only as a secondary concern. The novel pits Hopkins's Edwardsean Calvinism against a more humane version of the kind that Henry Ward Beecher was preaching,[23] which would replace a rigid insistence on the inefficacy of faith and good works with a more flexible plan that would allow more than a minute number of predestined souls to gain admittance into heaven. *The Minister's Wooing* has not received nearly the amount of critical attention that *Uncle Tom's Cabin* has: this novel does not seem that relevant to us because its obvious concerns no longer resonate as *Uncle Tom's Cabin*'s concerns about race and slavery do.

The novel seems stubbornly time-bound in another way. Unlike another novel set in Puritan times that takes place in one small village and features a rather hapless Calvinist minister, it resists being taken symbolically. It is mired in the actual and is "first of all a glimpse of the everyday" (Duguid, no pagination). It is hard to abstract from such quiddities as "the hours meals were eaten and the proper time for retiring, the normal preparations for quiltings and wedding celebrations, and a list of the characteristic topics at parties" (Duguid). Though many critics have insisted that Hawthorne's *The Scarlet Letter* (1850) offers an accurate portrayal of the Puritans and though critics like Walter Benn Michaels have also linked Hawthorne to specifically nineteenth-century concerns,[24] Hawthorne's novel seems always to speak to its readers, whichever generation they may belong to. *The Scarlet Letter* appears to say something about human nature or the workings of patriarchal authority or the nature of representation in ways that seem either timeless or peculiarly pertinent to any given critic's own moment.

It has always been more of an effort to make Hawthorne's novel topical to either the time in which it takes place or the time in which it was written than otherwise. But I do not think that this is simply because of the critical tradition that we have inherited about the novel; it is also a result of the way the novel is written, its absence of everyday detail, for example, and its insistent ambiguity. *The Minister's Wooing* seems immovably historical (although it seems to be as much about nineteenth-century New England life as about eighteenth-century life). It is hard to make this novel into a recharging allegory for any given critic's contemporary time. Debates over predestination and grace through good works, details about tea rusks and snowy lawn tablecloths, lack the malleability required for timelessness.

Lawrence Buell has compared *The Scarlet Letter* and *The Minister's Wooing*. Though they both meditate on Puritanism, he sees them as very different from each other: "Hawthorne emerges as the more serious *student* of the New England past, who had to work his way back more deliberately into his subject than Stowe, whose more experiential knowledge of Puritanism equipped her better to provide an animated, closely textured documentary" ("Rival Romantic Interpretations" 94; emphasis in the original). Although Buell is at pains not to denigrate Stowe, his description does suggest the standard characterization of the sentimental as "documentary,"[25] leaving the designation "art" to the seemingly less autobiographical products of canonical authors. Buell states that Hawthorne struggled to capture his material whereas Stowe simply had to transcribe it. According to Buell, Stowe's own life determined her novel.[26] Hawthorne's experiences came indirectly from books, and his artistry transformed even them.

According to Buell, we can see an example of these different approaches in each novel's relationship to the past:

> [*The Scarlet Letter* reminds] us that the world being described really exists beyond our fingertips and must be retrieved painstakingly and imperfectly from printed sources. Stowe's narrators, on the other hand, while also conscious of a historical distance between themselves and their subjects, express no self-conscious reservations as to whether the past can be recaptured, as to whether they might be engaging in misrepresentation or conjecture. (82)

Buell is right that Stowe's narrator does not attend much to the difficulty of recapturing an earlier era. The narrator, in fact, is so cavalier about the difficulty of doing this that she ends up being inconsistent in how she represents the relationship between herself and the events narrated. At some points Stowe's narrator, like Hawthorne's, is an archivist, reconstructing events from old documents. Apropos of a letter that the temporarily reprobate sailor James has sent the pious Mary, the narrator notes in passing: "We got it out of a bundle of old, smoky, yellow letters, years after all the parties concerned were gone on the eternal journey beyond earth" (69). But notice how the sentence diverges from the thorny path of reconstructing the past in order to lift her readers up into the firmament. The sentence contrasts the transience of earthly cares to an eternal afterlife, which receives more emphasis. Elsewhere the narrator insists on the simultaneity of the narration and the events narrated. After telling the story of the slave Candace's resolution to believe in the catechism, the narrator, again in passing, relates: "While we have been telling you all this about her, she has fastened her horse, and is swinging leisurely up to the house with a basket on either arm" (140–41). Again, the sentence does not ask her readers to dwell on the time of narration but on something else, in this case on preparing themselves for the next turn of the story.

Both of these narrative interjections, though expressing different relationships between the tale and its telling, imply the reality of the events recounted. But even this is not consistent; at one point, the narrator admits that she has sent "unregenerate James" to sea "on purpose that our heroine may recover herself of that foolish partiality for him which all the Christian world seems bent on perpetuating" (181). As good readers of these kinds of novels, her intended audience knows that Mary is not going to marry her older suitor, Dr. Hopkins, whom she reveres but does not love. She is going to marry James. Furthermore, the comfy, mock-serious tone of Stowe's remark lets her audience know that she knows they know this. This quotation suggests that Stowe's readers might know the conventions of this type of novel. Thus Stowe assumes that her readers know this is a novel partaking of certain literary conventions, rather than simply a "documentary" recording of reality. Yet by the offhandedness of the remark she suggests that her readers do not really care. In fact, they are so far from caring that in this formulaic novel she can even expose her own hand in conforming to the formula: how she must stretch out the anticipation of James and Mary's eventual union. It does not matter that her intended readers know by page 26 that Mary and James will end up together. The pleasure of the text comes from experiencing the drawn-out process whereby Mary chooses her mate. Readers know that Mary is not going to marry Dr. Hopkins; Stowe knows that they know this. Yet she trusts that her readers will read on anyway.[27]

We can think about the relationship between formula and documentary in this text in two possible ways. Perhaps they work at odds with each other: the "documentary" quality of *The Minister's Wooing*, its insistent quiddities, cuts against its seeming like a formula. But I think that it is more likely the case that these formulas so structure the intended reader's sense of reality that to invoke them does nothing but ensconce this more firmly as documentary.[28] Stowe trusts that her audience reads these novels as though they are documentaries of what really happened even when confronted by admissions to the contrary. Yet this articulation does not capture what is going on for modern readers: for them, this is hardly a documentary.

Yes, Stowe is unselfconscious—to the point of blatant inconsistency—about the possibility of reconstructing the past. But it is blatant to us partially because we have been influenced by canonical male authors and their own set of concerns. Stowe's unselfconsciousness about representing the past becomes obvious only when we view the world through the lens of Hawthorne, who assumes it to be very difficult. Stowe simply does not see it as a problem or even as an issue. Her cavalier attitude to narration and her conventionality show her intended readers how much the story lives: her mistakes and her lack of singularity attest to her guilelessness. She is like the untrained orator, incapable of the studied effect. Her seeming lack of sophistication renders her all the more persuasive to an audience on the alert for sophistry. Respectful reader that he is, Buell makes a mistake in taking Stowe at her word. He loses the distance that a critic needs in order to recognize this as a move, the fundamental move of sentimentality in fact, rather than simply the result of Stowe's lack of artistry.

This novel is not a documentary in another sense. It prizes orality over the dead letter of writing. Hopkins, who does not fare well in the contest between orators, is associated with books and solitude: "[T]he place where our Doctor was happiest was the study" (91). Aaron Burr, who does the worst, is an inveterate letter writer. If letter writing revealed the characters' villainy in the early seduction novels, it has now begun to constitute it. But Mary—and she does well indeed in this rhetorical contest—flourishes in the realm of speech: "[N]or did [Dr. Hopkins] know why it was that the truths of his theology, when uttered by her tongue, had such a wondrous beauty as he never felt before" (93).

Yet an association with orality is not just something that allows us to distinguish this novel's characters: the text itself wants to be seen as "living speech." Note its cozy, conversational tone, its many apostrophes, and (as discussed above) the ease with which Stowe presents the past. No matter how many demurrals Stowe's narrator makes about her own contrivance, no matter how many times she suggests that the characters reside only in musty letters or never existed at all, her readers are not going to mind. Such admissions cannot overcome the overwhelming impression that this and other sentimental novels try to leave: one of immediacy and living presence. (In fact, the inconsistencies in the novel only add to the impression. As in a conversation, frame narratives shift or are forgotten; similarly, Stowe insists that the plot turns of this novel—like stories told in casual conversations[29]—cannot be predicted in advance, as the epigraph to this chapter shows.) This is a novel whose main effect is the kind of immediacy found in conversing with someone else. And this text literally began orally: unlike her other novels, Stowe dictated *The Minister's Wooing* to a secretary.[30] This text allows us to see that the dichotomy we commonly invoke between speech and writing might be permeable: just as some orators speak as some men write (the famed orator and Massachusetts legislator Fisher Ames mentioned in the previous chapter seems to have spoken thus),[31] so there can be written texts that want to be mistaken as speech, read as though they were being listened to or, even better sentimentally speaking, witnessed.

In *The Minister's Wooing*, Stowe wants us to believe that these characters and events exist apart from anything the narrator can say (or deny) about them: like the text itself, these characters do not want to be seen as crafted. Stowe has not created characters but revealed a set of people. To apprehend this novel as "documentary" is to read it as she wants it to be experienced. This novel is time-bound, but not just because it explores a dead religious question or long-forgotten New England customs. This novel embodies a particular nineteenth-century solution to problems in nineteenth-century rhetorical theory by insisting on its own artlessness.

Paradoxes of Sentimentality: Text as Oratory

This study proceeds chronologically, but a less obvious structure also guides its unfolding: a series of paradoxes. As we have seen in the preceding pages, sentimental rhetoric derives its shape from its solution to the problem of professional male rhetoric and oratory: sentimental novels feature orators whose persuasiveness can be trusted. Yet what do I mean by calling a character in a novel an orator even though the novel does not announce that as her profession (in fact, there were very few women orators in this period)? In what sense, beyond the conventional situation of characters trading dialogue, is she speaking? And, even more absurdly, what do I mean by suggesting that these sentimental texts are themselves oratorical productions in some sense? In sum, how can text be oratory? I have alluded briefly above to how *The Minister's Wooing* wants to be seen as oratory, but I want to offer a fuller discussion of the question of written text as oratory, using *Uncle Tom's Cabin* as my example.

Let me begin with the fact that *Uncle Tom's Cabin* was frequently heard as well as read because of the practice of families reading it aloud to each other in the Victorian parlor. It was read publicly as well: a few years after the novel's publication, Stowe commissioned Mary E. Webb, an early African-American professional performer, to read selections of the novel to audiences in the United States and England.[32] Although Stowe changed the text of *Uncle Tom's Cabin* in the process of preparing it to be read publicly, the novel already possessed many oratorical characteristics.

Like nineteenth-century oratory, *Uncle Tom's Cabin*'s aim is persuasion: characters want to persuade other characters to adopt a particular worldview, and the novel as a whole wants to do the same thing to the reader. The diminutive Mrs. Bird, trying to persuade her husband (Senator Bird) of a higher law that reveals slavery to be immoral, is a stand-in for the diminutive Stowe, who wants her intended audience to adopt this view themselves. Stowe renders these scenes orally: although many actual people in the nineteenth-century presumably were persuaded to adopt different political positions through reading or reflection, characters within *Uncle Tom's Cabin* change their minds through other characters' speaking. For example, Mrs. Bird's act of persuasion happens orally, even though it is rendered textually. That is, characters persuade other characters by speaking to them—even when they "speak" through their bodies and not their words.

If we look closely at these and other scenes of characters trying to persuade other characters, we might notice something beyond their oral dimension: although sentimental novels are known for their intrusive narrators who try to mold their readers' reactions at every turn, these scenes are rendered with a minimum of authorial intrusion. For example, the scene of Mrs. Bird's persuading her husband of the immorality of the Fugitive Slave Act, passed in 1850, is rendered as a series of quotations.[33] This scene offers an example of what Gérard Genette would call "reported speech," the most mimetic way of rendering speech (as compared to what Genette calls "narrated speech," which occurs when the narrator records a character's speaking without indicating the character's actual words: for example, "Then Mrs. Bird took her husband to task for his support of the Fugitive Slave Act"). But it is reported speech of a particular radical kind: with two exceptions, the series of quotations is unmarked even by phrases like "he said" or "she replied." Genette associates the abolition of such "narrating instances" with modernist novels (173), yet here we find it in a novel that few have characterized as being formally avant-garde. Reported speech offers a pure form of mimesis: it allows the reader to witness, minus the mediating presence of the narrator, what really transpired (that is, what really transpired in the fictional world of the novel, whose fictionality this scene and others are trying desperately hard to make the reader forget). It puts the reader in the presence of Mrs. Bird and her speech. This is an oratorical scene because it strongly evokes the presence of the speaker.

If we turn to the two exceptions to the rule of reported speech within this scene, we realize that these moments of narrative intrusion, although they mediate Mrs. Bird's presence, add to the oratorical nature of the scene in other ways. The only narrative intrusion in this series of direct quotations that follows the conventional form of "he said" is followed by a telling phrase: "'Of course, it would be a very painful duty,' began Mr. Bird, *in a moderate tone*" (73; emphasis added). Certainly this adverbial phrase gives us information about Mr. Bird's character: he is or at least fancies himself to be a man of moderation. It also alludes to the problem with Mr. Bird and other "moderate" men: the Fugitive Slave Act should elicit strong emotion. But the phrase also provides oratorical information: it shapes how the reader hears Mr. Bird's voice in her head. The other narrative intrusion in this series of quotations is a paragraph detailing Mr. Bird's character and his reaction to his wife's speech: we learn that "turning away anybody that was in trouble never had been [Mr. Bird's] forte" (73) and "that his wife knew it. . . . So he had recourse to the usual means of gaining time. . . . [H]e said 'ahem,' and coughed several times. . . . Mrs. Bird, seeing the defenceless condition of the enemy's territory, had no more conscience than to push her advantage" (73). By positioning Mr. Bird as the recipient of Mrs. Bird's "assault," the paragraph reinforces the impression that she is the speaker and he the audience, thus reinforcing the impression that this scene is less a dialogue than a speech.

The paragraph also forges a relationship between Mr. Bird, the direct addressee of Mrs. Bird's speech, and the intended reader, a less direct but even more important addressee. This paragraph has as its intended audience both a male and a female reader (not that an actual female reader cannot adopt the male intended reader subject position and vice versa). Stowe assumes that the intended male reader wants, like Mr. Bird, to be seen as a good Samaritan. Forged in the first sentence, the relationship between Mr. Bird and the male intended reader grows more complicated by the end of this paragraph. On one hand, this reader might, like Mr. Bird, continue to fortify himself against Mrs. Bird's speech. But the passage also mocks Mr. Bird, thereby creating a distance between Mr. Bird and the male reader: Mr. Bird has become an unreliable narrator in the sense that his self-presentation is at odds with his internal beliefs (the narrator reveals that Mr. Bird is not as tough as he wants to appear). The intended male reader, audience to both Mrs. Bird's speech and the narrator's comic revelation about Mr. Bird's unreliability, is gently encouraged to desist from his own support of the Fugitive Slave Act and adopt the proper view of the matter. It invites the male reader both to identify with Mr. Bird and to improve on him. In other words, this paragraph-long narrative intervention pays sustained attention to the audience of Mrs. Bird's speech. If this scene were being filmed, this paragraph would translate into a reaction shot: what effect does this speech have on the audience, Mr. Bird, and by extension the male reader, who is figured, through the existence of these direct quotations (these speeches), as another auditor of the scene?[34]

In fact, similar "reaction shots" pepper sentimental scenes of persuasion. Later in *Uncle Tom's Cabin*, when the angelic Eva finally persuades the slave girl Topsy to be good, another series of quotations (though qualified with markers as to who is speaking) is punctuated by a paragraph detailing Topsy's reaction to Little Eva's words:

> The round, keen eyes of the black child were overcast with tears;—large, bright drops rolled heavily down, one by one, and fell on the little white hand. Yes, in that moment, a ray of real belief, a ray of heavenly love, had penetrated the darkness of her heathen soul! . . . [T]he beautiful child, bending over her, looked like the picture of some bright angel stooping to reclaim a sinner. (258)

Here the narrator shows how Topsy, the audience for Eva's persuasive speech, reacts to it. But something different is going on here than in the case of Mr. Bird. The paragraph, with its insistent color-coding, seems to label Topsy as different from the intended reader (although many actual black readers read *Uncle Tom's Cabin*, as Robert Levine notes, the intended reader is white). Yet the last line confounds that division: Topsy morphs from a "poor [black] child" (158) into a "sinner." We might read this as equal in its offensiveness to the narrator's description of Topsy's "heathen soul." I would argue for a contrary reading, however: Topsy's blackness does not distinguish her from the white audience of intended readers here; instead it allows her to become representative. That is, what is so offensive to modern readers of Stowe, the equation of black skin with ignorance or taint, here binds Topsy with the white intended reader, who is also a sinner as long as America countenances slavery. Like Topsy, the intended reader must learn to be good.

Why pay so much attention to the audience's reaction? It is an oratorical trope in the nineteenth century that the most eloquent orators inspire strong feeling in their auditors—to the extent of making people forget what was actually said. Here, for example, is Thomas Jefferson's reaction to hearing Daniel Webster's speeches: "When [Webster] had spoken in opposition to *my* opinion, had produced a great effect, & I myself been highly delighted & moved, I have asked myself when he ceased, 'What the Devil has he said,' & could never answer the enquiry" (qtd. in Looby 276; emphasis in the original). Eloquence cannot be captured by words alone, but words can compensate by both using what Christopher Looby calls the "trope of inexpressibility" (275) and expressing instead the effect of such eloquence on the audience member. These sentimental "reaction shots" testify to the power of the speaker, but at a deeper level they are meant to evoke the oratorical situation itself.

I have been discussing how *Uncle Tom's Cabin* figures some of its scene as orations diegetically, but it also figures itself as oratory at the extradiegetic level. Jane Tompkins notes how "[g]roups of characters blend into the same character, while the plot abounds with incidents that mirror one another" ("Sentimental Power" 134). Less sympathetic readers simply find the novel unbearably repetitive. Tompkins attributes this repetitiveness to Stowe's typological way of structuring the plot. But we might also attribute this repetition to the text's commitment to orality. Alessandro Portelli names some of the qualities associated with orality: "incorporeal, ephemeral, mutable," against writing's association with "the lasting, the tangible" (15). Oral performances disappear, cannot be referred back to (except in memory), and thus often employ repetition as a way to engrave themselves into a reader's mind. Stowe tells the same stories over and over again from scene to scene: for example, endless variants on how slavery rips apart the black family. Certainly repetition is just a feature of any pedagogical project, but this repetition might also be a function of how often pedagogy is delivered orally and how much it responds to the oral situation: for example, professors today might be especially inclined to repeat important ideas when they know that their students are not particularly avid note takers.[35]

Uncle Tom's Cabin repeats itself; it also, on an extradiegetic level, directly addresses its audience. I have described how much of the narration in *The Minister's Wooing* is rendered colloquially, as if the narrator is chatting rather than writing to us. I have also mentioned the apostrophes that speckle that novel. *Uncle Tom's Cabin* is similarly speckled but also features a sustained apostrophe at the end, in its "Concluding Remarks," where the narrator, whom we are meant to see as Stowe herself, defends the veracity of her novel and offers a passionate plea to the reader to take a stand against slavery. In *The Pursuit of Signs*, Jonathan Culler discusses apostrophe in the context of Romantic poetry. He associates apostrophe with voice and presence. Referring to the "O" that often precedes a direct address, Culler writes that "[t]he poet makes himself a poetic presence through an image of voice, and nothing figures voice better than the pure *O* of undifferentiated voicing" (142). He goes on to say that "[a] phrase like 'O wild West Wind' evokes poetic presence because the wind becomes a *thou* only in relation to a poetic act" (141–42; emphasis in the original). Apostrophe evokes presence because the addressee of the apostrophe is conjured through the act of apostrophe itself, which is the act of a poet speaking.

Yet the situation is slightly different in Stowe's case, and not just because we are dealing with prose, not poetry. Culler is concerned with apostrophes addressed to inanimate or nonhuman objects; Stowe addresses the apostrophes in "Concluding Remarks" to different groups of people: "To you, generous, noble-minded men and women, of the South" (403); "Farmers of Massachusetts, of New Hampshire, of Vermont, of Connecticut" (403–4); "Christian men and women of the North!" (405). These living but absent addressees do not need to be summoned to sentience by a poetic act; they need only be called together to hear the narrator's speech so that they might change their sentiments regarding slavery. Stowe's apostrophes not only bind a fragmented regional populace into a national community (brought together through their commitment to eradicating the sin that affects all of them, not just Southerners) but, more basically, gather an audience together to hear the voice of the narrator rouse them to action. Unlike the diegetic scenes of persuasion where the narrator must massage the actual addressee of Mrs. Bird's speech (Mr. Bird) into a proxy or goad to the intended reader, the addressees of the narrator's apostrophes in the "Concluding Remarks" *are* the members of the intended audience. Mrs. Bird's act of persuasion and the "Concluding Remarks" offer a sharp contrast in terms of narrative intrusion. This differencc affects the reactions of contemporary readers: the former scene barely registers as noteworthy because we are so used to scenes of reported speech, whereas the latter can strike many readers as annoying or odd ("Don't tell me how to think!" or "How old-fashioned this way of writing is!"). Yet we should note how similar they in fact are: what unites them are the characteristics of oratory that they both possess, in their evocation of voice and presence. In "The Concluding Remarks," it is as if Stowe's own voice can be heard by the reader beyond the confines of the page.

But it still is an "as if." Threaded throughout Culler's discussion of apostrophe is the question of why contemporary literary critics find apostrophe an embarrassment. He finds that the answer lies in its artificiality: "This trope proclaims its artificial character rather too obviously" (152). That is, it too thinly disguises that poetic presence is the result of a mere figure. The final chapter takes up the embarrassing nature of sentimental prose in more depth, but for now I would like to pursue this idea of a textual object pursuing an impossible goal of vocal creation. Textual objects cannot really summon an audience to hear their persuasive speech. Yet a textual object like *Uncle Tom's Cabin* sets the stage for such a self-transformation by making a case against textuality within its own pages.

Sandra Gustafson offers a heuristic for understanding the complicated relationship between text and speech in Western culture: "Text that is privileged for its permanence and stability is set against the ruptures effected by demonic speech. When the powers of the living voice are celebrated, they are imagined triumphing over the dead letter" (xvi). In other words, text and speech are always opposed, but the privileged term can shift: sometimes writing is held up above speech and vice versa. When speech is celebrated, it is celebrated for its immediacy; when it is condemned (in favor of writing), it is characterized as dangerously seductive. Sentimental rhetoric, influenced by both nineteenth-century evangelism and the discipline of rhetoric and oratory, commits itself to the celebration of speech.

Uncle Tom's Cabin celebrates the living voice, and it does this by making an argument against the dead letter. Let me demonstrate this system of values via a brief tour through some actual letters (both alphabetic and epistolary) that show up in *Uncle Tom's Cabin* in order to show how the novel wants us to embrace a paradoxical illiteracy, what I call antiliteracy. This novel comes out against the letter. As critics like Houston Baker have noted, Frederick Douglass's *Narrative* intertwines his freedom with his literacy. *Uncle Tom's Cabin*, however, views literacy with suspicion. At one point, Tom and Little Eva try to write a letter to Tom's wife, but they produce something that looks "quite like writing" (216). This phrase is worth mulling over: in *Uncle Tom's Cabin* writing is always "quite like writing": a fake, a thing that promises knowledge about the world but instead acts as a barrier to it.

At the beginning *Uncle Tom's Cabin* sets Tom on the path to literacy. The son of Tom's master, George, has begun to teach Tom the rudiments of reading; but just as the novel takes Tom farther and farther South, toward worse and worse masters but ultimately toward Redemption, so the novel unravels the little bit of literacy that Tom has attained, toward something better. The following passage takes place on the boat to New Orleans that takes Tom away from his first, most benevolent master. Here Tom engages in a strange method of reading:

> It had been his custom to get the Bible read to him by his master's children, in particular by young Master George; and, as they read, he would designate, by bold, strong marks and dashes, with pen and ink, the passages which more particularly gratified his ear or affected his heart. His Bible was thus marked through, from one end to the other, with a variety of styles and designations; so he could in a moment seize upon his favorite passages, without the labor of spelling out what lay between them;—and while it lay there before him, every passage breathing of some old home scene, and recalling some past enjoyment, his Bible seemed to him all of this life that remained, as well as the promise of a future one. (132)

So Tom does not read the letters on the page but the strong marks and dashes (reminiscent of breathing marks that orators use to mark up their speeches), which evoke voices: they "gratified his ear." And these voices call to mind not the passages themselves but living pictures.[36] But why then mark the passages at all? Why not just remember scenes when he was read to and dispense with the book itself? Stowe seems to be saying that readers need the passages themselves to remind them of the pictures: in Tom's case, the letters on the page—because he does not read them—must themselves form a kind of picture that spurs his memory. To be effective, letters must become pictures.

The novel actually literalizes this desire, as we can see from one of its supposed comic interludes. Master George has written Tom a letter, which Tom loves so much that he wants to turn it into a picture: "He . . . even held a council with Eva on the expediency of getting it framed, to hang up in his room. Nothing but the difficulty of arranging it so that both sides of the page would show at once stood in the way of this undertaking" (236). And if this seems just an odd throwaway, at another moment in the text, letters (this time in the sense of written characters) do become pictures. Here the narrator is describing Senator Bird's ideas about fugitive slaves: "[B]ut then his idea of a fugitive was only an idea of the letters that spell the word,—or at the most, the image of a little newspaper picture of a man with a stick and bundle, with 'Ran away from the subscriber' under it. The magic of the real presence of distress . . . this he had never tried" (80–81). As in Stowe's description of Tom's antiliteracy, "real presence," which distinguishes eloquent orators, is opposed to the false letter. Letters morph into pictures, and for Stowe pictures are irresistible. This quotation about letters morphing into an escaped slave shows that Tom's strange antiliteracy is a recommendation for the reader; Stowe does not envision her audience to be illiterate slaves, but she certainly imagines some of them to be eloquent white men; and for both, letters need to become pictures.

Recall Stowe's plan for *Uncle Tom's Cabin*: to write a novel that is actually a series of pictures. Although Senator Bird's defenses were weakened by the speech of his wife, what finally convinces him of the higher law assumed by his wife is the picture of the recently escaped, half-dead Eliza in the Birds' kitchen: Mr. Bird "started, quite amazed at the sight that presented itself:—A young and slender woman, with garments torn and frozen" (74). Eliza here stands as one of Stowe's mute and highly persuasive orators. Stowe's characters learn how to read words as pictures that attest to "the mute appeal" of the orator. Her intended audience is to do the same. To be moved by *Uncle Tom's Cabin* is to show how you have learned this lesson, how you have become a different sort of reader: an antiliterate one.

Gustafson continues her discussion of speech-text opposition by noting that this "set of mutually constituting symbolic categories . . . produces speech and text as performatives that signify through the very choice of medium" (xvi). But what should be done in a case of a text whose choice of medium contradicts its allegiance to the living voice? Rather than undermine Gustafson's heuristic, *Uncle Tom's Cabin* shows how strongly it flourishes in the nineteenth century. So strongly were sentimental readers convinced of the power of "living speech" that they could forget the textuality of what they were reading (but thought they were hearing or witnessing). In this sentimental novel, far from the medium being the message, the medium is undermined and—if all goes well—transformed by it. The pinnacle of sentimentality saw readers accepting this transformation and being transformed by it in turn.

3

The Art of Character in Louisa May Alcott's Work

The Minister's Wooing charts the triumph of the sentimental orator; Henry Ward Beecher embodies his downfall. But Louisa May Alcott has already foretold his defeat. Only a decade and a half separates *The Minister's Wooing* from the "scandal summer" of 1874, when the alleged affair of Henry Ward Beecher with one of his parishioners riveted the nation and made people regret their previous susceptibility to this silver-tongued preacher. A few years earlier, Louisa May Alcott's *Work: A Story of Experience* (1872) was published in a magazine edited by Beecher. Alcott did not single-handedly undermine the authority of the sentimental orator, but her novel allows modern readers to understand why this figure would soon meet with such skepticism. In this chapter I offer an explanation of why sentimentality loses its persuasiveness in the last third of the nineteenth century and how this process is hastened—rather than hindered—by some of its own practitioners.[1]

One of my claims in this chapter is historical: certain cultural developments in the last third of the nineteenth century led readers and listeners to distrust sentimental rhetoric. I show how the entry of middle-class women into the workforce,[2] the new interest in parlor theatricals and dramatic training,[3] and, more abstractly, the shift from "character" to "personality" are reflected and reinforced in Alcott's and Beecher's sentimental writings. Yet my account avoids pinpointing whether the waning power of sentimental rhetoric during this period is caused by elements outside sentimental texts or by elements within it. The extrinsic and intrinsic cannot be separated because the historical developments that I focus on—such as the popularity of François Delsarte's acting method and the decreased attention paid to "character"—register *within* these texts. It is also plausible to suppose they are reinforced or hastened by them. These new textual themes come more and more to preoccupy their readers and cause them to question their previous susceptibility to sentimental rhetoric.

Yet to suggest that sentimental stories and novels disappear toward the end of the nineteenth century or that sentimental rhetoric loses its ability to persuade each and every one of its readers even in this period of lessening influence is to speak falsely: Alcott's *Little Women* has never gone out of print, and Beecher retained his ministry even after his trial. It seems more accurate to say that the power of sentimentality oscillates, and in the last part of the nineteenth century texts employing sentimental rhetoric did not move readers to the extent or on the scale that *Uncle Tom's Cabin* had.

The second claim of this chapter is a literary-critical one. If I am right about the oscillating power of sentimental rhetoric in the nineteenth century (specifically why this power falters once working women and white men start using it), we might want to revise what was itself already a revision in critical thought about these popular nineteenth-century American women writers. The historian Barbara Welter started what amounted to a critical industry with "The Cult of True Womanhood" (1966), which described how nineteenth-century Americans idealized the white middle-class woman into a pious, submissive, sexless creature. Literary critics took this idea of "true womanhood" and linked it to the "scribbling women" writers, whose apparently "separate sphere" allowed critics to discern the hidden rebellion that lay below the surface conformity of their writings.[4] The "separate spheres" paradigm began to be strafed in the late 1980s and came under increased attack in the late 1990s. In 1989 the historian Laura McCall suggested that Welter had cherry-picked her sources when it came to identifying "The Cult of True Womanhood" and its four pillars of piety, purity, domesticity, and submissiveness; Cathy Davidson began dismantling this model as well as the association between women writers and sentimentality in a special issue of *American Literature* (1998), asking "why is the metaphor of the separate spheres both immediately compelling and ultimately unconvincing as an explanatory device?" (444). Collections like Mary Chapman and Glenn Hendler's *Sentimental Men* (1999) and Millette Shamir and Jennifer Travis's *Boys Don't Cry?* (2002) continued the job.

But it has always troubled me that the wholesale rejection of the separate spheres model has a hard time explaining any way but condescendingly why the initial model ever looked good. It seems that these earlier feminist critics were simply blinded by their commitment to cultural feminism. But what if this initial insight really has merit? Let me tread lightly: "True Womanhood" was not the name of a nineteenth-century club that actual women knew the name of and could join (only middle-class and white women need apply); nor were the virtues associated with it as straightforward as Welter suggests. Using Stowe's and Alcott's work as well as that of Stowe's sister Catharine Beecher as data, "submissiveness" never involved actual passivity on the part of women: it involved the semblance of adhering to the wishes of men while using women's moral influence to sway them. Or as Catharine Beecher wrote in her *Treatise on Domestic Economy* (1841): "[N]one will deny, then to American women, more than to any others on earth, is committed the exalted privilege of extending over the world those blessed influences, which are to renovate degraded man" (37). American women may not be fighting on the battlefields or offering orations on the Fourth of July, but they are still able to exercise their power (which takes the form of "influence") on the men around them, who only seem to hold all the power.

We might still gingerly use the term "true womanhood" with some caveats in mind: not as a lived reality but as an ideal accessible to some women and not others (working-class women, women of color),[5] as a regional rather than national phenomenon,[6] and as involving a complicated version of submissiveness. We might also rescue the separate spheres paradigm to the extent that we can begin to see that—while sentimental rhetoric is not inextricably tied to the domestic, pious, pure, and "submissive" woman—she does allow it to flourish.[7] Working women as well as white men (neither of whom are domestic) can use sentimental rhetoric, but they do so only at the risk of sullying its reputation.

Alcott, Delsarte, and the Working Woman

When Christie Devon, the protagonist of Louisa May Alcott's novel *Work: A Story of Experience* (1872), addresses an audience of working women at the end of the novel, she is a huge success, "an example to comfort, touch, and inspire them" (333). We know that Christie is electrifying because Alcott tells us that she is. Yet Alcott does not reveal to us what this female orator actually says.

One critic has explained Alcott's omission in terms of a contemporary notion of feminist teleology: he implies that Alcott lived too early to know how to depict an empowered female voice:

> [T]he scene of [Christie's] great triumph, which would seem to cry out for dramatic representation, is reported in brief summary, and we never hear Christie's new voice. It is evident that Alcott does not know what that voice would sound like, and that the fantasy of a mediating woman's voice, which ought by virtue of much labor to be Alcott's own, is only fantasy after all. (Wallace 272)

In fact, we do know what Christie's voice sounds like. Alcott has described it to us: "then in a clear, steady voice, with the sympathetic undertone to it that is so magical in its effect, Christie made her first speech in public since she left the stage" (332). It might seem as though I am quibbling. Obviously Wallace meant that we never hear Christie's words. But his substitution of "voice" for "words" deserves attention because it performs the same substitution found in *Work* and in other sentimental novels. These novels believe that a character's voice is much more persuasive than her actual words.

This critic is making the same sort of substitution that the novel does, yet he criticizes sentimentality for not being effectively political. He is not alone in either move. "Voice" has become a key term in cultural feminism,[8] yet many cultural feminists share in the contempt that accrues around the label "sentimental." As noted, Elaine Showalter, who wrote the introduction to *Alternative Alcott*, prefers to call Alcott's writing "realist," explicitly rejecting "sentimental."[9] Ironically, Alcott's *Work* paves the way for this kind of rejection. It reveals a crack in sentimental rhetoric: when too much pressure is applied, sentimental rhetoric crumbles before the growing skepticism of its reader. In order to make *Work* seem valuable to such a reader we must claim that it is not sentimental. *Work* causes this collapse not by satirizing sentimental conventions (as Mark Twain would do) but by embracing them and trying to adapt them for new kinds of speakers.[10] By being *au courant* in terms of its depiction of a protagonist who is a working woman rather than a true woman, it demonstrates (as explained later in the chapter) why true women were natural orators and working women could only appear to be so.

Despite Showalter's demurral, it seems to me that Louisa May Alcott is self-consciously working in the sentimental tradition. *Work*, in fact, had the backing of two famous sentimentalists. Begun in 1861 and originally entitled *Success*, Alcott's novel, retitled, was serialized in 1872–1873 in the *Christian Union*, which was edited by Henry Ward Beecher. Louisa May Alcott had the imprimatur not just of Beecher but of his most famous sister as well, as we can see in a passage from a letter that Harriet Beecher Stowe wrote to Alcott a few months before her brother began publishing *Work*: "In my many fears for my country and in these days when so much seductive and dangerous literature is pushed forward, the success of your domestic works has been to me most comforting. It shows that after all our people are *all right* and that they love the right kind of thing" (qtd. in Saxton 314; emphasis in the original). *Little Women* had just been published in 1868–69 and had made Alcott famous. Stowe approves of Alcott. But what is it that she approves of?

Stowe could simply mean that she likes the way *Little Women* ends with everything tied up in a domestic bow (despite how disappointed many readers felt, even at the time, in Jo's choice of mate). Yet Stowe does not point to particular plot elements. She emphasizes the emotion that Alcott evokes in her audience. Alcott assures Stowe that the American people "love the right kind of thing." The reassurance that Alcott provides echoes Stowe's own suggestion at the end of *Uncle Tom's Cabin* about what individuals can do in the face of slavery: "they can see to it that *they feel right*" (385; emphasis in the original). This is the desire that readers have faulted Stowe for ever since, accusing her of caring more about people's feelings than about political action. Yet it is an unfair accusation: the two were not separable for Stowe and for many of her contemporaries. Rejecting the pertinence of the "catharsis" model for nineteenth-century American readers, Robyn Warhol writes that "from the Victorian perspective, crying over *Uncle Tom's Cabin* or *Little Women* did not drain a reservoir of stored feelings, nor did it debilitate readers from taking action in the extra-textual world" ("As You Stand" 114). For Stowe, who is also following nineteenth-century theories about psychology, people will act only if their emotions have been touched. The masses need to be more than convinced; they need to be persuaded.

Work tells the story of Christie Devon, who is ultimately a master persuader but who begins as an orphan raised by an ineffectual aunt and an acquisitive uncle in a New England village. She leaves her home for the city and after a series of different jobs—servant, actress, governess, companion, seamstress—marries the son of a good Quaker woman. Soon after the marriage, Christie's husband is killed in the Civil War. The novel ends (as noted earlier in the chapter) with Christie's attending a meeting to address the plight of working women and experiencing a "sudden and uncontrollable impulse" (332) that compels her "to rise in her place and ask leave to speak" (332). She is a sensation, "where more impressive than any thing [*sic*] she said was the subtle magnetism of character" (333). Like other sentimental novels, *Work* foregrounds the "natural" over the highly trained speaker. *Work* loves especially a speaker who has suffered. The working women who make up Christie's audience know that "[h]ardship and sorrow, long effort and late-won reward had been hers" (333), and this knowledge connects Christie to them. Hepsey, an ex-slave whom we meet much earlier in the novel while Christie is working as a servant, shows even more clearly this predilection on the part of sentimental novels. Hepsey is unschooled in all but the pain she has experienced. She becomes a model of persuasiveness. Alcott notes that "[h]er story was like many another, yet, being the first Christie had ever heard, and told with the unconscious eloquence of one who had suffered and escaped, it made a deep impression on her" (26).[11]

If sentimental novels favor inarticulate people who are not in control of their own words, even better are people who do not need to speak at all. Mrs. Sterling, Christie's eventual mother-in-law, "influenced others by the *silent* power of character" (222; emphasis added). A speaker gains power in proportion to how little she consciously strives for effect. Mrs. Sterling could not strive less. She has no control over her effect on other people; it comes from the exudation of her essence.

Even when a speaker has to take recourse to speaking, it is much better when she speaks without any thought about what impression she might make. Thus we have this description of Christie's own unconscious eloquence as she recounts the death of her Aunt Betsey to a suitor, Mr. Fletcher:

> Mr. Fletcher tried not to smile as Christie sobbed out the old-fashioned name, but a minute afterward there were actually tears in his eyes, for, as if won by his sympathy, she poured out the homely little story of Aunty Betsey's life and love, unconsciously pronouncing the kind old lady's best epitaph in the unaffected grief that made her broken words so eloquent. (56)

Here too Alcott pairs unconsciousness and eloquence. There is nothing calculated about Christie's delivery. In fact, she seems to lack control over it. Orators at the mercy of their emotions could not possibly deceive their audience. Thus Christie's tears only add to her eloquence. The fact her words are broken by grief—this lack of fluency—makes her persuasive. The quotation seems proof of the Scottish rhetorician Thomas Sheridan's remark quoted in the previous chapter (which will be referred to again), about the power that the inarticulate and pained wield over us, the power of their "inarticulate sounds."

If Christie resembles no one so much as Mary Scudder of *The Minister's Wooing*, a parallel can also be drawn between that novel's Aaron Burr and Mr. Fletcher.[12] Like Burr, Fletcher is marked as an "aristocrat" (52). Like Burr, he has a habit of observing those around him, of standing a little apart, as revealed in his first reaction to Christie's story about her aunt's demise ("[he] tried not to smile" [56]). Like Burr, Fletcher is adept at conversation: "he exerted himself to be as brilliant as possible, and succeeded admirably" (244). Yet here we have the kiss of sentimental death. People must never exert themselves to achieve a certain effect.

The novel explicitly compares Christie's two suitors, the polished Mr. Fletcher and the workmanlike David Sterling, Christie's eventual husband. It initially seems to render Mr. Fletcher's and David's differences as aesthetic ones:

> [David's] simple English sounded harsh, after the foreign phrases that slipped so easily over the other's tongue. . . . More than once he was right, but failed to prove it, for Mr. Fletcher skilfully changed the subject or quenched him with a politely incredulous shrug.
>
> Even in the matter of costume, poor David was worsted. . . . Christie used to think his suit of sober gray the most becoming man could wear; but now it looked shapeless and shabby, beside garments which bore the stamp of Paris. . . . David's tie was so plain no one observed it. (244–45)

The aesthetic quickly merges into the nationalistic: Alcott makes a point here about the contrast between manly American straightforwardness and effeminate European urbanity. Yet these sartorial differences do not just register patriotically. They signal great differences in these two men's styles of persuasiveness. David lacks style altogether. Like his tie, he disappears into the crowd. He is just like James in *The Minister's Wooing*: plain-speaking (though like James he also has education and money). Sentimentality cultivates a style that aspires not to be recognized as one. It wants no textual obstacle to come between itself and the reader's experience of it. David cannot hope to best Fletcher in a contest of verbal fluency, and this deficit is why the novel shows its preference for him in having Christie choose him as her husband.[13]

I have been trying to interpret Mr. Fletcher's and David's differences as differences in kinds of persuasiveness. Yet we might argue that they are simply differences in class. When it comes to white men, the sentimental novel prefers common to elite, hard-working to wealth-inheriting—in other words, middle-class energy to aristocratic anomie.[14] I am not denying this. What I am trying to argue is that the sentimental author prefers these things as a result of a prior commitment to a certain kind of persuasion. David's workmanlike clothing does not signify merely "common man" but "sincere man" and hence "good speaker."[15] The sentimental novel is trying to change the world not through a redistribution of wealth but through a redistribution of eloquence (the redistribution of wealth will follow).

Yet there is something curious about this redistribution. As we have seen before, in the sentimental novel the most powerful eloquence comes from those lacking traditional kinds of power (thus David can be a good speaker but not a great one). In the sentimental universe, the traditionally powerless reign: women, children, and slaves. Their power as speakers comes from their exclusion from traditional sources of cultural capital like the universities, the site of conventional oratorical training. But this redistribution leads to an odd static that we modern critics experience when we try to listen sympathetically to these sentimental novels. Christie is at her most eloquent, as was Mary Scudder, when she is at her most inarticulate, as we can see when she talks, brokenly, about her Aunt Betsey. Christie is at her most eloquent the less she says and the more she simply *is*. She mostly *is* sympathetic, both toward others and as an object of sympathy herself. But the more she relies on this sympathetic essence, the less of an individual with distinctive characteristics she becomes.

Glenn Hendler has noted Christie's blankness, the "link between sympathy and the loss of individuality" exemplified in *Work* ("Limits of Sympathy" 693) and traces it back to contemporaneous notions of proper femininity.[16] True women were meant to be self-effacing. But we might also see it as an outgrowth of sentimentality's relationship to professional male oratory. Sentimentality is motivated by the fear of deceit: an orator can seem as if he is trustworthy yet be motivated by self-interest. In that case, he will say what the listener wants to hear rather than what is true. In response to that fear comes the sentimental author's adoption of a common trope of the time: the orator who knows not what he speaks is transported out of his own narrow self-interest while possessed with the spirit of eloquence—in other words, the orator as cipher.[17] Christie's most eloquent moment, her address to the crowd of working women, involves just such a lack of self-possession: "What [Christie] said she hardly knew" (332). She later describes how she does not "deserve any credit for the speech, because it spoke itself, and I couldn't help it" (342).

The successful orator becomes just the person the audience desires her to be. Eloquence elicits projection. Christie's working-woman audience "saw and felt that a genuine woman stood down there among them like a sister, ready with head, heart, and hand to help them help themselves" (332). Christie becomes an extension of the audience: instead of setting herself up as someone who can provide these working women with answers that they lack, Christie will "help them help themselves" (333). The audience, that is, projects onto Christie qualities that she then allows them to recognize in themselves. Their projection registers spatially as well: these working women imagine Christie among themselves, not up on a platform as the narrative previously explained she was. The audience can know who Christie is just by looking at her because she is just like them: in other words, eloquence erases any differences between the orator and the audience (and among members of the audience themselves).[18]

In *Work*, Christie's apparent self-loss disguises no hidden motives: she remains blankly philanthropic. Alcott does not go so far as to suggest that sentimental eloquence might provide a comfy persona for a gifted scoundrel, but she does pave the way for such a man. Alcott's rendering of sentimental persuasion opens up what it tried to foreclose: the possibility of disingenuousness. Here is how it happens. For a novel that stakes everything on the transparency of the orator, *Work* is notably preoccupied with acting. Christie's second attempt at a career has her working in a "respectable theatre" (30). It makes sense that the profession of acting would arise in this novel in both a biographical and historical way: Alcott and her sisters engaged in parlor theatricals growing up, and Alcott remained entranced by the theater as an adult. In this the Alcott sisters were not alone: parlor theatricals arose as an American middle-class pastime in the 1850s, as Karen Halttunen has documented. Yet *Work*'s interest in the theater also makes sense in a symptomatic way: acting raises the question of ingenuousness and disingenuousness, seeming versus being, the problematic with which Alcott, as well as other sentimentalists, is preoccupied. It seems no surprise that it would show up in this novel. How can someone tell whether the orator is acting or whether he is sincere? In the 1870s, the audience might refract this question through the lens of acting.

We might expect that a sentimental novel like *Work* would insist on a clear distinction between acting and eloquence, a distinction that would easily be apprehended by the audience. Stowe's novels, for example, make it immediately clear to their readers (if not immediately to the more innocent characters) in coded descriptions or asides or even apostrophes when characters are trying to deceive those around them as to their true character. For example, on the first page of *Uncle Tom's Cabin*, Stowe's reliable narrator announces with genteel distaste that the slave trader Haley "did not seem, strictly speaking, to come under the species [of gentleman]" (1). It is inconceivable to imagine a sentimental novelist creating a character like Melville's Amasa Delano (discussed in detail in chapter 5), whose trustworthiness is asserted by his fellow characters and the narrator but possibly undermined by the implied author. Delano is a man whose character, if not indeterminate, is extremely hard to determine.

Work initially seems to cleave to the distinction between acting and eloquence. At first Christie does not seem to be a very good actor: "She had no talent except that which may be developed in any girl possessing the lively fancy, sympathetic nature, and ambitious spirit which make such girls naturally dramatic" (37).[19] Even in her earliest acting turn, Christie's "natural grace made it easy for her to catch and copy the steps and poses given her to imitate" (34). It turns out that she does have some talent but that the right kinds of roles are required to bring it out. In the words of her acting mentor, she makes a "capital character actress" (40). The novel wants us to understand that Christie can excel at playing roles that reflect who she already is, as when Alcott implies that Christie can play characters out of the novels of Charles Dickens because "[s]he loved those books, and seemed by instinct to understand and personate the humor and pathos" of them (39). Christie's travails, too, have been marked by both pathos and humor.[20] It seems that Christie can play only herself. We might see her as a very early method actor. Christie needs to find some personal connection to the characters in order to portray them.

Yet the differences between what Christie does and what a method actor does are illuminating. Constantin Stanislavski provided the theoretical underpinnings for Method Acting, the American translation of his system. He believed that actors act better when they draw on their own experiences in order to create a unique character rather than try to mimic the external manners that they imagine the character would have: a character is formed from the inside out. Actors mean to create a character that, though recognizable, is uniquely their own.[21] No longer is there a generic "Stanley Kowalski" to envision; now there is "Marlon Brando's Stanley Kowalski." But Christie does not strive to create a distinctive character, either in her acting or in her eloquence. Who is

Christie playing when she plays herself? If she were a method actor, she would be playing a character created out of her inner life. In *An Actor Prepares* (1936), Stanislavski famously wrote, "Through conscious means we reach the subconscious" (191). But Christie does not aim to access an inner life; nor is it clear that she has one. As her mentor comments: "When her parts suit, she *forgets herself* entirely and does admirably well" (40; emphasis added).[22] Her most effective acting occurs, the novel tells us, in a scene where "she comes like a good angel to the home of [a] poor play-wright, [and] she brought tears to the eyes of her audience" (44). Yes, Christie is playing herself, but not in the way of a method actor.

During the times when she acts well, Christie draws on herself, yet what she is drawing on is her skill at becoming sympathetic both to the character and to the audience. She "personates" the character that she is playing rather than presents her own interpretation of her: she manages to "catch and copy the steps and poses" (34) and by such a lowercase method becomes that character. She follows the method laid out by the French actor and teacher François Delsarte, whose work was promulgated in the United States starting in the 1870s and was adopted by both actors and elocutionists. According to the historian Mark Salter, by the 1870s "the so-called 'Delsarte System of Expression' was probably the most popular method of speech training in the United States" (qtd. in Suter 98)—and this movement quickly became a female one.[23] Delsarte proposed a method that turns the Stanislavski Method "on its head," according to Robyn Warhol ("As You Stand" 113): "For Delsarte, then, the gesture not only expresses the motion and the state of mind, it brings them into being" ("As You Stand" 114). Character is formed from the outside in. Christie's skill at being sympathetic involves emptying herself out, allowing herself to be taken over by what she imagines the character she is playing to feel. Christie's act of sympathy triggers the same response in her audience. Presumably they are engaged in a similar self-dispersal, allowing themselves to become suffused with the emotions of the characters they are viewing.[24]

Acting provides Christie not just with employment; it offers her training for the novel's most cherished career for her. Christie's moment of oratorical triumph depends on her having been trained as an actor: "That early training stood her in good stead now, giving her self-possession, power of voice, and ease of gesture; while the purpose at her heart lent her the sort of simple eloquence that touches, persuades, and convinces better than logic, flattery or oratory" (332).

The assumptions made in this description might remind us of those found in the professional oratorical manuals described in the first chapter: training is what leads to "ease" and allows Christie to appear natural to her audience (unpracticed speakers appear stiff or idiosyncratic). Yet some elements of this passage pull against the professional oratorical ideal: "the purpose at her heart"—the fact that Christie feels something deeply—remains apart from her training and translates into "simple" eloquence (as opposed, presumably, to the "oratory" of men like Daniel Webster). Christie seems to have it all: both art and artlessness, cultivation and guilelessness. It is possible that this mix of characteristics could blend into a seamless whole for at least some of Alcott's contemporaneous readers. For this mix to do so, readers must be able to believe in the tenet of professional male oratory and the Delsarte System that training can enhance naturalness. But the interesting thing about this passage is that Alcott herself seems unable to believe it. If she did, the sentence would not be a balanced set of contrasts with training on one side and naturalness on the other. Training and the heart pull in different directions, as this passage performs with its own syntax: its neoclassical contrast, with its matching set of threes (self-possession, power, ease versus logic, flattery, oratory), seems a far cry from "simple eloquence." This tension can also be seen in the way "voice" is described in the passage: "voice" is a result of training, not an emanation of the character's essence as it was in earlier sentimental novels. The description of Christie's speech registers a tension that Alcott seems only faintly aware of. But Alcott has created a snarl of contradiction for many modern readers. Is Christie self-possessed or is she self-effacing? Is she an actor or is she sincere? It seems impossible for the modern reader to see her as both.[25]

In *Work*, the elements required for good acting and for eloquence are *exactly the same*: for one thing, they both depend on the same trope of self-forgetting. Sentimental novels require their heroes and heroines to forget themselves at the moments when they are most persuasive in order to assure us that they are not being disingenuous, not motivated by self-interest. Yet Alcott's novel, with its inability to untangle acting and eloquence, prepares the way for speakers who will only act as if they are forgetting themselves. The figure of Ion, the canny orator of Socrates, rears his charismatic head. For most of the dialogue, as discussed in the first chapter, Ion has claimed that he forgets himself when he performs; but we should remember that at one point he reveals that he has not given up control of the effect he is making.

The problem I have just limned—the question this novel raises of whether an orator might be acting as if sincere—had been handily solved by the older sentimental novels. Stowe's novels, for example, believe in good character, the idea that a person has an essential core of integrity. Stowe's readers can believe in good character because they believe in the link between true womanhood and essence. True women have good characters because they are domestic creatures. They exist in their homes and also through them. Lori Merish has examined the "[t]he dynamic interplay between . . . middle-class interiority and the middle-class interior" (140). This relationship, broadly speaking, is a familiar idea even to modern readers, who with varying levels of cynicism acknowledge the way that houses and their contents express their owners' identities or at least their aspirations. But the relationship between domesticity and interiority for middle-class women was even tighter in the early and mid-nineteenth century: the home did not just express a previously formed identity but constituted it.

Essence connotes something that is both dematerialized and concentrated. The architecture of the ideal middle-class home both etherealized and distilled the true woman. It did the former through what was removed or hidden in the house (the dirt, the slops). It did the latter by embodying the same values that she did: "When, therefore, the wise woman seeks a home in which to exercise this ministry [of training her children], she will aim to secure a house so planned that it will provide in the best manner for health, industry, and economy, those cardinal requisites of domestic enjoyment and success" (Beecher and Stowe 27). In other words, the middle-class home was essential for the true woman. It was not just the base of her power, but the base from which her power would radiate outward.

Those idyllic scenes that I have documented here and in the previous chapters in which a true woman is least verbal, most powerful, and most essential are domestic: the Quaker Rachel Halliday in her kitchen; Mary Scudder in her garden. In *Work*, Mrs. Sterling, David's mother, exudes "the silent power of character." Mrs. Sterling's case of exuded essence is not linked to a particular domestic space but to an *eternal* one. Explaining Mrs. Sterling's essence, Alcott has this to say: "As George MacDonald somewhere says, 'Her soul seemed to sit apart in a sunny little room, safe from dust and noise, serenely regarding passers-by through the clear muslin curtains of her window'" (222–23). Here we have the clearest demonstration of the links that the earlier sentimental novel made between true womanhood, domesticity, and an essential character that people can trust.

Yet who is Christie exactly? What guarantees her essential goodness? The novel wants to rescue Christie from both disingenuousness and erasure by highlighting the "subtle magnetism" of her character (333). As discussed above, sentimental novels imagine people in terms of "essences." What makes an orator persuasive is her good character, which is apprehended by the audience as a kind of essence; the orator is not a scholar with an argument to make. It is not a coincidence that Christie's moment of oratorical triumph cannot be recorded. The words do not matter; in fact, the words get in the way. What matters is her *voice*, a much more effective vehicle to convey Christie's essence than any contingent words that she could utter.

Yet *Work* troubles this notion of sentimental essence because of its cultural currency—because of work. Work brings middle-class women outside the home. Christie's home while she works is mostly a room in a boarding house, furnished impersonally by the aptly named Mrs. Flint. Earlier sentimental novels did not have to prove that true women stayed the same despite their contexts because their contexts remained the same and guaranteed their characters. But *Work* does have to prove this. Christie, like many other young middle-class women of her time, decides to go out and work. She no longer has a domestic sphere in which to ply and prove her essential nature. Yet the novel still retains the idea of "essence," which allows the working-woman heroine both to remain the same despite her changing jobs and to be terribly persuasive.

Christie's "essence" in the absence of a domestic context is something that has to be asserted rather than assumed. Her essence, as we have seen, is conveyed most noticeably when she is being eloquent, but the novel equates eloquence with acting. In *Work*, essence as an exudation of character threatens to become the studied effect of a crafted persona. I would like to suggest that this association between acting and eloquence, as inadvertently and unevenly as it appears in *Work*, might be related to a broad culture-wide shift in America toward the end of the nineteenth century that the cultural historian Warren I. Susman has described. Looking at a wide array of self-improvement literature, Susman describes the shift in America from a culture of character to one of personality. The difference has been deftly caught by Henri Laurent: "Even as character may be good or bad, so Personality may be famous or infamous" (iv). Susman goes on to say that "[t]he social role demanded of all in the new culture of personality was that of a performer" (280). His summary of what he calls the new "personality literature" shows how "voice," once the guarantor of character, has become the instrument of a self-conscious performer: "Every work studied stressed the importance of the human voice in describing methods of voice control and proper methods of conversation or public speaking" (280).

This shift from character to personality reinforces the system that Delsarte outlines, where performing a certain gesture or striking a certain pose leads the actor to the appropriate emotion rather than the other way around. How do actors choose the appropriate pose or gesture? In the absence of a dramatic script, they look to the social script: "What would the person I am trying to impress expect me to be feeling? Then let me mimic that person's 'steps and poses.'"

Delsarte's protocol finds its way into *Work* in such a line as "So let me seem until I be" (248), which we find toward the end of the novel. Here is the context: Christie and David are staring into a mirror together. When she asks him what he sees, he replies: "A good and lovely woman, Christie" (248). Christie then says to herself: "So let me seem until I be."

Alcott does not seem upset by Christie's behaviorist utterance: she does not seem to realize that it undermines her own logic of sentimental essence. Alcott's unselfconsciousness makes sense because a tradition of mentorship can be found in earlier sentimental novels: Gerty in Maria Susanna Cummins's *The Lamplighter*, for instance, must copy the habits of her true-woman friend Emily before she becomes a true woman herself. This sentimental behaviorism might also seem like a minor problem because it surfaces only occasionally in *Work*.[26] Yet in *The Lamplighter*, the protagonist was imitating a real true woman; *Work* suggests that Christie's becoming a good woman will involve studying herself in the mirror as she practices certain expressions and gestures.

Alcott's "sentimental behaviorism," an outgrowth of her preoccupation with acting, destabilizes the older notion of character that she wants to cling to.

Delsartism arrived in America around the time when Alcott was writing about Christie's experiences in the theater.[27] An early notice of it occurs in an article entitled "Delsarte" that appeared in the *Atlantic Monthly* in 1871 (followed a few articles later by "Our Whispering Gallery, V," which features Nathaniel Hawthorne saying that Bronson Alcott was "one of the most excellent men he had ever known" [649]). At first, Delsarte's system seemed a naturalistic alternative to the melodramatic acting style that characterized the theater in this period (what theater historian Roberta Pearson terms the "histrionic" style), because Delsarte encouraged actors to observe how people acted in real life and then copy those gestures on the stage. Pearson quotes one of his American disciples, Geneviève Stebbins, to this effect: "The actor's art is to express in well known symbols what an individual man may be supposed to feel. . . . But unless the actor follows nature sufficiently close to select symbols recognized as natural, he fails to touch us" (qtd. in Pearson 22). As Delsartism became popular in the United States, its practitioners began to ignore its enjoinder to base their gestures on observation. Instead the system hardened in the theatrical realm into an exercise in memorizing a codified set of gestures. The gestures came to stand in for the emotion rather than express it. A similar thing happened in the oratorical realm. In *Delsarte System of Oratory* (1892), a textbook much used in the late nineteenth century, Delsarte delineates the gestures needed to convey different emotions. Here are the directions to convey devotion:

> This gesture embraces seven movements:
>
> 1. This consists in raising the passive hand to the level of the other hand, but in an inverse direction.
> 2. This consists in turning back the hand toward one's self.
> 3. This consists in drawing the elbows to the body, and placing the hands on the chest.
> 4. This is produced by taking a step backward, and turning a third to one side; during the execution of this step, the elbows are raised, and the head is lowered.

5. This consists in drawing the elbows near the body, and placing the hands above the shoulders.
6. This consists in developing the arms.
7. This consists in developing the hands. (no pagination)

The shade of Gilbert Austin has returned in this new codification of "natural" bodily movements. The cycle of disingenuous eloquence has begun to accelerate.

Sentimentality and Delsartism are not just parallel historical phenomena. In fact, they are intimately related: sentimentality's loss of power around this time seems in part caused by Delsartism. Delsartism seemed able to justify "sentimental behaviorism," until the self-conscious craft it enjoined its followers to embrace undermined its promise to merge seeming and being. In our era the consensus seems to be that "Delsarte devised an elaborate system of acting based on purely mechanical techniques" (Hatlen 265). This characterization contradicts one made by Robyn Warhol, who touts Delsarte for understanding that emotion often follows gesture ("As You Stand"). Warhol's characterization flies in the face of our modern "commonsense" understanding of emotion, where emotion is seen as giving rise to gesture, which will otherwise be taken as "mechanical." Contemporary neuroscience seems to support the Delsartean notion of ex post facto emotion, but that does not, I think, contradict the fact that this model compromises sentimentality toward the end of the nineteenth century.

To see just how "sentimental behaviorism" compromises sentimentality, we must turn away from Alcott, who only occasionally counsels its use, to Henry Ward Beecher, whose success depends on it. Alcott's *Work* produces, as I said, a crack in sentimental rhetoric in its preoccupation with acting and its inability to distinguish between acting and sentimental eloquence. But the undermining work that this novel does is more subtle than not. Alcott still manages to move her contemporaneous audience—both fictional and actual—with her sentimental eloquence.[28] Henry Ward Beecher continually urges the orator to act as if he felt certain things that he does not really feel because eventually such acting will bring the existence of those feelings into being: the orator will become the person he impersonates. The crack is about to widen.

4

Henry Ward Beecher and the Fall of the Sentimental Orator

Christie is a transitional figure on the way toward Henry Ward Beecher, whom Sinclair Lewis called "a combination of St. Augustine, Barnum, and John Barrymore" (qtd. in Hibben viii).[1] From 1847 until 1887, the year of his death, Henry Ward Beecher was the wildly popular minister of Plymouth Church in Brooklyn (he was less popular after 1874), famous for his support of both abolition and the "woman question."[2] Beecher was a man who spoke from the heart and not from the head. He made his audiences cry. As his contemptuous biographer Paxton Hibben wrote, "[W]hen he raised his voice in prayer, the tears streaming down his full cheeks, he could hear the little staccato sobs of women and the harsher sobs of men from every corner of the vast house" (189). Beecher's popularity arose out of the intensity of his feeling—or, as his detractors would have it, out of the semblance of it. E. L. Godkin, editor of the *Nation* during Beecher's ascendancy and also his cousin-in-law, went from believing Beecher to be "the most remarkable preacher of his time, the most popular, the most influential" (qtd. in C. Clark 2) to condemning him during his trial, because "[w]hat he has most encouraged . . . is vague aspiration and lachrymose sensibility" (Godkin, "Chromo-Civilization" 89–90).

This charge sounds almost identical to later condemnatory evaluations of the "scribbling women."[3] This is no coincidence, because Henry Ward Beecher is himself a sentimental author and orator, becoming in real life what his sister Harriet could only aspire to be.[4]

Godkin was not the only one to revise his opinion of Henry Ward Beecher. After Beecher was accused of committing adultery with one of his parishioners, Libby Tilton, the wife of a close friend, the whole nation turned its horrified, titillated gaze on him. His trial in 1875 ended in a hung jury, with nine of the jurors supporting Beecher. Many, including Stowe, would not even entertain the thought that Beecher might have been drastically different from the way he appeared. "I cannot hear the subject discussed as a *possibility* open for inquiry without such an intense uprising of indignation & scorn & anger as very few have ever seen in me in these late years," Stowe wrote (qtd. in Hedrick, *Harriet Beecher Stowe* 378; emphasis in the original). Not everyone felt the same. The *Louisville Courier Journal* called the Reverend Beecher "a dunghill covered with flowers" (qtd. in Korobkin 59). Many reveled in the thought that this paragon might have been a sinner, that Beecher's constant references to his own virtue provided a cover for his self-serving activities. Some found the uncovering of what seemed like such massive hypocrisy delicious.

We should not see Beecher as a self-righteous prig exposed. His most recent biographer, Debby Applegate, makes a persuasive case that Beecher *was* guilty of committing adultery (and fathering Libby Tilton's youngest child), even though it seems impossible to find out what exactly transpired between them amid the swirl of conflicting testimony.[5] The story should not end there. More interesting than whether or how many times Beecher committed adultery (which I would not deny is quite interesting) is the way the trial produced contradictory responses. It made the public vacillate, certain one minute that he was as guilty as sin, the next that he was wrongfully accused. Laura Korobkin, who has written extensively on the trial, calls it "an increasingly undecidable interrogation of hypocrisy" (61). The trial cast doubt not just on the integrity of a revered person but on the populace's "own methods of judgment" (Korobkin 61). The trial puts sentimental methods of judgment in doubt: ways of judging the trustworthiness of other people that novels like *Uncle Tom's Cabin* both cultivated and reinforced. The public found that what had seemed like enough evidence to judge Beecher—his ability to make them cry, the vivid picture of goodness he presented—was not sufficient. The trial of Henry Ward Beecher reproduces in miniature all the doubts that sentimental rhetoric as a method of persuasion would inspire in a large number of its future audience.

The contradictory versions of Henry Ward Beecher that the trial created foretell the divergent characterizations that nineteenth-century sentimental novels have produced among contemporary literary critics: the sentimental author as guileless and unfairly attacked versus the sentimental author as self-indulgent and manipulative. For an influential example of this tension, we can compare the way Jane Tompkins rails against those who have prevented us from "recognizing and asserting the *value*" ("Sentimental Power" 123; emphasis in the original) of sentimental texts to the way Ann Douglas dismisses them as self-indulgent (4) and deceptive (12).[6] As to Beecher himself, Douglas characterizes him much as she does the sentimental authoresses—as "careless and prolific souls" (83). Just as contemporary literary criticism has trouble deciding on sentimentality's true nature, so both contemporaneous and modern critics have trouble determining Beecher's. Douglas uses another term to characterize him: she speaks of his "amorphousness" (243). Beecher inspires grave doubts in his audience, arising in response to his writings done before the trial, not just as a result of the trial itself. The trial, in other words, could not have happened to a more deserving man, whose efforts to extend the provenance of sentimental oratory went quite a way toward destroying its power.

Here is how Korobkin describes the strategy undertaken by Beecher's defense attorney, William Maxwell Evarts:

> If Beecher's alleged corruption can exist without any hint tainting his publicly available behavior, if "there is no necessary connection between character and conduct," then our own judgments, based on similarly external "evidence," are unreliable, and we may well be unknowingly surrounded by diabolical confidence men. . . . The only way to solve the problem, argues Evarts, is to take a stand for the reliability of outward appearance and to refuse even to investigate accusations that, if true, would undermine the assumptions that prop up our own lives. (77)

This defense expresses a strange logic: we can assure ourselves that no confidence men are in our midst not by exposing them but by assuming that they do not exist in the first place. At least three of Beecher's jurors decided not to uphold a system so clearly flailing.

Beecher contains elements of two orators that I have juxtaposed above. Unlike E. T. Channing, Beecher is a riveting speaker, who, like Mary Scudder, is able to use his physical presence as a kind of eloquence: "[i]t was simply necessary to look into his face to see how full of sympathy and kindness was his heart," as the Admiral David D. Porter eulogized him (5). But like Channing, Beecher is an instructor in oratory. It is this dual position—as both practitioner and instructor of sentimental eloquence—that gives Beecher his amorphousness. In codifying what he wants his audience to see as spontaneous, he suggests how he has self-consciously become what they desire rather than what his essential character would dictate. He allows us to see how codification leads the audience to sense inauthenticity, to suspect that the sentimental orator is merely an actor. Sentimentality cannot be taught, a state of affairs that embroils men in particular in a bind.

Since men lack the requisite essence to be sentimental orators, they have to work at it and be mentored in it. This situation leads its contemporaneous audience to suspect that true women had to work at it too. For most of the modern literary critical audience, this suspicion has hardened into a certainty. In some ways sentimental rhetoric becomes a victim of its own success. Other men wanted to learn to be as eloquent as Beecher, and he was happy to teach them how to do so. Yet as soon as sentimental rhetoric seems to be a product of learned behavior rather than the spontaneous outpouring of a full heart, it is open to charges of disingenuousness. Even apart from Beecher's explicit teachings about preaching and oratory, we can start understanding why he was so effective at undermining sentimental rhetoric by looking at his one fictional work, the sentimental novel *Norwood*, whose didacticism erodes the notion of sentimental essence.

Beecher wrote *Norwood: Or, Village Life in New England* at the insistence of his friend Robert Bonner, who serialized it in the *New York Ledger* in 1867. It offers a portrait of a New England village focusing on two families, the Wentworths and the Cathcarts, who produce the children whose eventual marriage ends the book. The novel is very like

Uncle Tom's Cabin in the way it represents a cross section of the population, conventionalized into a similar array of types to those of his sister. These include the proud and scheming characters, whose schemes are eventually discovered (Judge Bacon); the efficient Old Maids, whose iron rule is belied by a tender heart (Agate Bissell); and the comic characters, who are uneducated and nonwhite (Pete Sawmill).

Beecher has another affinity with his sister. *Norwood*, like *The Minister's Wooing*, devotes an astonishing number of words to the proposition that the best sort of eloquence is of the silent variety.[7] Beecher disavowed, charmingly, his similarity to his sister: "People used to accuse me of being the author of 'Uncle Tom's Cabin'—until I wrote 'Norwood'" (qtd. in Hibben 190). Yet *Norwood* similarly puts forth as its winning orators the people who speak the least. *Norwood*'s Rachel Liscomb, pillar of virtuous womanhood, "was one of the few without gifts of speech, whose bearing and looks are a full equivalent for them" (9). Beecher believes that bodies speak louder than words: "Words are of the flesh, opaque. Looks are of the spirit, luminous" (467). Here he is talking about the glances that lovers cast at one another, but the statement also works in its other sense: as with Stowe, it is possible to determine people's trustworthiness by looking at them.

But if Stowe and Beecher both assert a preference for wordlessness in the midst of their extremely wordy novels, they differ in their choice of spaces where this wordlessness takes place. For Stowe, eloquence takes place in domestic interiors (with the exception of Mary Scudder's conversion speech to Madame Frontignac); but Beecher's most profound scenes take place outdoors, in nature.[8] Clifford E. Clark, a biographer of Beecher, comments that, of all Beecher's works, "the connection between faith and nature was most fully developed" in his one novel (188). Readers cannot get far in *Norwood*, whose introduction involves a lengthy paean to the New England elm tree ("The Elms of New England! They are as much a part of her beauty as the columns of the Parthenon were the glory of its architecture" [5]) without noticing that in this diffuse and episodic novel nature exists at the center of many different plots. Yet to say "nature" so casually is to suggest that modern readers know what "nature" is, but Beecher's "nature" is infused with properties that the modern audience does not generally associate with it.

The natural world that Beecher creates in *Norwood* waits in quivering anticipation for people to observe it. Trees, rocks, and other inanimate things yearn to lay themselves open to human apprehension. On the long-awaited day of the protagonists' wedding, the church bell abandons its usual "measured, doctrinal ring" (546) and gives out a "real, out-springing, merry ring, as of a bell that would like to kick up its heels and dance on the green with the best of them" (546). Like his sister's, Beecher's cozy humor relies on the anthropomorphization of objects that seem to like nothing better than to participate in human affairs. Yet this passage and the many like it are meant to be more than humorous: Beecher believes that inanimate objects and nature really do "speak" to people (while at the same time avoiding words).

Objects speak to people because they do not argue. Beecher does not like arguments. Parson Buell, this novel's Minister Hopkins—all head, no heart, a man devoted to argument and logic—gets a lecture on both nature and arguments from Beecher's stand-in, the affectionate, outdoorsy Dr. Wentworth. Buell has been arguing with the doctor over whether "[i]magination is the very marrow of faith" (52), a position that the logical Dr. Buell rejects. Dr. Wentworth contends that both Buell and another Norwood resident, the hardheaded Judge Bacon, are wrong in their commitment to argument:

> [B]oth of you insist upon reducing all truth to some material equivalent before you are subject to conviction. A truth which does not admit of a logical statement, seems to you a phantasy. You believe not upon any evidence in your spirit, but upon the semi-material form which language and philosophical statements give to thought. The further you can bring a truth from its spiritual condition, and the more nearly it is incarnated, the more satisfactory is to you the evidence of its existence. But, with me, I accept facts which appeal to my senses as the lowest possible truth, and as appealing to the lowest avenue of my mind. Nature is more than a vast congeries of physical facts, related to each other as cause and effect, and signifying nothing else. (52)

This exposition is dry stuff, which halts the story in its tracks (a habit of Beecher's). But it holds its own fascination: for modern readers, a strange realignment of categories is taking place. Argument and logic have been linked to the material, what can be apprehended by the senses, while nature has been lifted out of the empirical realm. The cause of this strange realignment has to do with words. According to Beecher, the necessity of embodying thought in language brings it down into the world of material things, which are of the earth and all that is mortal. Words stand opposed to the divine. Nature, because it can be apprehended without being incarnated into language, gives us access to the divine realm. For Beecher, words are something to be avoided.

Beecher makes this position clearer a little later in the dialogue when Dr. Wentworth adds that "there are great truths of the affections seeking an inlet upon men, which flow from God, and which reach men, rightly sensitive, through the doings and appearances of what we call Nature" (52). Beecher, like Channing, believes in the existence of mental faculties, but for Beecher it is the *imaginative* faculty that promises salvation: "No man without imagination can by any possibility be an acute observer" (56). Nature gives unmediated access to the truth because it cannot be contained in logical propositions, boiled down to cause and effect.

Beecher uses nature as one more line of defense in the war against disingenuous eloquence. Nature makes visible the workings of both the divine and human nature, and it is impossible to read nature incorrectly. How difficult it is for us to believe in this. It is not even that the novel *insists* that what someone takes to be a sign found in nature will have a single, apprehensible meaning or that readers are not projecting their own desires onto nature. The thought never even comes up. Recognizing natural signs—which to us might seem arbitrary in the extreme—comes to be a matter of training the proper faculties. Like Channing, Beecher believes that a person will come to the correct interpretation once the faculties have been trained.

Interpretation has a different meaning in *Norwood* than it does for the modern critic. Our modern literary-critical sense of interpretation hinges, in the wake of pragmatism and reader-response criticism, on the idea of our own active involvement in making sense of things. Many of us take this a step further, as Roland Barthes did in "The Death of the Author": we proclaim our inability to fix a final, incontrovertible meaning to a given text,[9] yet these ideas are utterly foreign to Beecher.[10] The difference between him and us lies not in his notion that someone needs to be properly trained to make the proper kinds of interpretation. This is not a foreign idea to us, as our many graduate programs in literature attest. The difference lies in the belief of this sentimental author that, once properly trained, people will interpret things exactly the same way.[11]

Interpretation for Beecher, as for E. T. Channing, corresponds to the eighteenth- and nineteenth-century concept of "taste," which was put forth by rhetoricians like Lord Kames and Hugh Blair (see chapter 1). Taste needs to be trained because proper training corrects defects. The ramification of this idea is that perfect taste exists. If everyone is properly trained, all differences in aesthetic estimation will be eliminated. Interpretive consensus is a difficult concept for us to credit, but in the case of *Norwood* it verges on the absurd. We have read endless stories mocking people's tendency to read things into nature, trying to make it conform to a human scale. To find *Norwood* persuasive, the reader must put aside that long-fostered skepticism and instead embrace the idea that nature begs us to understand it and that it will lead us gently but ineluctably (like Henry Ward Beecher) to the things it wants us to know.

If we spin out this idea of what might be called "sentimental non-interpretation," we realize how short a distance lies between the sentimental novel and the Gothic. Both kinds of novels fetishize objects by attaching tremendous affect to them. The hank of hair that summons up the dead plays a role in both Gothic novels and sentimental ones. In both genres, objects come alive at the drop of a hat. We might think that the difference lies in the way in which the Gothic takes these things literally: a bit of hair really can summon ghosts (as opposed to simply calling up vivid memories of the deceased). Inanimate objects really can come alive, an animation that is not just a humorous convention or, as Merish would argue, a way of affirming the connection between psychological and domestic interiors.

Though the sentimental novel does not feature the literal reanimation of corpses or the summoning of actual ghosts, it does, like the Gothic, literalize psychological defense mechanisms and complexes.[12] The Gothic draws from a whole range of defense mechanisms and complexes, from the castration complex to repetition compulsion. So, for example, the protagonist in Edgar Allan Poe's "Berenice" becomes fixated on recovering the teeth of his dead fiancée, who was the symbol of his manhood; the protagonist of Poe's "The Black Cat" finds himself repeatedly trying to get rid of an unwanted feline, sign of his own guilt.

But the sentimental novel specializes. It occupies itself with literalizing one psychological defense mechanism over all others: projection.[13] When a character imbues an inanimate object or a wordless character with certain motives and desires, the novel does not want readers to doubt that what they are seeing is really there. Even though it is difficult to believe that the interpretation of nature in *Norwood* is ever anything but psychological projection, the novel absolutely discourages this reading. It is a radical reading against the intention of a sentimental novel to diagnose a character's propensity to read truth in nature (or in a dying, crying woman) as his own fantasy. This is not to say that these texts do not invite such a reading from modern readers but that this reading seems wholly against the grain.

In contrast, the Gothic relies on ambiguous interpretation. The characters in a Gothic story often doubt their own perceptions, just as the ideal reader of the Gothic is similarly left in doubt as to the status of the events just recounted. For example, H. P. Lovecraft's protagonists often do not know if they are dreaming (modern Gothic tales often feature another twist: a character who decides that he has dreamed the whole thing wakes up to find a material souvenir from his "dream"). Poe's characters often wonder if they are deranged (and modern Gothic tales often literalize that doubt, presenting the protagonist as having been institutionalized). Gothic tales tread the line between projection and an actual malevolent external reality. Hawthorne's Gothic-inflected tales and novels quite self-consciously and provocatively lay out the idea that we are merely displacing our own fantasies onto our surroundings. *The Scarlet Letter*, for example, casts doubt on the appearance of the scarlet letter on Arthur Dimmesdale's body, a mark that "[m]ost of the spectators testified to having seen" (174). "It is singular, nevertheless, that certain persons, who were spectators of the whole scene, and professed never once to have removed their eyes from the Reverend Mr. Dimmesdale, denied that there was any mark whatever on his breast, more than on a new-born infant's" (174). Hawthorne lets us dwell in doubt; the sentimental author wants all doubts as to the true appearance of things removed.

Yet Beecher shuts down the notion, crucial to the Gothic, that the signs that its characters find in nature are open to interpretation in the modern sense. For sentimentality to be powerful, we must never doubt that things are what they appear. Stowe's novels, for example, afford no possibility of interpreting the wordless women, the dead or dying children, differently from the way the text obviously wants us to see them. I am not saying that modern critics do not offer readings of these sentimental orators that go against the grain—they do this all the time. See, for example, Hortense Spillers's interpretation of Little Eva in "Changing the Letter." But making such an against-the-grain interpretation undermines a sentimental text's ability to move that reader. It is not just the contents of Spillers's interpretation of Little Eva as a pimp-in-the-making that is damning. The moment that Spillers and other modern literary critics embark on any nonobvious interpretation of a sentimental orator—in other words, one that sees her as something to be analyzed rather than simply experienced—the sentimental orator has lost her intended audience. The ideal reader of *Norwood* similarly is a noninterpreter: it has no need, it claims, for such an argument-making personage. It is impossible for a person who has the proper imagination to get nature (which speaks wordlessly, along with certain true women, in *Norwood*) wrong.

Yet this insistence on the needlessness of interpretation in *Norwood*, its legacy from successful sentimental novelists like Beecher's sister, comes into tension with his desire to democratize sentimental rhetoric. *Norwood*, unlike *The Minister's Wooing*, tries to teach people explicitly how to become sentimental orators. Two particularly didactic moments in *Norwood* demonstrate what happens to readers when sentimental techniques are made explicit. These moments function like the dramatic tableaux so popular in late nineteenth-century dramatic productions: they isolate and freeze the techniques of sentimental persuasion.

At one point in the novel, Dr. Wentworth tells his little daughter, Rose, some stories about nature. One of them is called "The Anxious Leaf." In this story a "little leaf" is afraid of the time when it will be blown from the tree and thrown "to die on the ground" (108). The twig it is attached to tells it not to worry: "you shall not go till you want to" (109). When October comes around, the leaf sees all the other leaves around it "becoming very beautiful" (109) and asks why. The tree replies: "All these leaves are getting ready to fly away, and they have put on these beautiful colors, because of joy" (109). The little leaf begins to want to go too, and eventually "a little puff of wind came, and the leaf let go without thinking of it . . . and fell into a dream and never waked up to tell what it dreamed about!" (109). This story is blatantly didactic. But the reason it is effective, so Beecher's thinking would go, is that it does not simply involve Dr. Wentworth telling Rose: "Little girl, do not fear death because you will not die before you are ready. In addition, death is like a dream." The story gains its persuasive power from the idea that this is a little leaf and not a person: the leaf is anthropomorphized but still retains its leafness, its difference from the human. And this difference lies in the falling leaf's inevitability, its freedom from thought and the fallibility of argument (as the wordless true woman is free): leaves do not think, they just are, and nature runs round its seasons not after long deliberations but because that is simply how it is. Yet it is hard for the modern reader to imagine that anyone but a little child would not see through this fable to its schoolroom wiles; using a child as the reader's stand-in seems symptomatic of the condescension that infuses Beecher's project.

What exactly is the danger that this little leaf poses? Sentimental novels insist on the naturalness and inevitability of their persuasive techniques (crying people do not lie; nature clamors to reveal to us truths about God and humans). When sentimental persuasion is at its most powerful, we accept at that moment the idea of a world free from the need for interpretation. Yet our willingness to believe in the naturalness and inevitability of these methods of persuasion goes only so far, as long as the sentimental novel resists self-consciousness. As soon as the sentimental novel reveals its own techniques, it fails. Sentimental persuasion needs to be thought of not as a particular technique but as something natural and spontaneous. Yet it becomes increasingly hard with regard to Beecher's novel and other writings to believe that sentimental persuasion is anything but a particular technique that is learned rather than something that is exuded.

Beecher himself suggests the idea that sentimental persuasion requires the auditor to suspend disbelief:

> Rose knew as well as her father that leaves never talked. Yet, Rose never saw a leaf without feeling that there was life and meaning in it. Flowers had stories in them. The natural world stole in upon her with mute messages, and the feelings which

> woke in her bosom she attributed to nature, and the thoughts which started she deemed a revelation and an interpretation of truths that lay hidden in creation waiting for her. (109)

In the hands of George Eliot or Henry James, this passage would suggest Rose's misapprehension of reality: we would read it along these lines: "Here's how Rose thinks, but we readers, schooled in the complicated irony these authors deploy, know to question, if not completely dismiss, this way of thinking." This is most definitely not the unironic Beecher's meaning. It is his misfortune that his writings reveal the restrictions that readers must place on the range of their reading practices if they want to find sentimental rhetoric persuasive.

Much more than his sister, Beecher wants to teach others how to become sentimentally persuasive rather than simply persuading them about the cause at hand. He faces problems similar to the ones that Channing faced. Channing had to figure out a way to justify the teaching of an art that is supposed not just to seem but to be natural. Yet both Channing and Beecher believe that untaught, "natural" men tend to get things wrong. We can see this elitism if we turn to Beecher's portrayal of a "natural man," which is, among other things, unabashedly racist. *Norwood's* Pete Sawmill "was a huge fellow, black as night" (83). As one villager comments, "Pete don't know much . . . but what he does know comes to him mighty natural" (84). Pete is uneducated, with a great affinity for all of nature, to the point where he himself is consistently described as an animal. One character comments about Pete: "Then he has a natural turn for horses, specially if nobody else can manage 'em. Pete, somehow, gets in with 'em as if they was related" (84). The narrator himself notes that "Rex, a Newfoundland dog . . . seemed to be another Pete running on all fours" (90).

Though Pete does demonstrate qualities that Beecher valorizes (dog-like ones: "simple affection and fidelity" [544]), he never ceases to be a comic character. It comes as a bit of a shock, then, that Pete turns out to be an oratorical ideal—not the ideal orator, as he might have been for Stowe, but the perfect audience for one. Toward the end of the novel, the heroine Rose tries to convert Pete. She despairs of his occasional bouts of drinking and calls him to her. This second tableau of sentimental rhetoric that I analyze here provides new possibilities for democratizing sentimental rhetoric and is therefore even more damaging to it than the first scene was:

> Instead of expostulating and reasoning with him, as heretofore, Rose on the last occasion had burst into tears.
>
> "Oh, Pete! you behave as if you cared for none of your friends. . . . I can't bear it, Pete; I can't bear it;" and Rose's tears fell fast.
>
> Poor Pete was never before conscious of being an object of such special regard that any human being would cry for him. . . . He shuffled his feet and fumbled with his hands, and felt deeply in his pockets for something that was not there . . . and blubbered and sputtered in the most distressing manner, till the whole contrast was too inexpressibly ludicrous for Rose, who covered her face with her handkerchief, and bit her lips to keep from audible laughter. But to Pete this covering of Rose's face was the last affliction. He thought that he had done some great damage to her, and he exploded in an extraordinary mixture of crying, confession and howling. (544–45)

It is Pete's misunderstanding of Rose's true feelings, his mistaking of hilarity for pain, which leads to his final conversion: "I ain't goin' to have no more rum; it's making *her* cry" (545; emphasis in the original). This is another comic moment, but it is telling. Here a conversion is effected not by a crying woman but by a woman that another character has wrongly taken to be crying. Pete is converted, which presumably excuses the moment of misinterpretation. The inverse situation probably would not hold: it would not be excusable for a person to mistake a character's gesture or facial expression so that his evil motive appeared to be a pure one. We could argue that Pete did not, in the end, misinterpret Rose: she did profoundly desire his conversion. Beecher has found a way to excuse the deceit that will ensue when sentimental orators start learning their trade rather than exuding their essence. Beecher clears the way for white men to be sentimental orators while at the same time helping to create the skeptical reader who will fail to be moved by them and, retroactively, by the women sentimentalists to whom Beecher owed such a debt.

In 1872, three years before his trial, Henry Ward Beecher gave a series of lectures to Yale Divinity School students entitled *Yale Lectures on Preaching*. He sought to give practical advice on preaching to supplement the students' other, more theoretical divinity classes. Henry Ward Beecher states the purpose of his *Lectures* at the outset: "The design of this lectureship is not to supersede the instructions given already by the incumbent of the chair of Pastoral Theology, but to intensify one portion of his teachings by bringing in from the field those who are actively engaged in the work of preaching, that you may derive from them the results of their observation and experience" (2).

Beecher trusts that these students' other professors will take care of the theory. But reading through the lectures creates the impression that Beecher's choice has less to do with a fear of duplication and everything to do with his own views on what matters when preaching. The stiff, official cadences of this opening passage are unique; everything that follows has a conversational tone, as when he reveals "I think [metaphysics] sharpens men, and renders them familiar with the operations of the human mind, if not carried too far" (*Yale Lectures* 93). The phrase "not carried too far" is striking because of its very offhandedness: in one quick stroke Beecher releases these students from the hard work of rigorous thinking that characterized the earlier Calvinist ministers, as Ann Douglas describes it.[14]

Beecher's offhand dismissal of metaphysics, "those subtle relations . . . that obtain among spiritual facts of different kinds" (*Yale Lectures* 93), is not nearly as surprising as a statement that he had made earlier in his lectures: "I have seen men who all the while produced the impression, God—God—God; there was nothing in them that breathed of gentleness, sweetness, or sympathy,—the very things that characterized Christ . . . and, if you will not misunderstand it, I would say that they failed because they had too exclusive a sympathy with God" (34).

Thus Beecher warns fledgling men of God away from too exclusive a devotion. What can account for such an odd statement? It marks his distance from the rationalistic preaching that grew out of the Enlightenment and that shaped Edwardsean Calvinism, which Beecher rejected in his movement toward an evangelical Christianity that appealed to the emotions (some disillusioned people described Beecher, after his death, as having preached a "Gospel of Gush" [Applegate, *The Most Famous Man* 354]).[15] But the statement also declares his allegiance to sentimental persuasion, which is influenced by its adherence and reaction to different preaching styles. Beecher believes that preachers should focus all their energies on "developing in [men] a higher manhood" (*Yale Lectures* 31), in "transforming men." He sounds just like Will in *The Minister's Wooing*, putting his finger on just what is wrong with Dr. Hopkins.

Dwelling on the fine points of theology does not engage the audience members, thus foreclosing the chance to convert them to a better life. Beecher has spent his life figuring out how to engage an audience, and an exultation creeps into his voice when he refers to his breakthroughs, especially the first "real" sermon that he ever preached: "I never felt so triumphant in my life. I cried all the way home" (*Yale Lectures* 12). Here Beecher reverses the usual sentimental process of persuasion: instead of the sentimental orator's tears drawing out his audience's, his audience's tears (which I am assuming he evoked) draw out his.

Not surprisingly, the means by which a young man comes to be a successful preacher do not involve an undue attention to study. Instead Beecher stresses that the effective preacher must be a good man: "There is no form of preaching that can afford to dispense with the preacher's moral beauty" (*Yale Lectures* 30). The preacher, as we have seen, must exude "gentleness, sweetness, or sympathy." The idea of "sympathy" is crucial to Beecher. But exactly what does this mean? It is similar to the "sympathy" found in *Work*. For Beecher, the apostle Paul embodies this idea. What characterizes Paul is his "willowiness" (*Yale Lectures* 36), his ability to bend himself into the shapes that will enable him to convert others. Beecher, as is his habit, not only gets into this biblical man's head but translates his thoughts into language that will be familiar to his auditors: "[Y]ou cannot find me a man so deep or so high, so blunt or so sharp, but I would take the shape of that man's disposition, in order to come into sympathy with him, if by so doing I could lift him to a higher and nobler plane of life" (*Yale Lectures* 36). Sympathy is an empathy so radical that people do not just feel what their object feels: they become what that person is.[16] Beecher closes his discussion of sympathy by remarking that Paul resembles nothing so much as a mother: "Paul, with that diffusiveness that he gave himself, that universal adaptation of himself—who *mothered* everybody, wherever he went" (*Yale Lectures* 36; emphasis in the original). Throughout these lectures, Beecher compares preachers to Christ and the apostles: "[y]ou must be . . . *little Christs*"

(*Yale Lectures* 66; emphasis in the original). And he compares Christ and the apostles to mothers.

The idea of a maternal Christ is not new. We saw it at the end of *The Minister's Wooing*, for example, and it is certainly a common trope in Christian theology. Yet both Stowe's and Beecher's ideas about motherhood partake of certain secular and religious ideas that are specific to their historical period. One of the most prominent theories had to do with women's malleability and selflessness, their ability to intuit the needs of those around them and fulfill them.

Beecher's reasoning begins with "moral beauty" and ends with "willowiness." Yet how can these two ideas coexist? With "moral beauty," Beecher assumes not only that a person has an inner essence but that this inner essence will be visible to all who see him. He assumes that the inside will be visible on the outside, an idea that the sentimental novel holds most dear. But with the idea of "willowiness," Beecher puts this idea of an inviolable inner integrity in doubt: what remains of a preacher if he is constantly adapting himself to be what others want? Christie Devon also found herself in this situation, and we saw how this resulted in the novel's inability to distinguish acting from eloquence. In *Work*, such a result seems inadvertent. With Beecher, such a result seems both conscious and an occasion for glee.

In a lecture given a year after his trial, upon the occasion of the third commencement of the National School of Elocution and Oratory in Philadelphia, Beecher deconstructs the category of "the natural":

> But it is said that this culture [training in the arts of oratory] is artificial; that it is mere posturing; that it is simple ornamentation. Ah! that is not because there has been so much of it, but because there has been so little of it. If a man were to begin, as he should, early; or if, beginning late, he were to addict himself assiduously to it, then the graces of speech, the graces of oratory, would be to him what all learning must be before it is perfect, namely, spontaneous. If he were to be trained earlier, then his training would not be called the science of ostentation or of acting. (*Oratory* 35)

It is not that this idea sounds foreign to modern readers; it becomes notable precisely in its appeal to modern ears, especially modern literary-critical ears. How many of the beliefs of modern literary critics—for example, beliefs regarding gender—grow out of the assumption that the category of the "natural" obfuscates what is in fact practiced, contingent, or socially constructed? The difference between this modern assumption and Beecher's is that he uses his deconstruction of the "natural" not to discredit the category of the natural but to celebrate it: "Consider this, audience: we really can achieve that wondrous quality of naturalness in oratory even if it doesn't come naturally!"

Here I come to that word again, which puts in relief the gap between a modern "actual" audience and the "authorial" (or intended) one, to use Peter Rabinowitz's terms. Beecher did not admit to his less-than-honorable actions concerning Libby Tilton; similarly, I imagine that he would not have admitted to his rhetorical inconsistencies if someone had been there to accuse him of them, not because he was a liar as well as a hypocrite but because he, unlike us, had not yet fully absorbed the consequences of his own sentimental pedagogy. He was still working at the tail end of an era where people believed in what Halttunen calls a "sentimental typology of conduct": "[Late nineteenth-century Americans] asserted that all aspects of manner and appearance were visible outward signs of inner moral qualities" (40). Beecher fully endorses this "sentimental typology of conduct" and makes it apply to prose style as well.

In "The Strange Woman," included in a collection of sermons entitled *Twelve Lectures to Young Men*, first published in 1844 (it originally featured only seven lectures), Beecher justifies what he calls "the plain and manly language of truth" (133). He associates this style with transparency. The sermon eventually rails against adultery and licentiousness, but at first it seems to be about something else. Beecher faced opposition in writing a sermon on this topic, and he begins by justifying what he is about to talk about: he believes that objections to speaking on this subject derive from a "false modesty" on the part of certain parishioners, who care "*how* you speak more than *what*" ("The Strange Woman" 128; emphasis in the original). Beecher hates indirection in prose, and this initial part of the sermon seems less about licentiousness than about how a person should use language: "The most dangerous writers in the English language are those whose artful insinuations and mischievous polish reflect upon the mind the image of impurity, without presenting the impurity itself" (128). Yet it becomes clear from the rest of the sermon that Beecher equates this "polished" prose style with the temptresses that he is warning his audience against. Young men must be told what these strange women are like: seductive without ("*Coverings of tapestry* and the *fine linen of Egypt* are hers" [139; emphasis in the original]), a charnel house within. While lecturing young men on avoiding certain kinds of women, he is also warning them against adopting the equivalent prose style. Beecher himself is committed to forging an oratorical style that leaves nothing hidden, whose *how* is equivalent to its *what*, whose outside is not a mask but a window. He implicitly sets himself up as the bearer of a prose style that will not deceive, and he does it here in an elaborate, metaphor-ridden, highly emotional sermon that comes out against the sin that he himself was forever marked by, adultery.[17]

In his defense of Beecher, Beecher's own lawyer asserted not just the possibility but the overriding need to believe in transparency. How do we read such an assertion? Halttunen reads it as evidence of a severe "anxiety" on the part of the middle class at the thought of being surrounded by confidence men. I think that we could also read it as evidence that the contradictions within sentimental persuasion have begun to be such a problem that they require the explicit naming of what is at stake. Yet what I find most interesting is that, despite our profession to value historical difference, we seem impelled to read such an assertion as evidence of hypocrisy. We assume that the makers of such assertions secretly knew that what they were saying contradicted the way things actually were.

Beecher himself lays bare the dilemma for the modern scholarly reader, the tension between our desire not to impose our modern understandings on a past culture that might not share our own critical predilections and our certainty about sentimental hypocrisy. Beecher sets our hypocrisy meters to level orange:

> Assume your position, therefore; and if a man says to you, "How is it you are so successful while using so little argument?" tell him that is the very reason of your success. Take things for granted, and men will not think to dispute them, but will admit them, and go on with you and become better men than if they had been treated to a logical process of argument, which

> aroused in them an argumentative spirit of doubt and opposition.[18] (*Yale Lectures* 125)

Of course, this statement about how a person should simply assert rather than argue contains an argument. The more Beecher reveals the self-consciousness of his performance—reveals that his performance is a performance—the less we can believe that he, as a sentimental orator, deserves our trust. In other words, I struggle to characterize him. The part of me that strives to become part of the "narrative audience" (the audience that believes what an author says to be true, not fictional) wants to exonerate Beecher from charges of hypocrisy, whereas the skeptical reader in me wants to condemn him. Let me split the difference and state that it is impossible for me to conclude whether Beecher is aware of the difficulties in which he embroils himself with his insistence that a preacher needs both to be and to seem sincere and that he should also plan to act spontaneously.

Beecher's *Lectures* offer two widely divergent solutions to the problem of an absent inner essence. The first one is suggested in his statement that "intuition is only a name for superior habit" (*Yale Lectures* 32). He offers a kind of behaviorist model of interiority. Again and again, the divinity students ask him what to do if they do not possess the requisite qualities for being a preacher. According to Beecher, if they act as if they do, the qualities will become part of them:

> One of my parishioners will say to me, "I have no benevolence, but you preach that I ought to give,—what shall I do?" I say to him, "*Give*, as a matter of duty, until you feel a pleasure in doing it, and the right feeling will come of itself." So, in addressing a congregation, a man may use the language of a feeling for the sake of getting and propagating the feeling. (*Lectures* 126; emphasis in the original)

This behavioral model is the opposite of the sentimental one, which assumes that the interior causes the exterior, which reflects it exactly. The behavioral model of personhood makes the interior a function of the exterior. Inner essence is determined by external actions. This is a solution to the position that we saw Stowe take in *The Minister's Wooing*:

that persuasiveness was largely a matter of genetic inheritance. With Beecher's behavioral model, anyone—even a white man—can become a sentimental orator.

The ramifications of this new model are too radical; this is a solution that Beecher will not pursue. Instead he goes down the opposite path. He tries to find a way to rescue the sentimental paradigm. One way he does it is through an endorsement of phrenology; "it has been the foundation on which I have worked" (*Yale Lectures* 94). Why is phrenology so appealing? Because it assures us that what we see on the outside reflects what is going on in the inside: "I see a man with a small brow and big in the lower part of his head, like a bull, and I know that that man is not likely to be a saint" (*Yale Lectures* 94). Phrenology gives a scientific reason, an immutable biological justification, for a reality that Beecher's own performativity threatens.

Unfortunately, however, Beecher cannot seriously offer the solution that all preachers become phrenologically accurate. But he can counsel that all preachers become like mothers. Phrenology and mothers had something in common in Beecher's time: each one gave biological assurance that the inner core matches the external appearance. Mothers possess a quality that is crucial for Beecher. People of the time believed that mothers acted on their impulses: "The mother makes haste to do those most offensive things for her darling child because she loves it" (*Yale Lectures* 36). Women's compulsiveness—the way they have no choice but to act out their inner feelings—guards against the possibility of hypocrisy that Beecher himself opens up with his insistence on preachers' "willowiness." Women, like spontaneous men, are under compulsion to act out their feelings. Beecher stumbles into the solution that Stowe finds in *The Minister's Wooing*. Yet Stowe cultivates this solution with much more success than her hapless brother does because she is not at the same time trying to codify how mothers and orators should appear.

Beecher shows us why the saintly Mary Scudder inevitably coexists with the devilish Aaron Burr. It is not just that Henry Ward Beecher himself is actually less like Will than like Burr. Beecher tries harder than anyone else to overcome the gap between seeming and being. Yet he reveals what happens when sentimental orators must both persuade an audience and teach it about persuasion. Beecher shows what happens when someone tries to codify the sentimental orator, to analyze her, to break down what makes her tick in order to teach others to become like her, other than simply allowing her to exist. By extension, he brings to the fore a tension in any sentimental work, between its persuasiveness and its self-reflexivity.

Beecher is a victim of his own success: he is the sentimental orator who aims to produce other sentimental orators. He is nakedly didactic, and his didacticism is not in the service of any cause greater than itself. Sentimentality without a cause greater than its own self-perpetuation founders. Thus we have come full circle since the beginning of this book: from seeing how the sentimentalists wrest oratorical power from the professional (white male) orators to seeing how one professional white male orator later tries to wrest it back for his brethren. But he cannot do it, because to democratize sentimental rhetoric is to undermine it.

In order to be sentimentally persuasive a person has to have no choice but to tell the truth. The sentimental system of persuasion does rely on practice, if not training. Madame Frontignac must spend a certain amount of time in Mary's presence before she can hear Mary's silent message; Dr. Wentworth has to be trained to hear nature's message and implies that others could be so trained ("Between Pete and you [Agate Bissell, a kind-hearted, crusty old maid], I hope to make a good girl of Rose," says Rose's father [*Norwood* 87]). But the system collapses when we suppose that there is nothing natural about sentimental persuasiveness, that the picture that someone presents to the world might belie what he or she really feels. This belief coalesces in modern readers and leads them to cry hypocrisy. Nor is it any better to suppose that how a person feels flows out of sentimental gestures and poses: we might no longer be talking about hypocrisy but something not much better, a case where it is quite possible that oratory has been inspired only by a desire to gain esteem or money.

The suggestion of the artfulness of sentimental persuasion first happens in *Norwood* as though through a mistake, when Pete takes Rose's laughter for tears. But this kind of potential mistake becomes foundational in putting forth a behaviorist model of good womanhood or sentimental oratory: for a little while at least, the hearts of good women and effective orators have not yet caught up with their outward demeanor. What appears to be a comic mistake in a not-very-successful sentimental novel actually foreshadows a necessity. When these new sentimental orators, working women or professional white men, need to persuade people of certain things, they rely on appearance rather than reality at least for a little while. That admission of what may be a small gap between what is meant by these orators and what is perceived by their audiences is enough for grave doubts to flower in the contemporaneous audience about the trust that these silver-tongued sentimental orators deserve. For modern readers, Alcott and Beecher inadvertently paved a way of reading sentimental novels from which most modern readers, especially modern literary critics, have yet to find an exit.

Where Does Emotion Come From?

The usual case against sentimentality emphasizes its sodden quality, its association with tears. Many canonical novels also inspire strong emotional reactions, however, so detractors have taken pains to distinguish the way in which the sentimental novels inspire emotion: through artifice and manipulation. In "What Is Sentimentality?" June Howard traces the animosity that sentimental novels inspire back to a distinction that modern audiences make "between manipulated sentiment and genuine emotion" (65). For most critical readers, sentimental novels are less genuinely emotional than manipulatively sentimental. Howard disagrees with this kind of dismissal. Drawing on research done by psychologists and anthropologists, she concludes that "neither the socially constructed nor the bodily nature of sentiment can distinguish it from emotion in general" (69). Feelings, according to Howard, do not "well up naturally inside individuals" as "the common sense of the modern world" would have it, although she acknowledges that "tropes of interiority and self-expression are difficult to resist" (65).

Howard lays out two different models of emotional expression: our commonsense model that sees emotion as something that is not manipulated, something that wells up naturally, versus an empirically true model, which the sentimental novels follow and which strikes us, ironically, as false. Complementing Howard's work, Warhol's "As You Stand, So You Feel and Are" historicizes two models of emotional expression that roughly correspond to Howard's models. Warhol traces a model of socially constructed (rather than internally driven) emotional expression to the latter nineteenth century, associating it with two thinkers, George Henry Lewes and a figure encountered earlier in this chapter, François Delsarte.[19] Like Howard, Warhol suggests that this is the model that nineteenth-century sentimental authors follow. According to her, the sentimental novelists understood the relationship between gestures and poses the way Delsarte did: "The sentimental novelist, like the Delsartean actor, relies on a set of 'mechanical' exercises (as Delsarte's detractors called his gymnastic drill for actors) to get the body of the reader into the pose that would generate real compassion, the pose of weeping" ("As You Stand" 114). Warhol goes on to describe the "mechanical cues" that sentimental novels provide for the readers, everything from a heightened poetical language to the assurance that our most beloved cultural myths are true. She shows how our modern commonsense model of emotions is not the only one possible.[20] Howard goes further, with her fund of empirical research, to show how this Delsartean model might actually be *right.*

If I am correct that Beecher's and Alcott's ideas about emotion follow this Delsartean model, then they might be right too. The irony, I would claim, is this: it does not matter. Knowing about the contingency of our modern model of how emotion arises—or even its falsity—does not necessarily affect our reading practices. If readers want to feel the power of Stowe's wordless, sentimental orators, they must forget what Alcott and Beecher have taught them about how sentimental orators manipulate their audiences. They must believe that Mary Scudder knows not of what she speaks and that Little Eva is not a heuristic device but a person; in other words, modern readers must believe that Stowe was not herself busily plotting how she could best manipulate her audience through the creation of such ingenuous characters. But this is very difficult for modern readers to do: knowing that there is no such thing as an "authentic" emotion does little to ease the readers' skepticism. Here is a thought experiment to get at the distinction I am trying to make. First, picture yourself witnessing a very young puppy being abused, kicked so hard he curls up in a ball and starts to whimper. Ask yourself this question: how would you feel? Now dissect an ad that was made for a local (conservative or liberal, whichever you like less) politician who is campaigning against animal abuse that features a very young puppy being so abused. Ask yourself these questions: why did they feature that cocker spaniel puppy rather than another breed? Why did they end the ad with that close-up of the puppy's mother? What effect does it have that Alicia Silverstone provided the narration? My suspicion is that you are more affected by the first exercise than by the second. The extent to which we focus on the mechanisms that sentimental authors use to make us cry is the extent to which our tears will dry up.

Reader-response criticism has allowed us to historicize different audiences. We are now aware of how past readers might have read differently from the way that contemporary readers do. Tompkins uses this insight to structure her famous defense of *Uncle Tom's Cabin* in "Sentimental Power": "If the fiction written in the nineteenth century by women whose works sold in the hundreds of thousands has seemed narrow and parochial to the critics of the twentieth century, that narrowness and parochialism belong not to these works nor to the women who wrote them; they are the beholders' share" (146). Tompkins implies that we can come to a newfound appreciation of Stowe's novel if we can only recapture the beliefs of that past audience. But knowing about how past readers read typologically does not necessarily translate into such a reading practice for ourselves.[21] Similarly, knowing about the extent to which emotion actually works from the outside in might not prevent us from associating nineteenth-century sentimental novels with manipulation. Warhol and Howard do not so much document a new (to us) way of conceptualizing the sentimental orator and author as confirm modern readers' suspicions of how they have functioned all along. In fact, we have come full circle: the association with craft and manipulation that dogged the nineteenth-century professional male orator has settled, in our own era, on the sentimental orator despite the fact that Stowe's version of this sentimental orator was created specifically to evade it.

In "The Paradox of the Actor," Diderot stages a dialogue between a man who believes that actors who are also "men of sensibility" will be the most accomplished. The other participant in the dialogue, Diderot's stand-in, sets him straight, arguing that great actors are ones with the coolest head, the most self-possession: "A violent man who's beside himself can never impose his will upon us: this is an advantage confined to the man who's in control of himself" (*Selected Writings* 104). Here we have an echo of Channing's distaste for the frantic man, whom Channing would bar from political assemblies. But in removing the man who has succumbed to his emotions from the stage, Diderot allows us to be moved by the morally unsavory among us. Diderot characterizes great actors (and, by extension, great orators) as having "few morals, no friends, hardly any of those sweet and sacred bonds which acquaint us with the pains and pleasures of another who shares our own. I have often seen an actor laughing off-stage, but I don't recall every having seen one weeping" (135). Actors' moral deficiency lies in their lack of sympathy, exactly what Stowe's and even Alcott's sentimental orators have an excess of. Though Diderot's actor can make the audience weep, he himself will remain unmoved. Diderot, like Channing, evokes Ion in his moment of selfish self-possession; Diderot, in fact, brings him to center stage.

Norman Hapgood, editor of *Collier's* and *Harper's Weekly,* drama critic and author of *The Stage in America, 1897–1900* (1901), commented on Diderot's essay in 1889. He takes Diderot to task for supposing that the best actor will remain unmoved by the emotions he pretends to feel. Hapgood quotes Charles Darwin's *The Expression of the Emotions in Man and Animals*: "He who gives way to violent gestures will increase his rage; he who does not control the signs of fear will experience fear in a greater degree" (qtd. in Hapgood 10). Hapgood builds on Darwin's claim by saying that "[t]he actor must have a double-consciousness, as we all have in daily life; he must be himself and another at once, must control himself and lose himself at the same time" (11). Hapgood does not enter into the debate over the actor and orator's moral character, but we can see how his understanding of the relationship between gesture and emotion would at least rescue a man like Beecher from charges of hypocrisy. Yet it is not enough. Opening up the possibility of the self-possessed orator, even one who starts to feel the emotions he is inducing in the audience and in himself, opens up the possibility of disingenuous eloquence. We can see a cycle forming: Diderot is countered by Channing, who is countered by Stowe, who is countered, however inadvertently, by Alcott and Beecher. A proclamation of the thorough-going artifice of the orator is followed by an attempt to downplay and justify that artifice, which is followed by an attempt to deny that artifice completely. This denial is followed by exposure. Howard and Warhol are part of a similar cycle: they try to justify the artifice that modern readers, legatees of Beecher's self-conscious sentimental orator, cannot help associating with Stowe. The problem is that this justification is not enough. Sentimental rhetoric requires us to read as if there is not any artifice at all.

Postscript

Sentimental texts eschew the written; sentimental authors craft works that reject the notion of craft and put forth as winning orators people who hardly speak. These are some of the paradoxes of sentimental rhetoric. As these last two chapters have shown, these paradoxes did not become debilitating until the latter part of the nineteenth century. Sentimental rhetoric solved the problem of disingenuous eloquence for a particular mid-century audience, which was not the audience that arose toward the end of the century. Even less so is it the audience for this monograph.

Walter Ong has made a useful distinction when it comes to talking about audience (a distinction that is nonetheless distinguished further in my final chapter). For now I think that it can serve to illuminate the variable credibility that the sentimental solution to disingenuous eloquence has for its different readers. In "The Writer's Audience Is Always a Fiction," Ong argues that authors do not write for actual readers; they ask readers to fictionalize themselves into the kind of audience the work requires. For Ong, the creation of an audience has to happen at a certain stage of narrative evolution: the reader-as-boon-companion that Ernest Hemingway creates, Ong points out, would have made no sense to an Elizabethan audience, who expected to be instructed as well as pleased (65). Hemingway's creation of a narrator who assumes that the reader is already familiar with what he is saying would have left them cold. One ramification of Ong's argument is that particular readers—removed in time from the original publication of a written text—might find it hard to fictionalize themselves in the way the text requires.

Indeed, this is what seems to have happened with the sentimental novels of Stowe and of her fellow "scribbling women," although Hawthorne's 1855 moniker requires me to complicate the notion of audience that Ong proposes (this is not at all an emendation "against the grain"): not all readers read alike even if they live during the same period. Just as there were skeptical readers of Stowe during her own time, so there are credulous readers of Stowe now, who have no problem taking on the vicarious witness role that she requires in her wrenching (to them) scenes of sentimental persuasion. In fact, the distinction that Ong takes as a founding moment of the fictionalized audience, the shift from oral to written discourse, is exactly the distinction that Stowe wants to deny. The audience that she fictionalizes must be able to conceive of a text as an oral act: the unmediated outpouring of one sufferer to another. I think that contemporary literary critics find it hard, in their roles as critics, to read this way.

Ong writes movingly at the close of his essay that "oral communication, which is built into existential actuality more directly than written, has within it a momentum that works for the removal of masks. Lovers try to strip off all masks" (74). This echoes a distinction made throughout Ong's article (and throughout his other work) between orality and literacy, the shift from the first to the second upon which his argument rests. Authors, unlike speakers, do not have their audience in front of them and thus must create it. Written communication requires masks, complicated contortions on the part of readers as we try to become who we are really not. Stowe aspires to orality and to strip her novel and its readers of pretense. And perhaps that implicit claim—that here be a text without craft; credulous readers wanted—is just what disables contemporary literary critics from fictionalizing themselves into who she wants us to be. The final two chapters take seriously the idea that contemporary readers, especially that subset made up of professional readers and teachers of literature, have trouble fictionalizing themselves into the proper audience for sentimental rhetoric. Yet rather than continue the story of sentimental rhetoric's fall that the past two chapters have offered, they show how sentimental rhetoric can nevertheless illuminate and reshape some of our current reading and writing practices.

5

In Defense of Reading Badly

The first four chapters of this book have created a picture of the sentimental reader. How was she meant to read? What was she meant to believe? What happens when she ceases to read a certain way and believe certain things? By establishing the character of this nineteenth-century reader, I believe that we might better understand our own. Chapters 5 and 6 explore how much our own reading practices have changed from those of the ideal nineteenth-century reader of sentimental rhetoric. Many would claim that they have changed radically. But I hope to convince readers that sentimental rhetoric is not as distant from us—or below us—as we might think. Sentimental rhetoric still has things to teach us.

This chapter applies a "lesson" of sentimental rhetoric to a contemporary problem in writing pedagogy: in this case, how to get novice English majors to read critically. (This problem leads to a question: just what does "critical reading" entail for English professors?) Here I defend a bad way of reading, which we often observe in students new to the discipline of English. Beginning students read fiction in order to identify with the characters. Thus it seems perfectly reasonable to them to dismiss a novel whose characters they find unsympathetic. They also "read to identify" when it comes to nonfictional or argumentative works. In this case, our students read to identify the commonsense lessons that they already believe in (or think they should believe in). Hence a nuanced text is reduced to showing readers that we need to strive after our dreams or that a person's hard work, regardless of race or gender, will be rewarded in the end. Avant-garde fiction or argumentative texts whose lessons cannot easily be identified are met with resistance.[1]

Mariolina Salvatori explains this bad reading process in detail, through the lens of Wolfgang Iser, who argues that the meaning of a text depends on the interaction between text and reader. Readers are not completely free to create the text out of the whole cloth of their particular context, but neither can they assume that the text's meaning exists "out there." Here is Salvatori, glossing Iser and going on to explain how students resist his model of reading:

> In the act of its reading, the work cannot, nor should, be reduced to one meaning, one perspective; the reader should not deny the possibility of subsequent revisions of meanings, subsequent modifications of perspectives. Unfortunately it is mostly against the indeterminacy and the dynamism of a literary work that our students defend themselves by reducing it either to the assumed reality of the text (i.e., the message, the information, the main idea, all conceived as stable, finite units), or to their own subjectivity (i.e., "I can relate to this," "I cannot relate to this," which are often spurious judgments based on ephemeral associations or pre-established perspectives). ("Reading and Writing" 660)

Salvatori does not use the term "identification," but I think that this is what she is describing. Students identify with the text in one of two ways: (mis)identifying its gist either in terms of the supposed similarity of a character with themselves or in terms of its simplified "message." Although Salvatori speaks only in terms of the violence that this kind of reading does to a text, she implies the violence that it does to the readers: it prevents them from ever being able to develop intellectually because they believe themselves, like the text, to be always already finished.

Beyond Salvatori's reader-response-inflected insight, why does "reading to identify" drive English professors crazy? It may help to bring in a phrase much used these days to describe what those at home in the discipline of English perform on their texts—"critical reading." Yet "critical reading" is not a neutral description: it performs crucial work for English departments by assuring skeptics that what we do is very hard, although teachable. It differentiates us from those reading amateurs out there, which is what our beginning students are. This phrase carries an aura, and it is not in our interests to pick it apart. In "Uncritical Reading," Michael Warner calls "critical reading" "the folk ideology of a learned profession, so close to us that we seldom feel the need to explain it" (14).[2] Instead he suggests that "critical reading" is most often defined in opposition to instances of noncritical reading, what our beginning students do and what it is our mission to train them out of.

Although we normally do not pick "critical reading" apart, I think that we can still get a sense of some of its sine qua nons by looking at how many of us go about training students out of their reading predilections. Salvatori and her colleagues at the University of Pittsburgh deliberately pick out difficult texts for their students to grapple with. In the words of David Bartholomae and Anthony Petrosky, "When we chose the essays [for the anthology *Ways of Reading*], we were looking for . . . texts that leave some work for the reader to do" (viii). In this predilection for difficult, "unfinished" texts, the Pittsburgh cohort is by no means alone. But they are distinguished by their translation of this desideratum into a set of well-thought-out, teachable practices.[3] We can infer from them what good critical reading looks like: a reading practice that asks readers to make connections between different aspects of a text or between the text and themselves that demonstrates critical reflexivity (readers strive to understand how they read as much as what they read) and that resists what Anne Berthoff, borrowing a term from psychology, has called "premature closure" (qtd. in Salvatori, "Reading and Writing" 662). Difficult texts are valuable because they force students to do what they should be doing even with ostensibly simple ones: resist a desire to foreclose the meanings that a text might have. Even if we do not assign difficult texts in our own classes, we still demonstrate that we share the aim of Salvatori and her colleagues when we tell our students that it is much more important for them to explore a good question than to answer it definitively. This high valuation of prolonged questioning rather than precipitous answering reflects the current thinking about writing (and reading) pedagogy in comp studies: exploration over assertion, process over product.

This understanding of "critical reading" with its prizing of difficulty sounds good to me (and, I hope, to you) because of my sympathy with this position—and not just because I cynically want to shore up my professional standing by insisting on the difference between what I do and what my first-year students do. My sympathy arises, in part, because of what I perceive to be the implicit politics of such a critical stance. Like most people, I believe that prolonged and self-reflexive analysis is necessary for good politics to happen.[4] Yet exactly how does critical reading lead to good political positions? We might see it by imagining how "uncritical reading" leads to bad ones. "[I]dentification, self-forgetfulness, reverie, sentimentality, enthusiasm, literalism, aversion, distraction" (15)—this is an inventory of "uncritical" reading practices offered by Michael Warner in "Uncritical Reading." They are all forms of readers' forgetting themselves in the face of an external authority—the text. And in a slippage that is as natural to English professors as breathing, "literary text" becomes a metonym for any external authority (which could itself be analyzed textually). In other words, uncritical reading forfeits autonomy in favor of unthinking obeisance to powers that uncritical readers assume to lie beyond the reach of their intervention.[5]

Is there anything to be said against critical reading or for uncritical reading? Lots, I hope. Warner himself notes that some kinds of "uncritical reading" are as exacting as the "critical reading" that we valorize. Moreover, by assuming that only critical reading practices are admirable, we tend to erase the presence of uncritical reading practices in figures of the past whom we admire. Warner brings up the Puritan author Mary Rowlandson, who is not a critical reader. In *A Narrative of the Captivity and Restoration of Mrs. Mary Rowlandson* (1682), she describes her reading of the Bible as though every passage her eyes alighted on was a personal message from God sent to her in her time of travail. Her practice of reading the Bible, however, is far from untrained or undisciplined; instead it is shaped by a large body of devotional manuals on reading scripture, relying on "repetition, incorporation, and affective regulation" (Warner 31). Yet critics, Warner notes, have rewritten Rowlandson in their own image: "the ritual gesture, when confronted with a Rowlandson, is to show that this apparently uncritical reading really was critical in some sense or another" (32). Look at how her way of reading allowed her to subvert ministerial authority. Look at how it was a necessary part of her self-positing (Warner 32).[6] We cannot ignore Rowlandson's uncritical reading practice without collapsing the present into the past.

This chapter aims to take up what Warner identifies as the barely begun project of reevaluating (and revaluing) certain "uncritical reading" practices. I focus here on the first uncritical reading practice that Warner names, "identification." "Reading to identify" might not always be the bane we take it to be. And "difficulty" might as often result in political paralysis as insight. I begin this reclamation project by exploring an earlier moment in the history of reading to identify, linking it to two often-taught nineteenth-century American texts about slavery, Herman Melville's "Benito Cereno" (1855) and *Uncle Tom's Cabin*. The first of these rejects identification, while the second embraces it. Stowe's antislavery epic depends upon identification in two senses. Her readers must be able to identify what her characters are like as a necessary precondition of their identifying with her characters' plight.

Many critics see *Uncle Tom's Cabin* as a very bad political novel, maybe even the worst possible in that its popularity enabled it to leave what they see as a murderously racist legacy. James Baldwin has argued that Stowe's insistence on identification (in the first sense) lies at the root of her bad politics. According to Baldwin, identifying people based on their membership in a particular group is denying them their humanity. The human being is not "merely a member of a Society or a Group" (533). For Baldwin: "He is . . . something more than that, something resolutely indefinable, unpredictable . . . only within this web of ambiguity, paradox, this hunger, danger, darkness, can we find at once ourselves and the power that will free us from ourselves" (533–34).

"Ambiguity, paradox, this hunger, danger, darkness"—why can Baldwin not settle on one precise term? Yet how could Baldwin identify a group of humans without destroying his own argument? If the sentimental way of characterizing people is so simple as to be clearly inaccurate ("their characters are flat and unrealistic" is a charge often leveled at the sentimentalists), Baldwin's solution is *not* to say "this is what these people really *are* like." As he said in 1989, forty years after "Everybody's Protest Novel," "[a]s long as you think you're white, there's no hope for you. 'Cause as long as you think you're white, I'm going to be forced to think I'm black" (qtd. in Miller 347). Baldwin denies that anyone could ever fully identify what blacks and whites are like—and certainly not by reading their surfaces. He does not name "difficulty" as the solution to Stowe's essentialist simplifications,[7] but the process that he lays out to counteract her way of reading is one that bears some resemblance to Salvatori's method of introducing students to texts (or people) that demand open-ended interpretations of their meaning.

Hortense Spillers has taken up Baldwin's call to arms against Stowe.[8] Spillers, like Baldwin, had no doubt where Stowe's path, paved with good intentions, leads. She calls *Uncle Tom's Cabin* "a lethal weapon" (547). At the root of Spillers's animosity toward this novel lies her claim that Stowe depicts her black characters as already fully identified. Stowe can confidently "explain . . . the central nervous system of the African" (543). She stands guilty of an epic act of hubris: just as she reduces individuals into "types," so she assumes that her own particular view of slavery is the only one possible:

> Stowe's view then, is not *the* "Gospel," already an Ur-text of polyvalence, but it is just *that*, a *view*, which, in its systematic assertions—and ironically enough, this is the foundation of its powers—*rivals*, even *analogizes*, in every sense, the omnipresent and univocal narrative structures in which "slavery" continues to arise in the fiction. In short, Stowe poses a purely local and quite particularistic notion *as* the place of an imagined and fictitious "universality." (552; emphases in the original)

According to Spillers, Stowe rejects any kind of complex interpretation, claiming that slavery (and the people it involves) is easily identified for what it is. For Stowe, it is not "slavery" but slavery. Her novel makes it seem as if "slavery" has only one interpretation—which really means that it needs no interpretation at all. Texts get no simpler than this.[9]

Spillers also takes up Baldwin's implied solution to this problem of simplicity. Like him, she touts a mode of representation that allows for human complexity. Spillers tries to neutralize Stowe's poison by administering irony in heavy doses. She champions Ishmael Reed's deeply ironic *Flight to Canada*: "For every single page of the 192 printed pages of the edition I am using, there could be as many source pages to read as the novel is long. This multiplying of textual allusiveness and the freedom of movement . . . would suggest that 'narrative time' for Reed is not imagined as a linear progression alone. It 'imitates' the tricks and intricacies of the loop" (566). Reed offers a corrective not just to Stowe's particular theory of blacks and whites but also to her implicit claim that slavery is not subject to complex interpretation. Having the power to loop back and forth in the story of racial injustice allows the readers to start anew and try out alternative paths, evading what these critics see as sentimentality's murderous legacy. For Spillers, Reed provides not just a corrective reading but a corrective lesson on how to read. Even more strongly than in Baldwin, we hear echoes of Salvatori's own recursive, self-reflexive pedagogical method.

I want to try to redeem "identification," which we can now see is not just a reading practice found in our students but one celebrated by Stowe and condemned by Baldwin and Spillers. I want to defend it on grounds that are precisely political: to show how it might be crucial, in fact, for taking a stance against racial injustice. I do this by comparing *Uncle Tom's Cabin* to another seminal nineteenth-century text about slavery, Melville's "Benito Cereno," which not only champions "critical reading" but specifically takes aim at reading to identify generally and American sentimental rhetoric in particular.[10] Contemporary critics of "Benito Cereno" notice its critiquing power, yet they do not notice how their own positioning of this novella as an antislavery text involves them in just such a practice of identification whose rejection they celebrate in Melville.

In what follows I make an implicit association between difficulty and irony. In fact, it is much worse than that: I would go so far as to name irony, "the mode of the unsaid, the unheard, the unseen" (Hutcheon 9), as the paradigmatic mode of difficulty. Let me try to justify this way of thinking. Lori Chamberlain, in her article on the teaching of irony, describes how difficult it is to contain irony, which has been variously characterized as a figure, a trope, a mode of discourse, and even a worldview. Irony spreads. Chamberlain touches on the politics of irony, suggesting that it is a discourse of the ruling class; but this containing move is undercut by Linda Hutcheon's view that irony is "transideological" (10), wielded as often by the oppressed as by the oppressors. This is not to say that irony can be anything to anyone. Part of the difficulty of ironic interpretation comes from the way that it seems at once to anchor the most radical reader-response theories in that the "*interpreters* [of irony] 'mean' as much as *ironists* do" (Hutcheon 12; emphases in the original) and to enable the most rigorous sorting of good and bad readers in that an ironic text always holds out the possibility of "not getting it." Irony seduces both poststructuralists like Hutcheon and taxonomizers like Wayne Booth, but one thing that it does not do is make for easy reading.

On its most basic level, an ironic text requires the reader to reject, at least in part, the surface meaning. No ironic text is self-evident or transparent or simple, all those qualities that characterize first-year students' assumptions about what they read. In fact, an ironic text attacks the holder of such assumptions. Reading an ironic text like Jonathan Swift's "A Modest Proposal" as transparent not only makes the reader appear foolish but invites comparisons between the naïve reader and the cannibalistic narrator. It seems that ironic texts might be ones to choose, as Lori Chamberlain has, when aiming to make students into critical readers. Just as irony is the paradigmatic mode of difficulty, "Benito Cereno" is a paradigmatically ironic text. Yet it is precisely the unrelenting irony, the unrelenting difficulty, of "Benito Cereno" that allows me to problematize "critical reading," with its celebration of readers who are prevented from identifying and readings that refuse to end.

Identifying Racism in "Benito Cereno"

Amasa Delano, the protagonist of "Benito Cereno," suffers from a compulsion to identify in two senses: he strives to identify what is happening on the ship that he encounters docked near an island off the coast of Chile and strives to identify with the sickly Spanish captain of this ship, Benito Cereno. The former compulsion, at least, is shared by first-time readers of this enigmatic story: like Delano, we struggle to figure out what is going on. Melville makes it difficult both for Delano and for us from the beginning. As is so often the case with Melville, metaphysical questions take physical form: Captain Delano's first glimpse of Benito Cereno's ship, the *San Dominick*, is obstructed by the "vapors partly mantling the hull" (38). Eventually, the narrator reveals what the ship really is: "Upon a still nigher approach . . . the true character of the vessel was plain—a Spanish merchantman of the first class, carrying Negro slaves, amongst other valuable freight" (39). Yet the book eventually undermines even this "true" appearance, revealing that the slaves have mutinied and taken control, with Babo, who masquerades as Cereno's body servant, as the leader. Yet until the very last minute Delano clings to the certainty that things are just as they appear.

Delano resembles first-year readers, with their almost physical aversion to digging deeper in their readings of the "texts" surrounding them. "All this is very queer, thought Captain Delano, with a qualmish sort of emotion; but, as one feeling incipient seasickness, he strove, by ignoring the symptoms, to get rid of the malady" (66). Delano attempts to cast off a suspicion that the situation around him is more complex than he has assumed. He holds on to his belief that appearance equals essence: Benito Cereno is indeed in control of a ship and its human freight that has foundered upon hard times. As Melville would have it, this, for one thing, makes him a fool. Melville takes quite particular aim at readers who read to identify by associating Delano's practice of reading with a much more objectionable characteristic than foolishness.

Delano is racist. His suspicions that something might be amiss are repeatedly quieted by evidence of the close relationship between Cereno and Babo:

> Sometimes the Negro gave his master his arm, or took his handkerchief out of his pocket for him; performing these and similar offices with that affectionate zeal which transmutes into something filial or fraternal acts in themselves menial, and which has gained for the Negro the repute of making the most pleasing body servant in the world; one, too, whom a master need be on no stiffly superior terms with, but may treat with familiar trust—less a servant than a devoted companion. (43)

According to Delano, Babo, like others of his race, is marked by his devotion to his master. Delano's characterizations of "Negroes" present them as simple, easygoing folks, with a gift for entertaining: "And above all [with "the Negro"] is the great gift of good humor, . . . [a] certain easy cheerfulness, harmonious in every glance and gesture, as though God had set the whole Negro to some pleasant tune" (73). But, of course, the twist of "Benito Cereno" gives the lie to these characterizations: the black characters are shown to be the shrewd ones, not just in their mutiny but in their ability to present Delano with the pictures that he needs in order to be persuaded that nothing is truly amiss. In "Benito Cereno," blacks do the reading instead of being read. Delano thinks that he can identify what the black mutineers on board the *San Dominick* are like just by looking at them: his identification relies on an ideology of white supremacy.

Defenders of the "transplanted African" like Stowe and Beecher emphasize this figure's innocent, animal-like qualities. Delano's depiction of the blacks on board the *San Dominick* seems to share in this conventional nineteenth-century trope:

> His attention had been drawn to a slumbering Negress . . . lying, with youthful limbs carelessly disposed . . . like a doe in the shade of a woodland rock. Sprawling at her lapped breasts was her wide-awake fawn, stark naked, its black little body half lifted from the deck, crosswise with its dam's; its hands, like two paws, clambering upon her; its mouth and nose ineffectually rooting to get at the mark; and meantime giving a vexatious half-grunt. (63)

Yet Melville takes the animal metaphor far enough to suggest motives other than tolerance in the minds of those who insist upon it. In the process, he suggests something unsavory about sentimental defenders of the slaves: their insistence on black people's family feeling—what they have in common with the whites—might derive from the assumption of their animal nature (one of Stowe and Beecher's favorite ways to characterize a black man, as we have seen, is as a big, friendly black dog). What seems to be an honest attempt by the sentimental defenders of the slave to show their white readers how similar blacks are to them (they also love their families) is at the same time a way of asserting their difference (black people love their family members out of animal instinct, not as white people do).

When Stowe focuses on scenes depicting the slave mother's maternal instinct or the natural devotedness of a male slave, she intends for the reader to see it through her eyes (that is, for the reader to assume that the narrator is her). But Melville filters such images through Delano, and the novella establishes a distance between Delano's perceptions and ours which becomes immense if we have already read the novella once. Like Reed, Melville provides loops for his readers. Melville offers us a retroactive guide not just to reading Delano but also to reading Stowe. This guide does not encourage us to reread with kindness. Melville provides his readers with enough distance so that they can reject the sentimental way of viewing slaves. "Benito Cereno" might even cause us to reread ourselves with a critical eye: to the extent that we accepted Delano's version of events, we must consider the idea that our own insistence on transparency may be linked to racism and an urge to dominate.[11] Even though we began in the same boat as Delano, at some point in the first section of this novella we are meant to want to disembark: to disavow this sentimental, racist man, who insists on easy identifications.

Readers of "Benito Cereno" must become "critical readers" or else. Melville shows us the misapprehension and racism that arise from insisting that everything means just what it seems to. Characters in "Benito Cereno" are *not* what they appear to be. Melville requires that, unlike Delano, we resist closing off our readings too early. Yet Melville's irony, the way in which he makes his text difficult, creates problems, being both bottomless and unstinting. It is not just that we cannot close off reading this novella too early; we can never close it off at all. We can never identify an appearance that we can know matches reality. Melville's irony riddles any ground we might have hoped to stand on.

Melville's story is ironic in different ways. It not only frequently uses irony as a trope but also exhibits an ironic attitude toward the world. First, let me discuss Melville's use of irony as a trope (a particular rhetorical device that defines a certain kind of verbal utterance): many of the lines in this novella are ironic. For example, the words scrawled underneath the canvas-wrapped figurehead on the *San Dominick*—"SEGUID VUESTRO JEFE" (follow your leader)—can be read straight only the first time, when they seem simply to refer to the way the crew members of a ship should follow their captain. But the second time we see the line we cannot take it at face value: a cable has whipped off the canvas that wrapped what Delano had taken to be the figurehead of the ship, "revealing . . . death for the figurehead, in a human skeleton, chalky comment on the chalked words below, FOLLOW YOUR LEADER" (88).

The skeleton belongs to Don Alexandro Aranda, Cereno's friend and the owner of Babo. The line suggests the threat that Cereno labored under: either he follows the orders of Babo or else he follows his friend into death. The line appears again briefly as a spur to Delano's men to attack and capture the *San Dominick*'s black mutineers (90). It reappears, in slight variation, as the very last words of the story: "Benito Cereno, borne on the bier, did, indeed, follow his leader" (104). Here its reconstructed meaning seems slightly harder to settle upon: it could mean that the deeply religious Cereno is following Jesus and thus could produce the feeling of an uplifting ending or could be interpreted as having a more sinister implication. Cereno has also followed Aranda and even Babo, who was executed a few months earlier.

But if the reconstruction of this line is difficult to pin down exactly, the sum total of these different reconstructions denies us any sense of a stable meaning. Certainly there is no one signifier:one signified, to use Linda Hutcheon's description of irony in general (13).[12] It is not that this line does not have a meaning, but that its meaning does not ever stay the same: the way readers interpret this line depends completely on context, and the context itself is not stable. "Benito Cereno" is a very different book depending on whether it is a first or second reading.[13]

Now let me talk about how irony is more than just a trope in this novella. David Holdcroft claims that "the proper way to understand an ironical text . . . is not in terms of the frequency of ironical utterances it contains, but in terms of its being an expression of an ironist's attitude to the world" (508).[14] "Benito Cereno" manifests this attitude. Melville refuses to indulge not just in any particular belief but in anything that might provide the grounds for belief. We can see this if we look at the narrator. Melville's omniscient narrator tempts us with epistemological certainty, but it is only a siren call.[15] The story is written in the third person, and the narrator has a distanced perspective from the events happening on board: "In the year 1799, Captain Amasa Delano, of Duxbury in Massachusetts, command[ed] a large sealer" (37). The narrator also seems to know more than any of the characters: for example, he mentions a detail that happens on board that goes "unperceived by the American" (82). He seems a source of firm, context-independent knowledge, a way out of the ironic hall of mirrors that Melville has set up.

The narrator of "Benito Cereno" is only sometimes omniscient, however—another way of saying that he is not. The narration sometimes seems focalized through Delano, although it is difficult to discern the borders of this shift. Upon observing the *San Dominick* and its inhabitants, Delano is dismayed at what he finds. The narrator describes his state of mind: "[S]urprise was lost in pity, both for the Spaniards and blacks, alike evidently reduced from scarcity of water and provisions, while long-continued suffering seemed to have brought out the less good-natured qualities of the Negroes, besides at the same time impairing the Spaniard's [Cereno's] authority over them" (42).

This passage records what are clearly Delano's thoughts. It is Delano even down to the characteristic hypocrisy of thinking the "Negroes" to be generally good-natured while at the same time fixating on the hierarchy that is necessary to keep them in line. The next words also seem to be filtered through Delano's mind: "But, under the circumstances, precisely this condition of things was to have been anticipated" (42). Even here, a little doubt might creep in about how much is Delano and how much the narrator. The next line is the one where it becomes extremely difficult to distinguish them: "In armies, navies, cities, or families, in nature herself, nothing more relaxes good order than misery" (42). Because this line generalizes where the previous lines kept to the particulars and strikes us as an omniscient narrator–like thing to say, our tendency might be to believe that it comes from the narrator, who is external to the story, and not Delano and thus is untainted by Delano's inability to see clearly. But we cannot be so sure: even if it comes from the narrator, it is clearly something that Delano would agree with. He has infected the narrator with his own biases.[16]

This infection continues throughout the story. Here is a description of the taking over of the *San Dominick* by Delano's crew: "Exhausted, the blacks now fought in despair. Their red tongues lolled, wolflike, from their black mouths. But the pale sailors' teeth were set; not a word was spoken, and, in five minutes more, the ship was won" (91). Delano is nowhere near, yet the narrator offers the kind of description that we expect from Delano, with his penchant for turning blacks into animals through his metaphors. By sharing Delano's perceptions, the narrator becomes fallible because part of Delano's unreliability as a source of knowledge about what is really going on has to do with his tendency to perceive blacks in animalistic terms. True, Delano (like Stowe and

Beecher) tends to see them more as big, black friendly dogs (73), but "wolf" is merely the obverse. Melville undercuts Delano's authority by revealing the bias that allows him to make such errors as an observer. So to the extent that the narrator shares this bias, his authority is undercut as well. Melville does not give us a stable point from which to figure out how we should interpret the mutiny and its aftermath. The omniscient, trustworthy narrator that we find in many nineteenth-century novels who might be counted on to do this has gone missing, though we might mistake his presence.

If, as I contend, there is no stable point from which to evaluate this text, then that means that we cannot assume even a most basic thing about it, such as its status as an antislavery text.[17] Exactly what kind of antidote to racial oppression does "Benito Cereno" offer? How are we to take that line that likens the slaves to wolves? We could easily argue that Melville and the narrator are *not* equivalent, but then another question arises. Where does Melville's point of view in this book lie, if not encapsulated by the narrator? Perhaps it lies in the ironic critique of sentimentality. It is embedded in the way the story reveals the insufficiency of Delano's vision and, by extension, that widespread bit of racial essentialist ideology common in the period, even among abolitionists, that blacks are not capable of great feats of intellect. "Benito Cereno" reveals that slaves are not mindless animals. But does revealing them as ingenious murderers really improve on matters? For this particular revelation supports another insidious bit of racial essentialist ideology: blacks are brutal savages. Peter Coviello and Ezra Tawil demonstrate the extent to which this novella critiques Stowe's romantic racialism, the "positive" qualities that she and others imputed to blacks. But romantic racialism does not exhaust the opportunities that nineteenth-century racial essentialism provided for whites to feel superior; it is just a subset. There is "unromantic" racialism, too, beliefs about black craftiness and savagery (which, in turn, fueled the proslavery argument about the need to civilize and Christianize the Africans brought over as slaves).[18] In fact, Melville's critique of romantic racialist thinking, I would argue, offers at least as much evidence for seeing this novella as critiquing the view that any ideology is trustworthy as it does for seeing this novella as antislavery.[19]

"Benito Cereno" offers no purchase, no place where the interpretive process stops and allows the critic to say "this I know to be true." For example, my own criticism of "Benito Cereno" is undermined to the extent that my claim to its ironic indeterminacy fixes the text. It is very hard to offer a satisfying reading of this novella. Notice how that claim is yet another attempt to find solid ground and remove myself from the sharp edges of its ironic undercutting. It is, to put it simply, quite hard to make "Benito Cereno" into anything but a critique, not least of the critic.

Yet the current critical consensus on this text does see it as antislavery in intent.[20] Many of these contemporary critics recognize the indeterminacy of the novella but assume that this indeterminacy ends right before the point where they claim the text takes a political stand. James Kavanaugh's article "That Hive of Subtlety" stands as a particularly interesting example, because much of it is devoted to the novella's indeterminacy. Moreover, Kavanaugh outlines the trap that Melville lays for the unwary critic. This article persuasively shows how the novella offers a critique of liberal ideology as embodied in the figure of the self-satisfied, self-deluded Amasa Delano, who becomes for Kavanaugh remarkably similar to the text's past critics. Kavanaugh begins his essay by faulting other critics for producing a discourse that falls right into Melville's ironic trap: "[T]his critical discourse recuperates his text as safe for 'our' civilization's new ideological and literary-ideological values and self-images, in ways that actually deflect the irony that such criticism explicitly claims to identify and affirm" (354). The usual critic thinks that he is offering a definitive description of Melville's ironic critique but through this self-confident description falls victim to the very irony that he hoped to domesticate.

Yet Kavanaugh's own essay ends like this: "We can hear 'Benito Cereno' say that the 'mystery' of violence and social oppression can only be disclosed through analysis and dissolution of that even more complex and malignant 'hive of subtlety,' which deliberately contrives its own confusions: the ideology of men like the 'good American,' Amasa Delano" (377). In this account, Melville's ironic critique can undermine Delano's liberal ideology, but it somehow ends before undermining Kavanaugh's. It is not that Kavanaugh's analysis seems off; to the contrary, it seems just right in many ways, not least in the antidote it offers to past critics who could not even see the novella as having to do with race. Kavanaugh faults these past critics not just for the content of their interpretations but for the certainty with which they proffered them even in the face of Melville's unsettling irony. Yet Kavanaugh himself brooks no uncertainty in offering his own reading of the message of the novella.

Exploring "Benito Cereno"'s stupendous powers of critique yet somehow stopping the critique before it can destroy the critic's own political claims about the novella is the paradigm that contemporaneous and more recent articles have followed as well. Joyce Sparer Adler sees Melville as undermining the idea that blacks and whites have inherent characteristics that make whites naturally masters, blacks naturally slaves. This undermining mechanism nevertheless results in Melville's own stance in the novella: "he is opposed to slavery whether white or black is enslaved" (92). Allan Moore Emery describes Melville's prescient critique of Manifest Destiny, his ability to undermine ideas of American exceptionalism. Emery does this while advancing his own article's "thesis, eschewing all manner of millennial optimism while exposing both the 'grand errors' of the contemporary American mind and the 'diabolic' permanences of human history" (111–12). Sandra Zagarell also sees how Melville launches a devastating attack on American exceptionalism—at the same time, according to Zagarell, demonstrating how America's hierarchical society is unstable. John Haegert documents Melville's resistance to narrative closure while also trying to show how Melville is insisting on the need for respectful silence when trying to tell the story of the Other. For Dana Luciano, "Benito Cereno" critiques totalizing monumental history in favor of countermonumental history, "insisting on the reparative possibilities of an understanding of history that sees time as discontinuous and fragmented" (34). Finally, Tuire Valkeakari sees Melville critiquing Delano's insufficient vision so that it can "evoke[] the antebellum North's insufficient understanding of its complicity in the economic and societal structuring of American life" (236).[21]

These are all close and convincing readings of Melville's text, but their ability to convince us is exactly what I want to call attention to. What unites all this criticism is identification: the way the critic identifies what the text is really about and identifies with Melville.[22] But in examining exactly how these critical identifications work—including a shared contemporary identification of this work as having everything to do with race and slavery—we should observe that identification is not quite the temporally straightforward process that we might take it to be. The critics have not "identified" what Melville actually believed in and then decided to identify with him. Instead, we have the feeling that they (unconsciously) take advantage of the textual indeterminacy of "Benito Cereno" to create Melville in their own self-image. The critics then conflate this constructed Melville with the actual Melville, who becomes the author of the text that the critics then interpret and discover therein Melville's admirable political beliefs, which, not coincidentally, mirror their own.[23]

I realize that I am performing an unmasking here that is in some ways unwarranted. We critics do not assert that our readings are definitive; most of us would concede that our readings do not exist "out there" but are a result (to modify Iser a bit) of an interaction between a particular text and a particular critic. In addition, the interpretations that I mention above all seem valid; that is, they take advantage of the formal indeterminacy in "Benito Cereno" to create plausible accounts of what the text really means. In fact, these interpretations are more than valid. They are admirable. In their effort to read Melville's text as politically progressive, they define what political progress entails (at least to contemporary literary critics). Thus it is unfair of me to cast aspersions on what these critics are doing by revealing the mechanism (identification) that allows them to come to these interpretations.

Yet this unmasking is warranted in the way in which we literary critics disavow how important a role "identification" plays in what we do. Instead I want to claim that identification makes our own work possible, especially in its political dimension. I would argue that "Benito Cereno" does not offer evidence for what kind of stand it takes toward slavery even though we want it to. How do I fancy that I can see so clearly in opposition to these other critics? To echo Socrates, my own advantage lies in my knowing that I know nothing (including what Melville really intended in this text): I can recognize the kind of identification that these critics are making and resist it. This allows me to make an alternative interpretation, but one that is very unsatisfying, in contrast to these other critics' readings, no matter how passionately I believe that I am right. "Benito Cereno" does critique bad political positions like Stowe's belief in romantic racialism, but this ruthless novella also attacks any position whatsoever that a critic might take.[24] It paralyzes the critic. My own interpretation of "Benito Cereno" paralyzes me too, in that it involves me in an endless assertion of my own awareness of the paradoxical status of my own interpretation, which tries to resist offering any final interpretation (except to the extent that this itself is a final interpretation).

Melville's novella binds racial oppression to questions of complex interpretation on all levels. The problems with Stowe, as we shall see, are undeniable: her simply untrue assumption that nothing in the world needs to be complexly interpreted and her embrace of degrading theories of racial essentialism. "Benito Cereno" exists as a negative force, critiquing not just these theories but the transparency that a novel like *Uncle Tom's Cabin* offers. "Benito Cereno" suggests that an insistence that questions of complex interpretation will never come up cannot make it so. But it also reveals that a reliance on unending interpretation as an antidote to racial oppression is no solution either. We must be able to identify if we want to take a political stand. To demonstrate this, I turn to *Uncle Tom's Cabin* and an often overlooked character in it, Augustine St. Clare.

Why St. Clare Must Die

Sentimentality works through a process of identification. Glenn Hendler explains sentimental identification:

> The reader is asked . . . to compare his or her emotional experiences analogically with those of the protagonist, but in a way that maintains a degree of difference between subject and object of sympathy. At the same time, sympathy demands a still closer connection between reader and character; the former is asked to feel *with* the latter . . . in order to transform partial sameness into identity. (*Public Sentiments* 5; emphasis in the original)

Sentimental authors try to forge a strong connection between reader and character even to the extent of insisting that they are identical to each other (and this is what gives a critic like Lauren Berlant pause).[25] But let me highlight a more basic sense of "identification" that defines the sentimental novel more fundamentally: we have to be able to identify what characters are like before we can safely identify with them.

With one exception, Stowe allows us to do this. To pick just one example, the slave trader Haley (whom we met briefly in chapter 3) dresses in a way that reveals his social-climbing pretensions: he wields a "heavy gold watch-chain, with a bundle of seals of portentous size" (1), among other parvenu accessories. But the interesting thing about Stowe's characters is that their insides are revealed not just sartorially but physically: Haley has "coarse, commonplace features"; his hands are also "coarse" (1). In the nineteenth century, people had little control over the shape of their body parts as opposed to how they dressed or even what expressions they wore. Stowe always worries that someone will learn to look like a true gentleman even though he is an arriviste. Her novel is motivated by the need to make sure that what we see is what we get. For Stowe, the physical is actually the ultimate line of defense in this war against open-ended interpretation, an insistence that the inside always match the outside. Stowe's system is founded on the axiom that "bodies never lie" (see chapter 2). We can see this axiom at work in a description of Miss Ophelia's embrace of Topsy: "Miss Ophelia's voice was more than her words, and more than that were the honest tears that fell down her face" (273). Words, then voice, then tears—this is the hierarchy of the sentimental novel. Words are always in danger of meaning something that they do not say: "voice" is better because it is partially outside our control, but "tears" are the ultimate guarantors of truthfulness. They literally bring the inside outside. Tears guarantee that questions of complex interpretation will not arise, because tears remove any discrepancy between how things seem and how things really are.

The problem is that Stowe imputes to various bodies all sorts of extra information: to black skin, a loving and child-like disposition; to white male skin, a penchant for rationality and coldness. Stowe's racial essentialism should disqualify *Uncle Tom's Cabin* from the approbation that Jane Tompkins and Jane Smiley have given it. Yet although racial essentialism indicates the extremes to which sentimentality is prone, it is not crucial to the sentimental depiction of racial injustice. The sentimental claim of transparency does not assume any particular qualities, just that the true qualities of the person will be manifested on the surface. The strategy (that claims not to be a strategy) of making everything apparent works particularly well when used to represent slaves. Stowe's strategy lays to rest a fear that abounded in her time. In the words of Thomas Wentworth Higginson, who was writing about the Nat Turner rebellion: "In all insurrections, the standing wonder seems to be that the slaves most trusted and best used should be the most deeply involved" (qtd. in Sundquist 181). Higginson raises the possibility that no one could ever know what plans are lurking in the hearts of slaves. Stowe puts down this fear by asserting that we always do. This generic strategy of sentimental authors—the drive to assure us that we can identify the motives that animate a person—has a particular resonance for the slavery question.

The sentimental mandate to have all revealed on the surface opens these authors up to another charge: they lack artistic ability. In these authors' hands, the world goes flat. I would like to suggest that this belief is incorrect. Augustine St. Clare shows that Stowe was not hobbled by lack of talent, assuming that literary talent at least partially involves creating round characters, rendering complex and ambiguous problems, and deploying irony. Yet Stowe decides to kill St. Clare off. It becomes not her burden but her choice to write the way she did. We should consider why she might have made what seems to be a very bad decision. St. Clare has not received the critical attention that he deserves;[26] to award it to him might provide evidence for an argument against "difficulty" and open-ended interpretations.

If St. Clare's death is attended to at all, critics account for it as a result of his vacillation on the issue of slavery, "a man who knows what is right but lacks the courage to act" (Ammons 161–62). While I agree that his passivity lies at the heart of the problem, it is merely a result of a bigger crime: his indulgence in a kind of rhetoric that Stowe finds dangerous. St. Clare *needs* to die because he brings up the question of endless interpretation in a book that wants to deny its existence. He makes everything—including the people around him—seem complex. Unlike the other characters in the novel, St. Clare molds his utterances to conform to what he thinks his audience expects. Here is how he responds to the slave trader Haley's panegyric about the "article" that he is attempting to sell and his daughter, Eva. The "article" in question is Tom. "All the moral and Christian virtues bound in black morocco, complete!" (135), St. Clare says, calling attention through this disturbing metaphor to Haley's tendency to objectify Tom. If St. Clare were simply sarcastic, saying the opposite of what he meant, he would be neither anomalous nor dangerous for Stowe.[27] But there is a difference between sarcasm, which is easy to decode (simply negate what is actually said), and what St. Clare does. This is irony of a particularly complicated and pleasurable kind. Gregory Vlastos would call it Socratic irony, an utterance that can be both true and not true at the same time: "[A]s when maintaining 'he knows nothing,' Socrates does and does not mean what he says" (Vlastos 41). The way St. Clare speaks makes us think that it is ridiculous to believe that Tom is so wonderful as to be made up of "all the moral and Christian virtues bound in black morocco." Yet *Uncle Tom's Cabin* tries and tries to make us believe that Tom is precisely that good. Here St. Clare voices a sentiment that most of Stowe's modern readers share—skepticism about the possibility of such a paragon. St. Clare has a knack for exposing the characters (and author) around him.

The novel offers another, astounding example of this "complexifying" (to use Linda Hutcheon's term) through irony. Miss Ophelia is horrified when she sees Little Eva kiss her slave caretaker, Mammy. Miss Ophelia explains her reaction to St. Clare:

> "Well, I want to be kind to everybody, and I wouldn't have anything hurt; but as to kissing—"
> "Niggers," said St. Clare, "that you're not up to,—hey?"
> "Yes, that's it. How can she?" (150)

"Nigger" is not a word that St. Clare normally uses: by choosing it he reveals the depth of Miss Ophelia's prejudice. She has not used that word, but it is the word that she surely means.

St. Clare performs an unmasking on Miss Ophelia, whom Baldwin, for one, has seen as a surrogate for Stowe. Yet St. Clare does not stop at pointing out Ophelia's hypocrisy about wanting to elevate slaves while not wanting to touch them. This is where it becomes extraordinary. St. Clare observes: "You would not have them abused; but you don't want to have anything to do with them yourselves. You would send them to Africa, out of your sight and smell, and then send a missionary or two to do up all the self-denial of elevating them compendiously" (162). This, of course, is *exactly what Harriet Beecher Stowe plans for the ex-slaves*, as she states at the end of *Uncle Tom's Cabin*, even to the last detail of sending two of her characters, George and Eliza, as missionaries (though Stowe later changed her mind about colonizationism). St. Clare is a dangerous man to have around. He has foreshadowed almost every other critic who does not like *Uncle Tom's Cabin*: they also focus on Stowe's plan for the freed slaves, to "let them go to Africa" (Stowe 405).

St. Clare casts doubt on Stowe's own solution, but more damaging is the way he casts doubt on the assumptions that sentimental authors make. He does not do this by suggesting that everyone can have hidden motives. Stowe concedes this too; in fact, she is preoccupied by this problem. Stowe responds by making sure that the hidden gets revealed on the surface. St. Clare's trick is to show that people cannot always see what is inside by looking on the outside. He does this quite literally at one point by not crying at Little Eva's death, even though he is devastated: "[W]ho could see that all this smiling outside was but a hollow shell over a heart that was a dark and silent sepulchre" (274). St. Clare's own body becomes a figure for the process of irony, the process of at least partially rejecting the surface meaning for a deeper meaning. St. Clare suggests that people cannot get away without reading below the surface: not everything is self-evident. Yet St. Clare's irony is not simply confined to particular lines that he utters or to his own body. As we can see from his interactions with the people around him, St. Clare manifests what Holdcroft describes as a "much deeper and systematic" irony (509). He has an ironic attitude toward the world, "general scepticism about claims to knowledge" (509). Because of this attitude, St. Clare suggests that interpretation might be an endless process.

It seems that we can do nothing more than celebrate irony and mourn the interpretive possibilities that pass away with St. Clare. Yet Stowe had her reasons for killing St. Clare, and I think that they are reasonable ones. I have suggested that St. Clare threatens the sentimental universe in general. This might make his death seem all the more tragic, depending on how much we dislike sentimental novels. But Stowe also suggests quite specific reasons for not liking St. Clare and his irony. As Ammons has said, St. Clare is plagued by passivity. We could forgive him if he were only unable to act on his convictions. The problem is not that St. Clare *knows* slavery to be wrong yet still does nothing about it. As I have described earlier, appeals to reason do not necessarily result in action, as understood in the nineteenth century. The problem is that

St. Clare also *feels* slavery to be wrong and still cannot act. As St. Clare's passionate denunciation of slavery attests ("His fine face . . . seemed actually to burn with the fervor of his feelings" [204]), he does not feel slavery to be right yet still does nothing effectual about it.[28] It is irony that short-circuits his system.

As St. Clare says of himself: "I became a piece of drift-wood, and have been floating and eddying about, ever since" (212). Stowe does not make the connection explicit between St. Clare's irony and his passivity, but she does make explicit the connection between his passivity and his lack of religion. And what prevents him from believing in the Word is his ironic worldview. Here is St. Clare's response to Miss Ophelia's question about whether he thinks that the Bible justifies slavery:

> "Well, . . . suppose that something should bring down the price of cotton once and forever, and make the whole slave property a drug in the market, don't you think we should soon have another version of the Scripture doctrine? What a flood of light would pour into the church, all at once, and how immediately it would be discovered that everything in the Bible and reason went the other way!" (168)

Like Spillers, St. Clare makes an assertion about the polyvalence of the Bible. For St. Clare, the absence of a text that is immune from complex interpretation leads to his passivity. He finds it difficult to act because no text and by extension no belief can warrant so much trust as to assure him that he is not mistaken in acting upon it. St. Clare is always finding out people's hidden motives, always finding that what seems apparent is not. The rug is always being pulled out from under his feet. St. Clare's ironic rendering of the world makes him passive.

We might then reevaluate the association of uncritical reading with passivity. In the case of St. Clare, it is precisely his impulse to read critically that makes him politically impotent. This is not, in the end, so hard to believe: as Stowe herself would have argued, we need to be moved as well as convinced in order to be driven to political action, but we also need to know that we can safely foreclose our interpretations. "Reading to identify" provides us with the affect and certainty that we need to carry through our political impulses.

Shifting the Grounds of Identification

Warner says that the first step in historicizing "critical reading" is to recognize "uncritical reading" practices as real rivals to "critical reading" practices. He tries to unsettle the opposition between critical and uncritical reading by showing that the latter should not be devalued. Instead I have tried to unsettle the opposition in another way: by showing that they cannot easily be disentangled. To the extent that "critical reading" wants to achieve some political purchase, it must take advantage of "identification."[29]

Yet we could argue that there is still a difference between the kind of identification that literary critics perform and the kind that students do. Marilyn Rye gives some examples of student interpretations taken from an exercise that seems like one that Salvatori might solicit from her students. It asks them to locate the parts of Bharati Mukherjee's *The Holder of the World* that they found puzzling. Rye found her students focusing on the mother Rebecca's decision to abandon her child Hannah in order to go off with her lover: in the words of one of Rye's students, "How can a mother leave a child and never get in touch with her again? Do you believe that there was more to this than we get from the story[?]" (23). A few other students grappled with this question, and I offer their responses in order to highlight how much a process of "reading to identify" motors their responses: "Maybe . . . Rebecca felt she was incapable to be [*sic*] her mother, and thought Hannah would be better off without her. Maybe she also felt that she was holding Hannah back" (24). Another wrote: "If her mother was anything like her [Hannah], she needed excitement in her life. She didn't just want to sit around the same old town,, [*sic*] she wanted to get out and be a part of some action" (24).

Rye offers these responses as evidence of "critical reading." Yet they still strike me as naïve, as engaging in a not particularly literary-critical kind of dialogue. We might think that that is because these students are so clearly "reading to identify." Even the initial question about how Rebecca could leave her child seems to come out of a "reading to identify" kind of premise: I could never leave my child, so how could this character leave hers? The responses to this question seem similarly immersed in identification: Rebecca might abandon her child out of motives that I have felt myself or assume to be true (we should not hold people back or people need excitement in their lives). Yet the problem, I would claim, is not identification.

Sophisticated literary critics read to identify as well. The difference comes not from the practice of identification but from the differing grounds of identification. Critics identify and students identify, but the commonalities that they find between themselves and the texts they read come from different places. The critic of Mary Rowlandson who is so ardently trying to remake her in his own image is identifying with her. But his identification grows out of his "recognition" that Rowlandson is a protofeminist or protopoststructuralist. His identification has its grounds in literary theory. Similarly, the critics of "Benito Cereno" that I have described are identifying with Melville out of similarly sophisticated political and theoretical commitments. In contrast, Rye's students are identifying with characters (and not, perhaps notably, authors) based on basic psychological or moral concepts, which sound like truisms in the hands of unsophisticated writers. The solution to these kinds of naïve interpretations is not to make students feel as if they have to abandon any sense of connection to the text (surely the critics of "Benito Cereno" who see in it a progressive call to action feel very connected to it) but to alert the students that the grounds of identification should stop following the template "What I would do in that character's place." What the new grounds of identification will be should grow out of the many alternatives for identification that we English professors are in the position to teach our students. I have been discussing a kind of political practice of "identification," which stems from a question like this: how do the racial/gender/class politics of the piece intersect with mine? But there are other alternatives: theoretical ones (e.g., how does this text intersect with my understanding of this theory?) and historical ones (e.g., how does this text intersect with my understanding of the era in which it was written?), to name just two. These alternatives are not mutually exclusive or exhaustive, of course, and the more of them our students have to choose from, the better. But the variety possible should not occlude the fact that all of these alternatives depend on identification: readers' attempts to recognize themselves (by which I mean less their "soul" and more their "beliefs") in the text being analyzed.[30] Nor should the familiarity of these approaches occlude that I am not simply advocating something we already do: introduce students to different approaches to analyzing literature. Instead I am advocating that when teaching these different approaches (or even when teaching a single critical article on a literary text) we make it clear that politically, theoretically, or historically oriented critics are still finding something in the text that resonates with their beliefs.

A problem with this way of modeling identification is precisely the extent to which it depends on the readers' beliefs: the student-readers' politics might be Manichean or their view of the past limited. But these are issues that can be addressed when understood (for example, through course materials that introduce students to the existence of competing sets of values or detailed accounts of the past). The advantage of touting "identification" lies in the way it allows experts in the discipline of English to connect what they do with what the beginning student already does and the way in which it motivates students to do something—analyze a text—that might otherwise seem to hold no stakes for them. By moving the discussion out of the realm of critical versus uncritical reading (at least in respect to "reading to identify"), I hope to show that the way to make students better readers is not to derogate their habits of identification but to explain the kinds of identifications that literary scholars embrace and the kinds that they do not and to provide students with the materials that they will need to make more persuasive ones. This chapter stands in a tradition, I hope, of demystifying the process of what English professors do and of understanding better what sets us apart from our students and what does not. As Gerald Graff (with whom I strongly identify) argues in *Clueless in Academe*, in making explicit what we do in the discipline of English, we might be sacrificing our priestly aura, but that loss is compensated by the increased competence and sense of belonging experienced by those new to our field.

6

The Problem with Being a Good Reader of Sentimental Rhetoric

ALTHOUGH SCHOLARS TRADITIONALLY HAVE BEGUN THEIR studies of the nineteenth-century "scribbling women" with a personal anecdote, I have saved mine to the end. When I was finishing graduate school and showed a draft of my dissertation on Harriet Beecher Stowe and Louisa May Alcott to a fellow graduate student, she fastened on the tone. "Why are you writing about texts that you feel so contemptuous about?" I had not been aware of my tone; though I was oddly proud of it once my friend brought it to my attention, I also worried that it would not please my advisor. I tried to erase it through a lot of strategic copyediting, though in rereading my dissertation now I see it creeping in at the edges.

The sociologist Howard S. Becker, who published a wonderful book on finishing long writing projects, claims that the problems that scholars encounter when trying to write on a given subject should not be evaded; they should be explored because they can yield valuable clues about the material (64–67). Why was contempt leaking into my writing about something that also fascinated me? In this final chapter, I face head-on a problem that I have treated glancingly up to this point: the complicated reactions that many modern readers, especially literary critics, have when reading sentimental fiction. In retrospect, my own contempt for these sentimental novels strikes me as an attempt to deny another reaction that I was having. Let us just say that I had gotten into the habit of using tissues as bookmarks. I suspect that many literary critics vacillate in their responses to sentimental rhetoric—just not in public. We represent different kinds of readers, which results in a confusing yet often pleasurable schizophrenia that is very hard to acknowledge in a critical article. Models of reading that assume we are members of only one interpretive community or imply that we cannot have conflicting habits of reading simplify the actual situation. It is likely that contemporary critics will experience a complicated reaction to sentimental novels like Harriet Beecher Stowe's *Uncle Tom's Cabin*. But it was much easier, at least for me, to focus on just one: contempt was a particularly gratifying choice. In this chapter, I not only pay attention to the varied responses that sentimental novels evoked in me but also explain why I still end up suspicious of some of them even as I recognize that readers who celebrate these novels, including many of my female students, deserve more credit than I once wanted to give them.

June Howard's plea that critics of nineteenth-century American sentimental fiction strive for neutrality—to avoid "slides into celebration or condemnation" (63)—testifies to a history of critical responses both emotional and extreme. Howard offers a glimpse into why such reactions arise: "[Sentimentality] is condemned so vehemently in part because its critics feel implicated in it" (69). This remark contains suggestive wording: what does it mean for critics to be implicated (as opposed to merely caught up) in what they study? What can sentimentality do to the critics to make them feel guilty?

Before I turn to that question, I want to repeat a claim made in chapter 3: how an audience reads a text changes over time. These changes can also be seen in a question that I have faced at almost every job interview I have ever had: "How do you get students involved in these nineteenth-century sentimental texts?" As we shall see, the better question might be: "How do you prevent students from getting overinvolved in these sentimental texts?" Many of my students, especially the female ones, become much more emotionally involved in these texts than I do. This last observation indicates that audience needs to be studied synchronically as well as diachronically: for example, how and why different contemporary readers react differently to a given text. To this end, I make use of a taxonomy of audience developed by the narratologist Peter J. Rabinowitz, particularly his distinctions among three different kinds of audience: actual, authorial, and narrative. I explain these terms more fully below, but for now let me say that every fictional text invites readers to become a member of the latter two kinds of audience (we have no choice but to be members of the actual audience). How people read and respond to a text depends on whether they choose to inhabit a given text's authorial and narrative audiences, although the "choice" often seems to take place unconsciously.[1]

Rabinowitz is concerned with readers in general; unlike him, I focus here on a particular group of readers: contemporary literary critics—specifically, feminist literary critics.[2] As described at the beginning of chapter 2, feminist critics rescued sentimental fiction from critical neglect and continue to be at the forefront in examining sentimental texts. Instead of continuing the tradition of examining sentimental texts through a feminist lens, I want to stand the tradition on its head and examine feminist literary critics by looking at how they read sentimental rhetoric. And that endeavor involves describing just what it is about this rhetoric that might both seduce and appall us.

Unmasking Sentimentality

Contempt for these nineteenth-century American women authors is not just widespread—it is enduring. If we turn to some early contemptuous criticism on sentimental rhetoric, we can gain insight into what makes this emotion arise. In a *Harper's* article from 1860 called "Sentimentalism," the Unitarian minister Henry Giles writes:

> Satan, we are told, can clothe himself as an angel of light; and so vice, by sentimentalism, assumes the guise of virtue. The sentimentalist is to ethics what the hypocrite is to piety, a striver after Falsehood; the one struggles to *feel* a lie, the other struggles to *believe* a lie: the lie may be at last believed and felt; but from the beginning both sentimentalist and hypocrite deceive themselves more than they deceive others—especially the sentimentalist deceives himself, almost intends to do it. (204; emphases in the original)

For Giles, the sentimentalist is not nearly as straightforward as a liar: the sentimentalist is a self-deceiver, especially pathetic and difficult for other people to recognize. But this is not difficult for Giles, who positions himself as the unmasker of "sentimentalism" and can cut through the web of false emotion that the sentimentalist spins. Giles sees "sentimentalism" at times as a ruse used by men to lure women to their doom: "[the male lover] was always self-possessed. . . . Yet to her it seemed sincerest eloquence, and it became deadly with a fatal power for wreck and ruin" (205). Giles has no problem in seeing through these male sentimentalists even when they become convinced of their own lies. His savvy comes from his certainty that any sort of rhetoric—especially rhetoric that strives to make the hearer forget its calculation—is inevitably tainted by the speaker's particular aims.

James Baldwin's excoriation of Stowe blurs the distinction that Giles sets up between impious hypocrite and unethical sentimentalist, but it performs a similar unmasking. Baldwin explains how Stowe's sentimental piety allows her cruelty against blacks to flourish. Here is how Baldwin explains why Stowe has Tom suffer so much: "born without the light, it is only through humility, the incessant mortification of the flesh, that he [Tom] can enter into communion with God or man" (535). Stowe's iconography—white as good and black as bad—provides a way for her to fool both herself and her contemporaneous readers, who would notice, in this traditional Christian color-coding, Stowe's piety rather than its implications for racial judgment. Stowe does not realize that her uncritical piety becomes the method by which she covers up (yet to modern readers reveals) her craven impulses toward blacks. Baldwin evokes the concept of the mask in order to explain that "[s]entimentality, the ostentatious parading of excessive and spurious emotion, is the mark of dishonesty, the inability to feel; the wet eyes of the sentimentalist betray his aversion to experience, his fear of life, his arid heart; and it is always, therefore, the signal of secret and violent inhumanity, the mask of cruelty" (533). Sentimentality appears to be one thing but is in fact another. It is the critic's job to tear the mask from the sentimentalist's face and from her prose.

This unmasking is a particularly delicious project when it comes to sentimental rhetoric, because its effectiveness depends on our forgetting how crafted it is. Authors of sentimental rhetoric want their writing to be seen as a spontaneous outpouring of emotion, not a crafted utterance from a morally dubious orator.[3] This desire accounts for why Harriet Beecher Stowe famously claimed that she did not write *Uncle Tom's Cabin*—God did. It is why Verena Tarrant, Henry James's sentimental orator in *The Bostonians*, claims to lose touch with her own personality when she addresses an audience. This is why so many critics read these novels as lacking artistry (although this accusation is like saying that Socrates has a very good pedagogical technique except that he asks too many questions).[4]

The idea of sentimental literature's false aspect—which enables the critic to remove the mask and reveal to readers just what lies underneath—has lingered into the present day. One last example, then, from another important work on the "scribbling women" (a wellspring, along with the Baldwin essay, for contemporary negative accounts):[5] in *The Feminization of American Culture* (1977), Ann Douglas's contempt for the sentimentalists, even apart from their negative effect on American culture, grows out of a personal animus arising from how sentimentalism once affected her as an initially unwary reader. As a child, she adored Little Eva. From her vantage as an adult critic, she needs to understand how the text tricked her to feel that way toward a heroine whose "only real demand on her readers is for self-indulgence" (4).

According to Douglas, sentimentality tricks us through a bait-and-switch technique: "[Sentimentalism] asserts that the values a society's activity denies are precisely the ones it cherishes. . . . Sentimentalism provides a way to protest a power to which one has already in part capitulated" (12). The content of Douglas's claim has to do with the way that sentimentality at once bankrupts and provides a cover story for mass culture, but notice, once again, its assumption about the structure of sentimentality. According to Douglas, "sentimentalism" is a bifurcated discourse: one thing on the surface and an opposing thing underneath.

Contempt is one natural result of this way of seeing sentimental literature as a bifurcated discourse: the critic sees through the sentimentalist's mask and looks down upon the sentimentalist for trying to put one over on her. Yet contempt is not the only result possible. Though I myself fell into the contemptuous camp, my reaction could have easily gone the other way. There is a tremendous similarity between contemptuous and celebratory criticism of the sentimental. This celebratory criticism casts sentimental fiction as a kind of roman à clef: instead of the characters translating into real people, the sentimental work as a whole translates into a subversive political screed.

Thus, even when we turn to celebratory works by Susan K. Harris and Elaine Showalter, we still find an insistence on a false aspect. Showalter, in her introduction to *Alternative Alcott*, writes: "Reading the work of this alternative Alcott also leads us back to her domestic romances with a sharper vision of their suppressed radical elements, and helps us understand similar divisions masked by domestic conventions in the writing of other nineteenth-century American women" (x). Once more we find the trope of the mask, once more the phenomenon of false aspect, except that what readers find under the mask is radical rather than repressive. Susan K. Harris sums up the idea of false aspect succinctly in the phrase that she coins to describe (and praise) a distinctive characteristic of the sentimental novels that she considers: the "coverplot." By this term, she means that the overt plot, which features elements like heterosexual marriage and female dependence, actually masks subversive elements that reside underneath and were meant to be decoded by the female reader.[6]

The difference between celebratory and condemnatory criticism of the sentimental lies in the critics' assessment of the motives behind the sentimentalist's false aspect: for the contemptuous critics, the sentimentalist sets out to make the reader (and possibly herself) believe some bit of dubious business; for the celebrators, the sentimentalist deliberately uses this false aspect to advance a liberatory project. But at bottom both the contemptuous and the celebratory critics are unmaskers. The former have contempt for an author who cannot acknowledge her own two-facedness; the latter celebrate the author's savvy at encoding her subversive message. Moreover, both the condemners and celebrators seem to be commenting as much on the method of reading that the feminist literary critic should employ as on the sentimentalists themselves: the feminist literary critic needs to expose the text's hidden agenda. Critics of both stripes revolt against the thought of an author whose text would prevent them from insisting upon a given text's rhetoricity, its constructed nature. They provide hidden depth to what some—including the authors themselves—insist is the flat landscape of sentimental rhetoric.

Sentimental Immersion

There are, of course, more than these two types of criticism,[7] and with a third type I think that we can gain insight into not just how feminist critics read sentimental rhetoric but how they generally do not. Joanne Dobson sounds nothing like the critics outlined above: she avoids performing an unmasking. Yet in her avoidance something interesting happens to her criticism. In "Reclaiming Sentimental Literature" (1997), Dobson argues that we can use formalist criteria to evaluate sentimental literature, identifying its own aesthetic goals and seeing how well it fulfills them. According to Dobson, sentimental literature uses conventional language and imagery in order to reach a mass audience. The following passage discusses Harriet Beecher Stowe and her depiction of Little Eva's pre-deathbed distribution of locks of her hair. This is where I think Dobson's criticism becomes extraordinary: "Eva's generosity is constructed within a cultural and historical context where all too often children *did* die, were snatched incomprehensibly from the arms of helpless families—as Harriet Beecher Stowe knew only too painfully" (273; emphasis in the original). Perhaps knowingly, Dobson has taken on the fervid tone, the impulse to paint pictures with words, even the punctuational predilections of the author she is writing about. Though she begins conventionally by speaking of Eva's constructedness, she ends emotionally, identifying with grieving families (by projecting onto them): they felt their children's deaths to be incomprehensible and almost too painful to bear. At this moment in her essay, Dobson wants to immerse us in the experience that she is describing. She wants us to identify with these families in their suffering. In so doing, she does not seem like a literary critic toward the end of this passage. She has lost her critical distance.

Thus it is not that critics of the sentimental always become unmaskers; at least one critic becomes a sentimentalist herself. But let us examine just what is different about Dobson. I have tried to show how the bulk of criticism on sentimental literature reads it as having a bifurcated structure. What sets Dobson's account apart is her rejection of this reading. Stowe has no hidden agenda: her conventional language and imagery exactly express both her true sentiments and social reality. But in rejecting the more common view, Dobson is in danger of losing her credibility as a critic.

Yet Dobson is the only one of the critics examined here who is a good reader of sentimental rhetoric, if we define "good" as a reader who does not read against the grain of what she is reading. Drawing from his article "Truth in Fiction," Rabinowitz would explain that she has become a member of the "authorial audience," the hypothetical audience that an author composes for, as opposed to the "actual audience," the flesh-and-blood readers who might come with quite different assumptions and reading protocols from the authorial one, especially if the actual audience is removed in time (an author who wants to sell a lot of books will try to make her authorial audience as close to her actual audience as possible).[8] Dobson tries to re-create the context in which Little Eva's death scene will resonate: small children often did die, so we can receive Little Eva's death as in some sense "real." Accepting her death as real allows us to become members of "the narrative audience," to use another term from Rabinowitz: we believe that the things being narrated are actually happening and are swept up in the world of the novel.[9]

Part of our training as literary critics involves developing an ability to read older and culturally distant texts both "authorially" and "narratively": if we want to do any sort of historical criticism, we must be able to read as the authors imagined their audience would read, even if our articles eventually go on to read against the grain. Similarly, much of our pedagogy involves animating older texts for our students, a task that often involves reconstructing the values and conventions of the authorial audience so that our students can become part of the narrative one. Yet this normally useful ability gets the critic into trouble when it comes to the sentimental text, for to read a sentimental text the way it wants to be read is to go against other implicit and mostly insuperable rules about what it means to read as a contemporary literary critic. Contemporary feminist critics of sentimental texts do not allow themselves to become part of the narrative audience or full members of the authorial one (see the discussion below). In the next section I explore why they do not, using my own responses as a representative (I hope) example.

How Critics Read

Jane Tompkins, one of the most well-known celebrators of the "scribbling women writers" as well as a reader-response critic, evokes the idea of the authorial audience in "Sentimental Power: *Uncle Tom's Cabin* and the Politics of Literary History" (1985). Arguing against the masses of critics who had dismissed *Uncle Tom's Cabin* as "trash" (123), her famous defense of this novel proceeds along these lines: if we can recapture the way that sympathetic contemporaneous readers read the novel, we might begin to value it ourselves. She claims that the "work of the sentimental writers is complex and significant in ways *other than* those that characterize the established masterpieces" (126; emphasis in the original). To value the novel, we need to shed our modernist bias, our desire for complex characters and formal innovation. This strategy should surely work: a contemporary audience often needs to understand the worldview and material circumstances of the actual contemporaneous audience in order to appreciate the work (assuming that the author was writing for an authorial audience not too distant from the actual one). We need to know contemporaneous attitudes about divorce to understand *Madame Bovary* and the arguments mounted by proslavery ideologues to gain a full appreciation of Frederick Douglass's *Narrative*. Literary critics seem well poised to embark on such an exploration. We are anxious, especially since the advent of historicism, to read sources that will illuminate the culture of the time. Then why does a historicist approach not work in the case of these sentimental texts?

To answer that question, I want to explore my reactions to an iconic sentimental scene from *Uncle Tom's Cabin* as a way of exploring the reading strategies that inform my own interpretive community ("presuppositions" about how to read a given text in Rabinowitz's terminology). I hope that this is not just a community of one but includes other contemporary feminist critics. Although Little Eva's deathbed scene has seemingly been picked clean by critics, it seems like a good passage to focus on precisely because it draws so much critical attention. I hope that I can add something new by giving a blow-by-blow account of the critical reflexes that it taps in me. Here is Stowe writing of Little Eva's death:

> "Hush!" said St. Clare, hoarsely; "*she is dying*!" . . .
>
> "Do you know me, Eva?"
>
> "Dear papa," said the child, with a last effort, throwing her arms about his neck. In a moment they dropped again; and, as

> St. Clare raised his head, he saw a spasm of mortal agony pass over the face,—she struggled for breath, and threw up her little hands.
>
> "O, God, this is dreadful!" he said, turning away in agony, and wringing Tom's hand, scarce conscious what he was doing. "O, Tom, my boy, it is killing me!"
>
> Tom had his master's hands between his own; and, with tears streaming down his dark cheeks, looked up for help where he had always been used to look.
>
> "Pray that this may be cut short!" said St. Clare,—"this wrings my heart."
>
> "O, bless the Lord! it's over,—it's over, dear Master!" said Tom; "look at her."
>
> The child lay panting on her pillows, as one exhausted,—the large clear eyes rolled up and fixed. . . .
>
> "Eva," said St. Clare, gently.
>
> She did not hear.
>
> "O, Eva, tell us what you see! What is it?" said her father.
>
> A bright, a glorious smile passed over her face, and she said, brokenly,—"O! love,—joy,—peace!" gave one sigh, and passed from death unto life!
>
> "Farewell, beloved child! the bright, eternal doors have closed after thee; we shall see thy sweet face no more. O, woe for them who watched thy entrance into heaven, when they shall wake and find only the cold gray sky of daily life, and thou gone forever!" (270; emphasis in the original)

Here are my reactions to this passage. First and foremost, I register how much Stowe wants me to cry. She describes the physical suffering of a child: Little Eva's physical pain and the allusion to her little hands. And the physical suffering of a child (or animal) appears especially keyed to eliciting emotion: suffering without being able to articulate it seems particularly horrible. The passage also provides proxies for the reader: St. Clare's appeal to Tom to show him how to act and Tom's copious tears in response. We are, after all, in the same position as St. Clare, watching helplessly as this beloved child dies and not knowing what to do. The scene contains many painful contrasts: between Eva's mortal agony and her spiritual peace, between the urge to want Eva to stay alive and the desire for her pain to end. This ambivalence culminates in Stowe's substitution of "life" for "death": the idea that we die into eternal life. These tensions beg for a release in tears—and a Christian understanding of what death means. Through identification, both with certain characters and with certain Christian understandings of the world, everything in this passage is meant to evoke and organize our emotions. In fact, we might see this passage as an emotion-generating and -shaping machine.

In Rabinowitz's terms, this description is a possible account of why the narrative audience feels the emotions that the passage seeks to generate (though the narrative audience is not, like me, becoming preoccupied with the actual mechanics). As a member of the actual audience, however, I do not cry but remain stone-cold.[10] In this case I am not able to enter the narrative audience effortlessly—or with effort—because my habits of reading make me so attuned to Stowe's attempts to make me cry: as soon as I become aware of them, I resist her rhetoric.[11] I resist because I start to notice how Stowe has made the scene resemble other sentimental scenes: how someone is always crying during scenes of great sentimental import; how Stowe uses apostrophe in order to script what we are supposed to recognize ourselves as feeling (and to help us out in case we are not experiencing what we are supposed to be experiencing); how Stowe uses her characters' suffering for didactic ends.

The problem is that the passage wants to hide its craft so that the narrative audience can read it as a spontaneous outpouring of emotion, not as a bit of artifice (or of art). The most persuasive orators are orators *in extremis*. Senator Bird, for example, cannot resist helping Eliza, the anguished, exhausted slave mother who is trying to prevent her son from being torn away from her. Similarly, the emotional and physical extremities undergone by the people in Little Eva's deathbed scene are meant to attest to the authenticity of the depiction, which is not meant to strike us as a depiction. In fact, Stowe emphasized "authenticity" so much that she thought of herself as providing not merely a "depiction" but unmediated access to events; as noted, she claimed that, more than "writing" about slavery, she was presenting "pictures" of it for her readers.

Stowe is following a tenet made explicit in the rhetorical theory of her time that people *in extremis* cannot help but speak the truth. Recall once again that passage from Thomas Sheridan: "[W]henever the force of these passions is extreme, words give place to inarticulate sounds: . . . sobs, groans, and cries in grief . . . are then the only language heard. And the experience of mankind may be appealed to, whether these have not more power in exciting sympathy, than any thing [*sic*] that can be done by mere words" (*A Course of Lectures* [1762] 102). Pained people have no choice but to speak the truth because they do not have the resources for calculation: crisis cancels craft. This tenet has lingered on as an intuition in our own day, activated in times of emergency in particular. For example, during the 9/11 attacks people did resort to inarticulate sounds, and it seemed that the only words they could utter bypassed the usual routes of craftedness and deliberation which conventional orators normally think they need in order to be persuasive.[12]

But my habits of reading, learned early on and reinforced throughout my formal schooling in literary criticism, block my access to this view of the emotions in the passage and thus to the narrative audience. I look right away for signs of craft and soon feel as if I am being manipulated by Stowe to respond in certain carefully scripted ways. So I resist her rhetoric. More specifically, in noticing how the passage resembles other sentimental scenes, I am following a reading protocol shared by critics and many amateur readers alike: linking similar scenes together in order to figure out patterns, which will help me know what to expect during such a scene in future readings (what Rabinowitz would call the reading rule of "configuration" in *Before Reading*). Yet in switching my attention to this process—and thus revealing this sentimental scene to be following a formula—I have undermined what would have made a contemporaneous audience become part of the narrative audience: the sense of crisis and emergency that this passage seeks to convey.[13]

It is very difficult to experience sentimental rhetoric as it is meant to be experienced. But some modern readers react differently to Eva's deathbed scene: they do cry. If forced to articulate why, they might say things such as "Stowe describes just what it feels like when a close relative dies" or "Religion can offer solace when someone is dying; it did for me." Note that these comments sound like Joanne Dobson's remarks asserting Stowe's fidelity to the way things really happen. They remove the distance between the modern reader and the sentimental author. In this respect, these comments show how fully these readers have entered the narrative audience of the passage; they then use that immersion as the basis for their positive assessments of Stowe as author. I have never found a critic other than Joanne Dobson who has made such claims in print (Jane Tompkins describes how Stowe's interpretive community would have read Stowe's novel but maintains enough distance to label these strategies as not her own in "Sentimental Power"). Yet I have read remarks similar to these in my students' papers to which I gave low grades. Given my habits of reading, I cannot help but find these kinds of remarks—this kind of reaction—uncritical.

People who would make these kinds of statements find such a passage powerful because it seems "real." They have no trouble inhabiting not only the authorial audience but also the narrative one and do not find it manipulative. Yet I do: I have a very hard time becoming part of the narrative audience, even if I can acquaint myself with the appropriate beliefs of the authorial one. This passage strikes me as fake not (mainly) because it is evangelical but because it seems crafted. It is not that I cannot imagine any passage that reveals its craftedness to be moving but that I cannot envision a sentimental orator *in extremis* passage to be so.[14] The passage's need to be seen as spontaneous cannot coexist with the way it strikes me as constructed. Because it is constructed but wants to be seen as spontaneous, it strikes me as manipulative—especially because it would exert tremendous power over me if it could trick me into seeing it as uncrafted. Manipulation, it seems, is less a quality that inheres in the sentimental text itself and more a reaction that characterizes the distance of the actual audience from the narrative audience. A work is unconvincing when readers choose not to join the work's narrative audience (Rabinowitz, "Truth in Fiction" 133); a work is manipulative when readers feel that the book wants them to join it using false pretenses.

Rather than become swept up in Little Eva's death, critics who share my reading habits identify the passage as the emotion-generating and -shaping machine that it is (and with easily replaceable parts). And because we recognize it as such—which is exactly opposite of how it wants to be recognized—we see through it. This vantage point, which allows us to see through the text's claim to uncraftedness to what is really there, allows contemporary critics to feel superior and puts us in the position of unmaskers. It also confirms our status as professional critics. This is what literary critics *do* after all: we break texts apart to see how they work. Here, then, is the sticking point in our becoming members of

Stowe's authorial audience: when we read as critics, we cannot recapture the sense that a fictional work can be uncrafted; and because we cannot, we cannot become members of the narrative audience and embrace the "reality" of the work. Dobson's description of Stowe's painful reality (which alludes to the loss of Stowe's son Charley in 1849) presents Stowe as a transcriber of reality: there is nothing crafted about the passage. It simultaneously revives the power of *Uncle Tom's Cabin* and limits Dobson's role as a critic—as well as undermining Stowe's status as an artist.

Canonical male authors are different. Mark Twain and Nathaniel Hawthorne give us texts that require readers to see them as crafted. If readers do not, the text makes them seem like idiots, the corollary to the characters in the novel who similarly fail to recognize artifice. Here is a case in point. Mark Twain, parodying sentimental conversion scenes, understands the contagious and manipulative potential of tears. Here is Pap, Huck Finn's father, putting one over on Judge Thatcher and possibly himself:

> And after supper [the judge] talked to [Pap] about temperance and such things till the old man cried, and said he'd been a fool, and fooled away his life; but now he was a-going to turn over a new leaf and be a man nobody wouldn't be ashamed of, and he hoped the judge would help him and not look down on him. The judge said he could hug him for them words; so *he* cried, and his wife she cried again. . . . Then the old man he signed a pledge—made his mark. The judge said it was the holiest time on record, or something like that. Then they tucked the old man into a beautiful room, which was the spare room, and in the night sometime [Pap] got powerful thirsty and clumb out onto the porch-roof and slid down a stanchion and traded his new coat for a jug of forty-rod. (48–49; emphasis in the original)

Twain is implicitly responding to the skepticism that sentimental rhetoric arouses in some contemporaneous and many modern readers. He mocks Christian platitudes ("the holiest time on record, or something like that"). He asserts the transient nature of sentimental conversions: tears are the tool and mark of the deceiver rather than the guarantor of sincere eloquence. Twain is in an interpretive community similar to mine, not just because of the content of his "message" about the sham nature of sentimental rhetoric. I can also, with a sigh of relief, sink into being a member of his authorial audience because I read the way he assumes that readers should read. Ah, finally, I think to myself, an indisputably bifurcated text (in this case because it must be read ironically): Huck Finn, the unreliable narrator, whose matter-of-fact description must be reconstructed—to borrow a heuristic from Wayne Booth—to reveal the "real" meaning. We must dig to find Twain's satirical message, which makes that message all the more compelling and brings attention by the very kind of reading that it encourages to the flat reading practice that sentimental rhetoric requires.[15]

Twain's passage has a deeper layer but an interpretation that we, as members of the authorial audience, can be fairly certain of. The following passage by Hawthorne, in contrast, seems even more self-consciously crafted, precisely because it calls into question the stability of interpretation itself. In a passage from chapter 12, "The Minister's Vigil," in *The Scarlet Letter*, Hawthorne offers us competing descriptions of a meteor and the shape it makes against the clouds. First, there is Dimmesdale's impression of it as tracing a giant "A," a message that he takes as the mark of his own guilt. Yet the narrator seems to undermine Dimmesdale's impression: "[I]t could only be the symptom of a highly disordered mental state, when a man, rendered morbidly self-contemplative by long, intense, and secret pain, had extended his egotism over the whole expanse of nature, until the firmament itself should appear no more than a fitting page for his soul's history and fate. . . . Not but the meteor may have shown itself at that point, burning duskily through a veil of cloud; but with no such shape as his guilty imagination gave it; or, at least, with so little definiteness, that another's guilt might have seen another symbol in it" (107). According to the narrator, the "A" is thus a clear case of psychological projection. We may agree—until the end of the chapter, when Hawthorne undermines this interpretation as well through a question put to Dimmesdale by one of his ministerial colleagues: "But did your reverence hear of the portent that was seen last night? A great red letter in the sky,—the letter A,—which we interpret to stand for Angel. For, as our good Governor Winthrop was made an angel this past night, it was doubtless held fit that there should be some notice thereof!" (109).

So what exactly is the status of Dimmesdale's perception of the scarlet "A" in the sky? Hawthorne gains the contemporary critic's self-congratulatory approval with his savvy-seeming awareness of a person's ability to project onto his environment what his presuppositions have already led him to believe will be there, a comment that has as much relevance for contemporary, self-conscious literary critics as it does for guilt-wracked Puritan ministers. How much more sophisticated, thus, does Hawthorne seem to us than Beecher. When Hawthorne, though, goes one step further and undermines the seemingly definitive theory of projection, he may earn not simply approval but awe. By suggesting through the minister's comment about Governor Winthrop that an "A" actually appeared in the sky, Hawthorne deliberately calls into question the narrator's own initial skepticism. What Hawthorne is doing here is quite complicated: by affirming the reality of Dimmesdale's impression, he ultimately suggests that sometimes the symbols that people project onto the world are, in fact, really there. Or does he? After all, the villagers see the "A" but read it differently (presumably it did not stand for "Angel" in Dimmesdale's mind). Or perhaps we are still meant to accept the narrator's seemingly authoritative initial statement that people tend to project more often than nature tends to reveal: the villagers are performing their own projection (wanting to believe that their repressive leaders are wonderful).

The problem comes down to our inability to determine what the narrative audience, which wants to read the text as a chronicle of what really happened, is meant to believe. If we are to believe that Dimmesdale is mistaken, are we to believe that the townspeople also are mistaken? The narrator craftily seems to leave room for both possibilities (that Dimmesdale and the rest of this Puritan community—like us—are wont to project), but what are we then to make of the coincidence of their both seeing an "A"?

This is reminiscent of that moment at the end of a horror story when the main character wakes up from what he and the narrative audience are concluding was a dream only to find clutched in his hand an object that featured in the dream itself, which now must have really happened. Is the "A" real? If so, the *narrator* must be seen to be unreliable or at least not completely trustworthy: he led us initially to disbelieve what Dimmesdale thought he saw. If the narrator is untrustworthy, what can we know with certainty? Is this uncertainty a comment on interpretation itself? Is Hawthorne suggesting that we should distrust how people—even seemingly omniscient narrators—describe the world around them, especially given their desire to convince us of their worldview?

The point is that Hawthorne leaves all of these interpretations open. From within the perspective formed by our dominant critical assumptions, regarding his text as meticulously crafted affirms Hawthorne's ingenuity and makes him a greater artist and thinker. He becomes more and more powerful as he undermines successive interpretations of the "A," moving from unreliable character to unreliable narrator to the uncertain status of interpretation itself. From this same perspective, however, regarding Stowe as offering a bifurcated text (not to mention a radically self-undermining one) makes her look like a sham, because the power of sentimental rhetoric lies in its ability to make us forget, in its urgency, its craft.

This forgetting is so hard for those of us within the dominant reading paradigm that we can even name what makes *Uncle Tom's Cabin* effective but mistake this for what makes it lame: "For the literary critic, the problem is simply how a book so seemingly artless, so lacking in apparent literary talent, was not only an immediate success but has endured" (qtd. in Flück 319). J. W. Ward assumes that artfulness makes a text retain its power over its readers. He even inadvertently explains his inability to fathom an alternative: his disbelief in the existence of artlessness (implied by his "seemingly") explains why he cannot grasp its power. I do not think that this kind of blindness derives from first aesthetic principles: that some people just hate sentimental rhetoric. I think that it derives from certain kinds of reading practices on the part of certain actual audiences, practices that actually precede what might seem to be first aesthetic principles. It is hard to read sentimental literature *as a critic* if we want to experience its emotional power fully or even if we want to understand how that power ever worked on other readers.

In order to do its work on us, sentimental rhetoric requires critics to read without critical distance, to read contrary to the reading practices that we have mostly adopted as critics. And it prevents our customary reading practices in a most uncompromising way by denying us that fundamental critical move of reading below the surface. I think that this denial is what makes us feel guilty whenever we succumb to sentimental rhetoric: we are participating in something that threatens to disqualify us as critics. The job of sentimental critics seems both hazardous and odd. They must either reject the premises of the sentimental text or endanger their status as critics.

Love and Politics

I have been talking at length about why sentimental rhetoric might strike us as appalling. But why is it also seductive? I have already implied some answers. On one hand, its seductiveness comes from the way it allows literary critics to accrue street cred as literary critics. We do not read the way sentimental rhetoric requires—far from it. Instead we read in such a way that we expose it for the sham it is. On the other hand, the requirements of historicist criticism provide a counterweight to this impulse, pulling us some way toward becoming members of its authorial audience.

But I have not yet alluded to another powerful source of seduction: the desire, especially on the part of some feminist critics, to read exactly the way sentimental rhetoric requires and thus redeem literary criticism from the divisive way it has conventionally been done. The editors of the feminist-influenced *The Intimate Critique: Autobiographical Literary Criticism* begin their book with the following epigraph from *Between Women*: "Women want to invent new types of criticism, alternate forms of cooperation" that are "less compulsive, aggressive, lonely, competitive; more communal, caring, and integrated with love and politics" (qtd. in Freedman et al. 1). These feminist critics want to remove the distance that grows up between critics who are all pushing their own "new" interpretations. This sentiment is echoed by Jane Tompkins in the oft-anthologized "Me and My Shadow": "[A] critique of the kind the [conventional] critic has in mind only insulates academic discourse further from the issues that make feminism matter. That make *her* [the feminist critic] matter" (169; emphasis in the original). Read sympathetically, sentimental rhetoric solves this problem of distance and alienation, not just between competing critics but between readers and what they read. Distance implies rationality and analysis; sentimental texts and the closeness they foster allow us to bring our feelings, this crucial part of ourselves, back into what we do.

I do not consider it a coincidence that Jane Tompkins is the author of both "Sentimental Power" and "Me and My Shadow," an essay that mixes the academic and personal and breaks many of the hygiene rules of academic prose (for example, by mentioning her need to go to the bathroom [173], Tompkins foregrounds her body). The essay contrasts what she perceives to be the impersonality and mean-spiritedness of academic criticism with a different, more human and caring, way of writing that she struggles to articulate in the essay. Even though Tompkins imputes her dissatisfaction with conventional literary criticism to personal psychological motives, we could just as well trace it back to the kind of reading practice that she turns to in her defense of *Uncle Tom's Cabin*.[16] Tompkins's impulse to bring to life the interpretive community of the nineteenth century in "Sentimental Power" is accompanied by a desire to adopt such a protocol of reading herself, which allows her to recognize *Uncle Tom's Cabin* as a profoundly powerful novel with "revolutionary potential" (145).

Such a reading protocol involves recognizing how much Stowe's novel necessitates "a change of heart" in the authorial audience (132s). More precisely, it involves not just recognizing this impulse but allowing the critic's own heart to be changed. We can see this shift from modern critic to emotional reader, this rejection of the dominant response of so many contemporary actual readers, in the last lines of the essay: "If the fiction written in the nineteenth century by women whose works sold in the hundreds of thousands has seemed narrow and parochial to the critics of the twentieth century, that narrowness and parochialism belong not to the works nor to the women who wrote them; they are the beholders' share" ("Sentimental Power" 146). The oddness of this sentence comes from the way in which Tompkins shows us that she has been transformed by the works themselves. Although she can identify the twentieth-century bias that leads critics to reject these works, Tompkins herself no longer shares it. She has transformed herself into a truly authorial reader. The change of heart that Stowe demands has happened, documented both in Tompkins's increasingly rapturous tone and in the implicit exclusion of herself from the ranks of twentieth-century critics. But although this essay marks her exclusion from the critical community, it signals her membership in a broader community: the authorial and narrative audiences of *Uncle Tom's Cabin*.

The third Tompkins essay that I want to consider, "Let's Get Lost" (1996), might be seen as the sequel to "Sentimental Power." Here we can see how the reading practice developed in that earlier essay (but not yet put into effect until the last line) has taken root. In "Let's Get Lost," Tompkins details her experience teaching a course called "American Literature Unbound," which provides students with an unconventional way to approach canonical American literature: "we would use the texts we read, *Moby-Dick* and *Beloved* (only those, for the course was to be uncluttered, unrushed, a pure opportunity for absorption in great works of literature—time to wallow in and be drenched by their beauty and profundity, nothing in the way) . . . [to] lead us into all kinds of experience, especially sensory, imaginative, and emotional experience—the kinds that usually get left out in school" (270). She takes this metaphor of absorption further when she describes a discussion of *Moby-Dick* conducted while she and the students eat brunch: "the language spills over everything, a rich, complex sauce"; or when she mentions how the prose of *Moby-Dick* is "in my bones" (272, 275). The text will become part of the reader (let us ignore for a moment the unwanted digestive entailments contained in these metaphors). Here Tompkins highlights the way the reader will "experience" the texts and absorb them; implicit in this description lies an unspoken contrast to "analysis," a technique that distances critics from what they read. Tompkins's technique is a sentimental one: valuing experience over analysis, providing opportunities for absorption, and using bodily metaphors to signal the proper relationship between reader and text.

The two texts that Tompkins picks, *Beloved* and *Moby-Dick*, do not themselves belong to the genre of sentimental fiction (although they both engage with that genre, sometimes explicitly); nonetheless, she can still remove the distance between herself and these self-conscious, formally unconventional works by refashioning them into sentimental literature. She refers over and over again to the emotions that they elicit and the effect that they have on the nervous systems of the readers rather than to their formal ambiguity or narrative complexities. She wants to remove the distances that open up when professors and their students read. Reading sentimentally allows these distances to be crossed. In a sentimental text, the implied author is the same as the narrator (the apostrophes come from "Stowe"), who is the same as the actual author ("children *did* die . . . as . . . Stowe knew only too painfully"), who is the same as the main characters (who share the same experiences as the author), who are the same as the authorial/narrative readers (who have also, it is assumed, experienced devastating losses and thus can feel along with the characters). Identification fuels these proximities.

It is not correct to say that *Adventures of Huckleberry Finn* and *The Scarlet Letter* do not offer opportunities for absorption (although I do not know if they are "pure"): as Rabinowitz has discussed, the internal ambiguities, including the ethical judgments that they ask us to make, draw us into these texts ("Truth in Fiction" 136–40). But we cannot read them without certain distances opening up: in the case of the passage from Twain, a distance between the authorial audience and the characters (including Huck Finn, the narrator). We are drawn closer to the implied author, who engineered this ironic passage, but our intimacy depends on the existence of an "out-group," hapless characters like Pap, the judge, and his wife as well as any earnest readers who do not get the irony. In the Hawthorne passage, the distances that open up are more profound: not just between the authorial reader and the characters but also possibly between the authorial reader and the narrator (who may himself be unreliable). And Hawthorne's text also opens up a distance between authorial readers, who seem justified in coming up with competing interpretations. A text like Hawthorne's, read authorially, gives rise to critics who are going to disagree about their interpretations. The kind of critical community envisioned by the editors of *Between Women* is hardly possible. Yet it is almost possible with *Uncle Tom's Cabin*: if we read Stowe's novel authorially, no interpretation is necessary both in the sense that we will experience, not analyze, the passage and in the sense that it has no hidden meaning. Communities of readers can be built on these canonical texts, but not without someone being left out and someone feeling superior. With the sentimental text, we have a community whose boundaries contain multitudes—except, of course, literary critics. Sentimental texts offer the chance for readers to forge a powerful community: just not one that most of us would regard as critical.

Dobson and Tompkins model a different kind of critical community from the one that we are used to: they are not just being historically minded readers; they are allowing themselves to feel the strong emotions called forth by the texts that they are reading and, even more bravely, allowing themselves to record these feelings in their criticism. Many critics desire to do so too, as a way, I think, to acknowledge all our different reading selves.[17] I am highly attuned to the dangers of such a desire and understand that fulfilling it may turn our criticism not so much utopian as uncritical.

Let me take advantage of this fragile detente by making a suggestion. We might stop seeing our students' growing distance from sentimental rhetoric—something that I used to think of as proof of a job well done—as an unmixed blessing. We should not let them forget or forget to value the kinds of reading practices that they give up when they emulate currently dominant critical habits. In fact, we can use these sentimental texts to begin a discussion about some things that have often gone unremarked, at least in my classroom: the distance that can exist between how a text wants to be read and how undergraduates and especially graduate students are trained to read it as well as the benefits and costs of being (or at least pretending to be) a single kind of reader.

The idea of the conflicted reader supplements a claim that runs through this book: that sentimental rhetoric oscillates in its power. We have seen sentimental rhetoric gaining power in the earlier part of the nineteenth century as an antidote to the craftedness of professional male oratory. Sentimental rhetoric begins as an anti-elitist mode of discourse (although the sentimental women authors were themselves from privileged backgrounds), available to the disempowered. But this is actually a crucial exclusiveness: sentimental rhetoric falters, later in the century, when it is adopted by speakers whose lives do not take place in the home or are not filled with pain. When Henry Ward Beecher, fatally capable of self-consciousness, attempts to codify its principles, we come full circle: sentimental rhetoric has become not the antidote to disingenuous eloquence but the thing itself. This is sentimental rhetoric viewed diachronically.

However, this oscillation occurs synchronically as well. From the beginning, nineteenth-century American sentimental novels had their detractors (see Hawthorne). Melville exposed the racism and near-fatal cluelessness that can come out of sentimental ingenuousness, and Stowe countered by showing the limits of an ironic worldview. Even today, amid the critical unmaskers of sentimental novels, some readers have no trouble becoming part of the narrative audience. In other words, actual audiences of sentimental rhetoric in both the nineteenth and twentieth centuries have always experienced diverse responses. But that means looking at audience as a collection of individuals and assuming that each individual has an unconflicted response. This is not always the case. In this chapter, I have tried to show that this same diversity can exist within a single actual reader, although the particular reader might deny even to herself the validity of a response that is looked down upon by her interpretive community.

An investigation into sentimental rhetoric allows us to glimpse our own complex identities as readers. Someone asked me a few years ago if other genres of nineteenth-century literature could be used to do this. Could we use literary realism or American Romanticism to explore how we read different texts and practice literary criticism? Herman Melville's and Stephen Crane's celebration of an ironic worldview and Hawthorne's withholding of the knowledge of what "really" happened are "lessons" that a modern critical audience has fully and self-consciously embraced.[18] One virtue of investigating sentimental rhetoric is that we imagine that we have moved beyond its lessons. Yet I hope that this book shows that we are legatees not just of the later nineteenth-century readers who read sentimental rhetoric skeptically but of the earlier audience of readers who found themselves persuaded by it to adopt positions that they would initially never have considered.

Appendix

The Scene from Uncle Tom's Cabin *Where Mrs. Bird Tries to Convince Her Husband of the Immorality of the Fugitive Slave Act*

On the present occasion, Mrs. Bird rose quickly, with very red cheeks, which quite improved her general appearance, and walked up to her husband, with quite a resolute air, and said, in a determined tone,

"Now, John, I want to know if you think such a law as that is right and Christian?"

"You won't shoot me, now, Mary, if I say I do!"

"I never could have thought it of you, John; you didn't vote for it?"

"Even so, my fair politician."

"You ought to be ashamed, John! Poor, homeless, houseless creatures! It's a shameful, wicked, abominable law, and I'll break it, for one, the first time I get a chance; and I hope I *shall* have a chance, I do! Things have got to a pretty pass, if a woman can't give a warm supper and a bed to poor, starving creatures, just because they are slaves, and have been abused and oppressed all their lives, poor things!"

"But, Mary, just listen to me. Your feelings are all quite right, dear, and interesting, and I love you for them; but, then, dear, we mustn't suffer our feelings to run away with our judgment; you must consider it's not a matter of private feeling,—there are great public interests involved,—there is such a state of public agitation rising, that we must put aside our private feelings."

"Now, John, I don't know anything about politics, but I can read my Bible; and there I see that I must feed the hungry, clothe the naked, and comfort the desolate; and that Bible I mean to follow."

"But in cases where your doing so would involve a great public evil—"

"Obeying God never brings on public evils. I know it can't. It's always safest, all round, to *do as He* bids us."

"Now, listen to me, Mary, and I can state to you a very clear argument, to show—"

"O, nonsense, John! you can talk all night, but you wouldn't do it. I put it to you, John,—would *you* now turn away a poor, shivering, hungry creature from your door, because he was a runaway? *Would* you, now?"

Now, if the truth must be told, our senator had the misfortune to be a man who had a particularly humane and accessible nature, and turning away anybody that was in trouble never had been his forte; and what was worse for him in this particular pinch of the argument was, that his wife knew it, and, of course, was making an assault on rather an indefensible point. So he had recourse to the usual means of gaining time for such cases made and provided; he said "ahem," and coughed several times, took out his pocket-handkerchief, and began to wipe his glasses. Mrs. Bird, seeing the defenceless condition of the enemy's territory, had no more conscience than to push her advantage.

"I should like to see you doing that, John—I really should! Turning a woman out of doors in a snow-storm, for instance; or may be you'd take her up and put her in jail, wouldn't you? You would make a great hand at that!"

"Of course, it would be a very painful duty," began Mr. Bird, in a moderate tone.

"Duty, John! don't use that word! You know it isn't a duty–it can't be a duty! If folks want to keep their slaves from running away, let 'em treat 'em well,—that's my doctrine. If I had slaves (as I hope I never shall have), I'd risk their wanting to run away from me, or you either, John. I tell you folks don't run away when they are happy; and when they do run, poor creatures! they suffer enough with cold and hunger and fear, without everybody's turning against them; and, law or no law, I never will, so help me God!"

"Mary! Mary! My dear, let me reason with you."

"I hate reasoning, John,—especially reasoning on such subjects. There's a way you political folks have of coming round and round a plain right thing; and you don't believe in it yourselves, when it comes to practice. I know *you* well enough, John. You don't believe it's right any more than I do; and you wouldn't do it any sooner than I." (72–73; emphases in the original)

Notes

INTRODUCTION: *The How of Sentimentality*

1. See, for example, Nina Baym, Joanne Dobson, Marianne Noble, Lora Romero, and Robyn Warhol ("As You Stand"). Dobson, Noble, Romero, and Warhol are discussed in more detail in chapter 6.

2. Andrew Lawson has also noted the derivativeness of Bowery culture in *Maggie* and attributes it to what he calls "class mimicry": the attempt of the lower-class slum dwellers to mimic the language and external attributes of the middle and upper classes. Class mimicry, according to Lawson, was what the "charitable visitors," middle-class women who visited the New York slums in the 1880s, tried to foster in the poor by making home visits and "performing middle-class identity" for the poor person's benefit (Lawson 604). In return, the visitee would perform her own "grateful" response: as a result, "character itself becomes artificial, hollowed out" (Lawson 604).

3. This is a rich simile: it evokes the same kind of hypocrisy—a so-called penitent whose physical grossness signals his duplicity—that we find the mother guilty of (while reminding us of her Catholicism). This also achieves another kind of irony. It reminds us of portraits of prosperous burghers and other figures of the bourgeoisie by painters such as Frans Hals, suggesting the distance between the milieu depicted in these portraits and that inhabited by Maggie and her family. It also underlines the futile aspiration of Mary and her friends to be "respectable," an aspiration embodied in the mock religious service that follows.

4. The scene does not just cannibalize "sympathy"; it also cannibalizes another preoccupation of sentimental novels. Sentimental novels abound in keepsakes of the dead, often a picture or a lock of hair. In *Maggie*, this keepsake comes in the

form of a wholly untranscendent "pair of worsted boots": "I kin remember when . . . her two feet was no bigger dan yer tumb, an' she weared worsted boots" (67). Mary wants to put the boots on her dead daughter, to which her son responds, "Dey won't fit her now, yeh damn fool" (68).

5. The famous phrase derives from a letter that Hawthorne wrote to his publisher William D. Ticknor in 1855:

> America is now wholly given over to a damned mob of scribbling women, and I should have no chance of success while the public taste is occupied with their trash—and should be ashamed of myself if I did succeed. What is the mystery of these innumerable editions of the "Lamplighter," and other books neither better nor worse?—worse they could not be, and better they need not be, when they sell by the 100,000. (qtd. in Frederick 231)

CHAPTER ONE

1. The subject of rhetorical training fascinated not just men but women (and not only upper-class women), as may be witnessed in Nicole Tonkovich's "Rhetorical Power in the Victorian Parlor," which traces the many articles by Sarah Josepha Hale, the long-time editor of the popular *Godey's Lady's Book*, that sought to teach her female readers how to have rhetorical power.

2. Channing is actually much more skeptical about electrifying orators—the classical irresistible orator—than his predecessor, John Quincy Adams, who held them up as an ideal. See Potkay for an examination of Adams's and Channing's very different attitudes about the ideal of civic eloquence.

3. Why, though, does the problem of disingenuous eloquence become such a problem in nineteenth-century America? Although I do not have the space to pursue this question in much detail, I think it is plausible to see the specter of disingenuous eloquence as a consequence of or parallel to the rise of the confidence man and other symptoms of American class mobility and increasing urbanization. The confidence with which earlier generations associated eloquence with virtue becomes increasingly hard to come by. For an argument about the way in which the American middle class changed in relation to ideals of sincerity and transparency in the nineteenth century, see Karen Halttunen's *Confidence Men and Painted Women*.

4. Lawrence Buell, in *New England Literary Culture*, as well as Gregory Clark and S. Michael Halloran, discuss the neoclassicism of nineteenth-century rhetoricians and orators. They also chart the decline of its influence as the century progresses. Buell sees neoclassical norms of speaking replaced by increasing vernacularization and hybridization, whereas Clark and Halloran see neoclassical values replaced by those of individualism and professionalization.

5. In his *Lectures*, Adams discusses "Quinctilian [*sic*]" and Cicero, the five "offices" of rhetoric (in Adams's terminology, invention, disposition, elocution, memory, and pronunciation), and the three different Aristotelian kinds (epideictic or what Adams calls "demonstrative," deliberative, and judicial). His work was not, perhaps unsurprisingly, a bestseller on the order of *Uncle Tom's Cabin*. Twenty years after its original publication in 1810, the initial printing was still not sold out.

6. This is an accusation that began to be leveled against American women orators who spoke to "promiscuous audiences" (containing both men and women) starting in the early nineteenth century, as Susan Zaeske reports. According to Zaeske, this warning "emphasized, in particular, the perception that woman by nature was irrational and could persuade only through seduction" (197). Although he does not make it explicit, Channing's portrait of the irrational seductive orator has a gendered cast. Implicitly, Channing's arguments reinforce the conventional prejudice against women speaking in public.

7. A development that furthered this association was the way in which Peter Ramus, a sixteenth-century French rhetorician and educational reformer, and his descendants modified the offices or canons of rhetoric: whereas the ancients focused on *inventio* (invention), *dispositio* (arrangement), *memoria* (memorization), *pronuntiatio* (delivery), and *elocutio* (style), Ramus restricted the study of rhetoric to the last two offices. He separated out "the conceptualizing part of the composition process," in the words of James L. Golden and Edward P. J. Corbett (6), a separation that abetted the sense of rhetorical study as study in the art of window dressing. E. L. Godkin, editor of the *Nation*, wants precisely to reverse this trend in his article "Rhetorical Training" (1875), when he enjoins his readers that such training should not assist the man in "glibness" (145) but "in the art of reasoning, in the arrangement of materials, in the quick perception of relations, and in penetrating to the heart of knotty questions and extracting essential facts" (146); in fact, we should not teach men how to speak at all but how to think ("the fluency, if it be not constitutionally wanting, is sure to come afterwards" [145]).

8. For Channing, insincerity is the same as deliberate falsehood. According to nineteenth-century rhetoricians, the orator always knows the truth; if he fails to reach it in his orations, he is acting out of self-interest not ignorance. Barnet Baskerville has characterized this period: "[T]ruth is readily ascertainable and has the same appearance to all men" (15).

9. The considerable influence of these rhetoricians on nineteenth-century American rhetoric is explored in Nan Johnson's *Nineteenth-Century Rhetoric in North America*: "Nineteenth-century rhetoric relied substantially on Campbell and Blair's innovations and on the subsequent extension of their revisions by Richard Whately" (Johnson 19).

10. The rhetorics that these three men wrote formed the basis of rhetorical

teaching in mid-nineteenth century America. Channing, for example, taught all three men: from 1819 to 1832 he had the freshmen and sophomores read Blair's *Rhetoric* (starting in 1827 almost all textbook study was confined to the sophomore year); from 1833 to 1839 the sophomores read Whately's *Elements of Logic*, after which it was assigned in the junior and senior years; Campbell's *Philosophy of Rhetoric* was used on and off until 1839, after which it was read every year by the sophomores (Anderson 70–71).

11. This link is a commonplace in classical rhetoric often repeated by eighteenth- and nineteenth-century American orators. Perkins, for example, in his 1794 Harvard commencement address notes that "eloquence can flourish only in the soil of liberty" (22). Baskerville, in fact, identifies it as one of the principal themes of nineteenth-century rhetoric. Later in the chapter, I quote a contemporary of Channing's who also voices this sentiment.

12. Much of Channing's oration seems to be a balancing act. In fact, the scale or balance seems to motivate Channing's own syntax: his balanced, hypotactic, neoclassical sentences. "We believe that the more perfect we are, the more intense will be our pleasures of taste, and that the more we cultivate the heart, the more thoroughly it will pervade and influence our opinions and characters" (*Lectures* 22). If Stowe's favorite mark of punctuation is the dash, Channing's is the semicolon: "I think it unquestionable, that the oratory of modern free countries is, in character, as precisely formed by and suited to our state of society, as that of the ancients was accommodated to theirs; and that it would be scarcely less ridiculous to lament over the decline of their oratory amongst us, than it would be to lament over the decline of good government, morals, and philosophy since the days of the triumvirate" (*Lectures* 12).

13. Yet character goes beyond assuring veracity: it also contributes to eloquence. Here is how Henry David Thoreau describes the eloquence of abolitionist Wendell Phillips at a lecture Phillips gave at the Concord Lyceum: "It is rare that we have the pleasure of listening to so clear and orthodox a speaker, who obviously has so few cracks or flaws in his moral nature—who, having words at his command in a remarkable degree, has much more than words" (qtd. in Warren 15).

14. How different this notion is from Stowe's in *The Minister's Wooing* (as we shall see): the character most marked by discernment and self-control is Aaron Burr, who is her villain.

15. F. O. Matthiessen has commented on the tendency of this age to conflate discourses that previous ages had held distinct: "[I]n [Emerson's] tendency to link poets and orators whenever he listed the various arts, he was responding to a . . . common and widespread belief of his time" (*American Renaissance* 22). Notice that in the case of Emerson oratory becomes associated with poetry. Channing,

too, wants to erase distinctions, but his erasure proceeds in the opposite direction: poetry (as a synecdoche for the irrational in rhetoric) becomes philosophy.

16. For an account of how taste functions to set groups (defined by age, sex, and class) apart, see Pierre Bourdieu's *Distinction*; Bourdieu also allows us to see how the concept of "taste" has changed from that set out by Lord Kames. As implicit followers of Bourdieu, modern readers will have a difficult time believing in the eighteenth- and early nineteenth-century sense of the liberatory potential of taste.

17. Dana notes in his biographical sketch that Channing evinced "a preference for the philosophy of Reid, from whose style of thought he seemed to receive peculiar satisfaction" (xvi).

18. We shall see that Henry Ward Beecher holds a remarkably similar view (chapter 4).

19. We can draw parallels, for instance, between Channing and Sandra Gustafson's portrait of Fisher Ames (1758–1808), a Massachusetts representative known for his congressional eloquence. Unlike Channing, for many (especially other Federalists) he was a riveting speaker, yet one quality of his speech foreshadows Channing's technique, according to Gustafson: Ames's copious use of literary figures as a way of distinguishing his own speech from that of the hoi polloi (236). But even beyond the similarity of their tropological preferences, Ames and Channing seemed to be in the business of both recognizing and cautioning against the destructive potential of the popular penchant for unrestrained and emotional speech. Ames embodied (and implicitly counseled) an "internalization of self-control rather than externalization of feeling in direct action" (Gustafson 241).

CHAPTER TWO

1. One of the most important articles limning a separate nineteenth-century American female literary tradition is Annette Kolodny's "A Map for Rereading." Yet the article is actually ambivalent about a distinct female tradition, as becomes evident when we look at her discussion of the relationship between Charlotte Perkins Gilman's "The Yellow Wallpaper" and Edgar Allan Poe's short stories. Kolodny discusses how Gilman's position in this Gothic tradition went unacknowledged by contemporaneous readers, who could not make sense of her story. This observation complicates Kolodny's claim that women were developing a tradition (or more accurately, according to her article, a "code") of their own. Instead it seems that Gilman was so radically adapting the (male) Gothic tradition that her contemporaneous audience could not recognize that the story belonged to it.

2. For an account of this transition from authorship as an avocation to a profession, see Michael Newbury.

3. According to Joan Hedrick, *Uncle Tom's Cabin* was inspired both by the passage of the Fugitive Slave Act and by the death of Stowe's son Charley from cholera in 1849 ("Stowe's Life").

4. Reading biographies of Stowe and her siblings creates a sense that this conversion narration (and the subsequent examination) required by Lyman from all his children could be seen by them as a kind of torture, most notably in the case of Lyman's oldest child, Catharine, whose own inability to narrate such an experience proved a long-lasting torment both to her and to her father (most recently, Debby Applegate discusses this impasse in her biography of Henry Ward Beecher). Exacerbating Catharine's distress, Lyman did not hesitate to pronounce Catharine's fiancé, Alexander Fisher, among the similarly damned; he had died when his ship sank off the coast of Ireland in 1823 before his own conversion. Fisher's tragedy and its effect on Catharine are seen, plausibly, to have inspired the part of *The Minister's Wooing* involving James Marvyn's supposed death and the torment that his dying unregenerate causes Mary Scudder and his mother; this section is also linked to Stowe's own recent loss of her son, Henry Ellis Stowe, who died while a student at Dartmouth College, also before being converted.

5. Kimberly VanEsveld Adams records the Beecher family's familiarity with the early writings of Jonathan Edwards, especially with his description of female conversions, including that of his future wife, Sarah Pierpont Edwards. Her article also offers a wonderful parsing of the various offshoots of Calvinism that engaged and enraged Lyman Beecher, his children Henry and Harriet, and Harriet Beecher Stowe's husband, Calvin Stowe. Gustafson discusses the rhetorical styles of the Great Awakening ministers George Whitefield and John Davenport as against the style of the antievangelical, well-to-do Boston minister Charles Chauncy, who seems like a forefather of E. T. Channing in Chauncy's elevation of "social deference over authenticity" (Gustafson 50). Gustafson also discusses the way that Edwards's written accounts of the female converts Abigail Hutchinson and Sarah Pierpont Edwards both enabled and forestalled their efforts to carve out a place for their own voices in the Calvinist tradition.

6. Hedrick describes Brace as "something of an eighteenth-century man" (*Harriet Beecher Stowe* 25) in his wide-ranging interests and commitment to reason. He taught the natural sciences, moral philosophy, and composition. Coming to remarkably similar conclusions as Channing would a few years later, Brace addressed students in 1816 and told them that their education had tried "to teach you to feel but to feel in subordination to reason" (qtd. in Hedrick, *Harriet Beecher Stowe* 25). Stowe loved him and was chosen, at age ten, to read one of her compositions at the academy's annual exhibition. The topic was "Can the immortality of the soul be proved by the light of nature?" (Hedrick, *Harriet Beecher Stowe* 26–27).

7. For example, the Victorian anthropologist J. M. Allan, who authored "On the Real Differences in the Minds of Men and Women" (1869), has this to say about women's higher faculties: "Even if woman possessed a brain equal to man's—if her intellectual powers were equal to his—the eternal distinction in the physical organisation of the sexes would make the average man in the long run, the mental superior of the average woman" (qtd. in Russett 30). Another anthropologist, Paul Broca, dismisses the "Negro race" in 1868 with the following words: "Never has a people with a black skin, wooly hair, and prognathous face, spontaneously arrived at civilization" (qtd. in Russett 27).

8. With this belief, Stowe parts ways with other nineteenth-century American feminists like the Grimké sisters and Elizabeth Cady Stanton. These factions left different legacies to modern feminism. The Grimkés and Stanton provide a feminism of the head and not the heart—they do not diverge from Channing and his modulated, bodiless orator as the sentimentalists do.

9. I am indebted in this formulation to Gustafson's heuristic for thinking about the relationship between written and spoken forms (xvi), which I discuss toward the end of this chapter.

10. Harris develops a technique of reading that justifies her turning away from the text's primary subject matter:

> By shifting focus from the text's explicit center to its margins, by re-viewing the major plot from the perspective of the minor, and by gathering together the text's transcendent moments, the alternate text that lies hidden, although not unexperienced, within *The Minister's Wooing* will be uncovered and the ways in which it functions to undercut the explicit valorization of heterosexual and hierarchical relationships in the novel will be unmasked. ("Female Imaginary" 182)

I contend that we can keep the book's primary concerns in mind yet still see how Stowe subverts conventional understandings of who holds the power in different religious and rhetorical situations.

11. See Jenny Franchot's "Unseemly Commemoration" for a fascinating discussion of the role of Catholic icons in *The Minister's Wooing* and George Washington Cable's *The Grandissimes*. Her argument posits a developmental narrative of the sentimental heroine as increasingly pure and disembodied, as opposed to the materiality and supposed carnality that these Catholic icons have come to represent in the post-Enlightenment West. Her account conflicts with my own account of the embodied nature of sentimental persuasiveness, although I admit that the bodies of sentimental heroines are frail and oddly spiritual things.

12. In the mid-nineteenth-century's prepragmatic understanding, the orator might choose not to tell the truth if he is a bad man. But if he is a good man, he will tell the truth, which will be true for everyone. Two assumptions are at

work here: the truth, like taste, is external to the orator: truth is not created by people. Second, if the orator wants to tell the truth, he will be able to: truth is readily accessible to everyone. I am indebted to Baskerville's "Principal Themes" for these formulations.

13. How the orator appears becomes very, very important to the sentimentalists, who would want readers to believe that this is because appearances never lie. Yet this sentimental prioritizing of seeming over being can be stated in another way that hints at why we might at times find sentimentality disingenuous: any system that claims that appearance equals reality puts itself at risk. As soon as someone begins to suspect the existence of a split between seeming and being, the sentimental system starts to collapse. See chapters 3, 4, and 6 for a fuller description of this phenomenon.

14. In *Daniel Deronda* Eliot compares Gwendolen Harleth to a picture. Gwendolen is staring at herself in a mirror. "'I should make a tolerable Saint Cecilia with some white roses on my head,' said Gwendolen,—'only how about my nose, mamma? I think saint's [*sic*] noses never in the least turn up'" (28). Mary Scudder also appears to be the picture of a living saint, but how different these two accounts are. In Eliot, it is Gwendolen herself who makes the comparison: her extreme self-regard is matched only by her trivializing of the spiritual aspects of life. In contrast, the narrator is the one who points out Mary's resemblance to a heavenly creature; Mary is not self-aware in the least. Eliot's novel associates pictures with artifice; Stowe characterizes pictures as a direct avenue to the heart.

15. Malapropping Chloe, Tom's wife, is the archetypal comic character. Wanting her owner, Mrs. Shelby, to come look at some chickens, Chloe wonders "If Missis would come and look at dis yer lot o' poetry" (232). Candace, a slave of the Marvyns, is the Chloe of *The Minister's Wooing*. Like Chloe, she is capable of occasionally persuasive pieces of eloquence. Candace chastises Digo, another slave, for appropriating the antislavery views of his master: "*You* a man, and not stan' by your color, and flunk under to mean white ways! Ef you was *half* a man, your heart would 'a' bounded like a cannon-ball at dat ar' sermon" (278; emphasis in the original). At other moments, Candace has a comic misunderstanding of the way words work, yet she becomes persuasive precisely because of her ingenuousness. She is also like James—or, rather, James is like her: both are inept at the finer points of language, thus fitted to be occasionally effective orators though never able to cast off their comic status. Their comedy ultimately hobbles them, bringing representation once again to the forefront.

16. *The Minister's Wooing* contains a steady stream of references to European culture: "she made a Faubourg St. Germain of the darkest room" (297). She also refers to various watering spots, as when the narrator interjects to ask us, "Do you remember, at Niagara, a little cataract on the American side?" (11) Stowe does

not see her audience as bumpkins but as members of the cosmopolitan leisure class. Richard Brodhead has characterized Sarah Orne Jewett's "local color" fiction as tourist literature and has shown how it was aimed at the genteel classes: that characterization holds for this novel. Hedrick confirms how much Stowe's own European tour led her to take on the role of the tour guide for the masses (*Harriet Beecher Stowe* 286).

17. I revisit the phenomenon of silly white men and its rhetorical ramifications in chapter 4.

18. Note the familiarity of the metaphors that the sentimental author turns to. "There are some people who receive from Nature as a gift a sort of graceful facility of sympathy, by which they incline to take on, for the time being, the sentiments and opinions of those with whom they converse, as the chameleon was fabled to change its hue with every surrounding" (*Minister's Wooing* 259). Stowe is not the first person to use the chameleon to evoke changeability—that is the point: the sentimentalists do not use metaphor to surprise the reader into recognizing a previously unnoticed quality in the thing being compared but to underline what the reader already knows to be true. The sentimental novel wants to be on exactly the same level as the reader.

19. This might explain, as well, sentimental rhetoric's fondness for fetishized objects, another trustworthy source, untouched by the verbal: "Have not ribbons, cast-off flowers, soiled bits of gauze, trivial, trashy fragments of millinery, sometimes had an awful meaning, a deadly power, when they belonged to one who should wear them no more, and whose beautiful form, frail and crushed as they, is a hidden and vanished thing for all time?" (*Minister's Wooing* 205).

20. Alcott's Jo is thus a breakthrough sentimental heroine in her sturdiness and health. Many people cannot countenance this, as can be inferred from Gillian Armstrong's self-consciously feminist film version of *Little Women*, which nevertheless cast the pale and waiflike Winona Ryder as Jo.

21. An unimaginable situation in the sentimental novel would be a fat sentimental heroine. For Stowe, bodies and character cannot be separated. What you see is what you get. Our usual distinction between inside and outside does not hold in the sentimental universe: the outside always conveys exactly what is inside.

22. See James M. Cox's "Harriet Beecher Stowe," in which he calls *The Minister's Wooing* a "pioneering [work] of the local color movement" (464). But the praise is faint, as is usual when labeling something "local color," and Cox offers it in the spirit of contrasting the novel's flickering power to that of the incandescent *Uncle Tom's Cabin.*

23. Adams, in fact, observes that James Marvyn is based on Henry Ward Beecher.

24. Walter Benn Michaels reads the genre of the romance (using the example of

The House of the Seven Gables) as exposing the cultural logic of nineteenth-century property rights. According to Michaels, the romance's vision of inalienable property results in a historical paradox: the separation of title from possession "turned out to be the condition that enabled speculators to flourish" out West (176–77). Michaels does not read Hawthorne as transcending history but as very much involved in thinking through nineteenth-century problems of selfhood and its relationship to the market.

25. Interestingly, this characterization of sentimentality as "documentary" coexists with one that views the sentimental as lacking proportion or realistic characters.

26. Really, who can blame Buell for thinking this? Stowe herself named the drowning of her son Henry Ellis Stowe as her inspiration for the novel, and the parallels between the religious debates in the novel seem to reflect the arguments among Henry Ward, Catharine, and Lyman as well as debates going on at the Andover Theological Seminary, where Stowe's husband worked. See Hedrick's *Harriet Beecher Stowe* as well as Adams's "Family Influences" for a fuller discussion of the parallels between Stowe's life and *The Minister's Wooing*.

27. Stowe has preempted a point that Janice Radway makes in *Reading the Romance*. Radway's romance readers see a given romance as a "novel" (it always comes as a satisfying surprise how the heroine ends up). But they also acknowledge that it functions as a myth (the reader already knows the ending); it is both real (these women claim that novels are real in their details, in their settings, and in the facts given to the reader along the way) and a fantasy (the same good things always happen). Though the romance readers admit that they may be fantasies, they like these novels because they seem, in fact, to be real.

28. Laura Korobkin suggests this possibility with her reading of the Beecher trial in *Criminal Conversations*.

29. Yet, of course, we know that conversational modes are not without their own formulas. For example, see Mary Louise Pratt's adaptation of William Labov's work on the six-part structure of oral narratives of personal experience, in *Towards a Speech Act Theory of Literary Discourse*.

30. As reported by Christopher P. Wilson, who goes on to comment on the conversational quality of the novel: "In part because this was one of the books she dictated to a secretary, and in part because the book first appeared in serialized form in the *Atlantic Monthly*, the narrative often adopts a disarmingly discursive candor. Aiming to give her narrative the aura of conversation, gossip, even intimacy, Stowe thereby downplays any conscious artistry" (560). Similarly, Dorothy Z. Baker points out how the novel is modeled on the "conversational" circular letters that the Beechers wrote to each other, where one member of the

family would respond to what another had said and then send it on to another family member.

31. Here is how Gustafson characterizes Fisher Ames's speech: "His characteristically elaborate figures and heightened tone reflect an influence of classical and English poetry so pervasive that in his conversation no less than in his oratory he spoke in language 'full of imagery, drawing similes to illustrate the topics of his discourse from everything about him'" (236). She goes on to characterize his speech in a way that links him to Channing as well as to John Adams: "His literary imagery made a social point. Like his fellow Federalist John Adams at the Boston Massacre trial, Ames employed a textual reference to distinguish his extempore oratory from the speech of the 'mob'" (236).

32. I am grateful to the University of Virginia website on *Uncle Tom's Cabin* for providing me with this information in a section entitled "The Christian Slave" (http://utc.iath.virginia.edu/uncletom/xianslav/xshp.html).

33. The scene is quoted at length in the appendix.

34. The "female" reader of this passage is encouraged to adopt the view that powerful white males, for all their bluster, are rather hapless and need a woman to lead them to the right path.

35. I have been discussing "orality" rather than "oratory" in this paragraph, but "orality" is obviously a crucial feature of nineteenth-century oratory. Yet they are not identical. Alessandro Portelli, for example, characterizes orality as often involving a back and forth between speaker and responder, who frequently switch places (18); however, nineteenth-century oratory includes speeches, where audience interaction is at a minimum (although audience reaction is at a premium).

36. Jane Tompkins has analyzed the scene of Little Eva and Tom reading the Bible together to demonstrate how the novel follows a typological structure; however, I would highlight how words continually morph into pictures in this scene:

> [Little Eva] read,—"And I saw a sea of glass, mingled with fire."
>
> "Tom," said Eva, suddenly stopping, and pointing to the lake, "there 'tis."
>
> "What, Miss Eva?"
>
> "Don't you see,—there?" said the child, pointing to the glassy water, which . . . reflected the golden glow of the sky. "There's a 'sea of glass, mingled with fire.'" (238)

CHAPTER THREE

1. Other critics have noted that this period, roughly defined, marks an end to the popularity and influence of the sentimental women authors. In her landmark study on nineteenth-century *Woman's Fiction*, Baym observes that the "genre had

run its course" by the late 1860s and 1870s (13); Gustavus Stadler notes how the *Atlantic* had spent the 1860s "excising a number of female authors from its list of contributors," including Stowe (657); Halttunen dates the demise of a sentimental culture of sincerity in dress and etiquette earlier, to the 1850s and 1860s. Warren Susman pinpoints the shift from "character" to "personality" (discussed in the course of this chapter as linked to the fall of the sentimental orator) to 1905. This capacious span of dates makes sense because the demise of sentimentality is a broad cultural phenomenon, registering in a variety of places (in the realm of the novel, the periodical, the conduct book, the advice manual, the sermon, the speaking manual, and the actual parlors of the middle class). It would be stranger to find that (*pace* Susman with his claim—facetiously made?—about 1905) that the waning of sentimentality during this period happened quickly or evenly.

2. Lynn M. Alexander notes that "[d]uring the last quarter of the nineteenth century the number of women employed outside the home skyrocketed" (593). An 1896 *New York Times* article, "Change in the Employment of Women," discusses how the percentage of women employed in "gainful occupations" increased 47.68 percent from 1880 to 1890 (noting that this is a significant number even if we take into account the 25 percent increase in population). Illustrating this phenomenon, the article comments that, however much images of "the superior sex" used to sell "the most esoteric constituents of women's attire," now it is the women themselves who are the salespeople.

3. In *Confidence Men and Painted Women* (see especially chapter 5), Halttunen charts the growing popularity of parlor theatricals and links their rise with the fall of sentimental culture, as evinced in the realms of clothing and etiquette. She sees sentimental culture as containing the seeds of its own demise, similar to the way I do. According to Halttunen, "[t]he quest for sincerity of form [e.g., the desire that dress match an individual's inner feelings] thus inevitably turned and destroyed itself, for when sincerity became a matter of style or of fashion, sentimental typology [the idea that physical appearance matches a person's character] was rendered meaningless" (189). Halttunen thus links the demise of sentimentality to its codification. A similar codification happens when one tries to widen the population that can harness sentimentality's tremendous powers of persuasion.

4. For example, Showalter enjoins modern readers to note *Work*'s "suppressed radical elements" (x).

5. Yet the class and racial exclusivity of "true womanhood" should not be overstated. The ex-slave Harriet Jacobs, for example, tries to win favor with her middle-class white readers in *Incidents in the Life of a Slave Girl* (1861) by asserting her likeness to them, stressing her religious commitment and her wished-for (but compromised) sexual purity. Although many critics have stressed Jacobs's fortitude

and determination in escaping from her sexually abusive master, we should note that her attempts are accompanied by a discourse of physical frailty. For example, Michelle Burnham locates Jacobs's power in a critique of a Foucaultian notion of agency, claiming that Jacobs instead finds "loopholes" in institutional structures. Yet we should note that Jacobs's account of her time spent in the attic of her grandmother's storeroom, which she calls "The Loophole of Retreat," is filled with the language of physical suffering: "Consequently, my clothes and bedding were often drenched; a process by which the pains and aches in my cramped and stiffened limbs were greatly increased" (117). However strategically she planted such allusions to her physical delicacy (in defiance of stereotypes of black people claiming that they did not feel physical pain the way white people did), the discourse of true womanhood was one that Jacobs felt was available to her.

6. For a discussion of how western women adapted the concept of true womanhood (which originated in the eastern part of the country), see June O. Underwood.

7. Stowe, like her nineteenth-century peers, did not use the term "true woman," but the characters who represent the female ideal in her work, like Mary Scudder and Rachel Halliday, exhibit at least three of the qualities that Barbara Welter uses to characterize this figure (as mentioned above, "submissiveness" is more complicated than Welter allows). If we turn to *Little Women*, we see that Marmee's domesticity is complicated by her charity work outside the home and her journey to visit her war-wounded husband; her piety is less discussed than that of Rachel Halliday (Marmee's purity is unquestioned, and her "submissiveness" is complex the way it is with many of Stowe's heroines). Thus I feel justified in discussing the "true woman" in reference to this work: even when the ideal is being redefined, it is also being registered.

8. Perhaps the most famous example of this use of "voice" would be Carol Gilligan's *In a Different Voice*.

9. See also Mary Rigsby's "'So Like Women!'" She asserts that *Work* lies outside the sentimental tradition (although she puts it in the "romance" tradition). In wording that echoes Showalter's, Rigsby writes that "Alcott prepares her audience for romance but delivers realism" (115). This kind of disavowal threatens to overturn the recuperative work that feminist critics have performed on sentimental novels. Many of Rigsby's conclusions about *Work* in fact echo claims made by other feminist critics in characterizing *sentimental* novels. For example, Rigsby's claim that *Work* values human connection is very similar to Joanne Dobson's claim about human connection being a central theme in *sentimental* novels ("Reclaiming Sentimental Literature").

10. In mentioning Twain I am thinking particularly of Emmeline Granger-

ford's potpourri of poems, which the reader is introduced to in chapter 17 of *Huck Finn*, including "I Shall Never Hear Thy Sweet Chirrup More Alas" (an ode to a dead bird) and "Ode to Stephen Dowling Bots, Dec'd" (who fell down a well from which "[t]hey got him out and emptied him / Alas it was too late" [113]).

11. In this novel as in other sentimental novels, what prevents most dialect speakers from rising to the rank of the most eloquent is their unwitting comic effect (see chapter 2). We can see this in the way that Alcott represents a white dialect speaker in the novel, Mrs. Wilkins. Mrs. Wilkins talks about leaving her portly husband Lisha after getting mad at him for slapping her, returning to him after they have both apologized: "[T]he good soul entered so heartily into her story that she unconsciously embellished it with dramatic illustrations. At the slapping episode she flung an invisible 'fork, dish, and pertaters' into an imaginary kettle . . . and uttered the repentant Lisha's explanation with an incoherent pathos that forbid [*sic*] a laugh at the sudden introduction of the porcine martyr" (150). The narrator makes Mrs. Wilkins into an unreliable narrator in the sense that we know something about her that she does not: that she and her "porcine" husband are ridiculous. Stowe achieves similar effects with Chloe, Tom's wife. In such portraits, we also see Alcott and Stowe creating one aspect of their "authorial" or "intended" audience: readers who are speakers of standard English.

12. There are other parallels between the characters in Alcott's novel and those in *Uncle Tom's Cabin*. Rachel Sterling seems to be a direct descendant of Rachel Halliday. Both are Quaker; both are intensely domestic; both influence others through their character more than through their words. And both seem to represent their author's ideal.

13. Many contemporaneous reviews of *Work*, however, find David unworthy of Christie. One reviewer comments that David "does not know how to love, and never can have experienced that passion in the masculine form" (from an 1873 *Springfield Daily Republican* review qtd. in B. Clark 190). The critic suggests a certain effeminacy about David, as does another reviewer who notes that David is "deficient in manliness" (from an 1873 *Daily Graphic* review qtd. in B. Clark 195). David registers on reviewers as a nonentity ("[Christie] marries David after a long and rather puzzling period of courtship, in which David does not figure to so much advantage as Miss Alcott meant, we fear" [from an 1872 *Springfield Daily Republican* review qtd. in B. Clark 191]). In the response to David's character we might glimpse another crack in the sentimental fabric: the qualities that Alcott values in David, his verbal and sartorial simplicity, are read by some of her contemporaries as effeminate. Earlier readers would have read Phillip Fletcher, the European-coded aristocrat, as effeminate.

14. We can see this commitment quite clearly in *Little Women*'s Laurie, who

is redeemed by being de-aristocratized over the course of the novel. Our first glimpse of him involves his lounging (the word "lounging" is a surefire clue to the presence of the aristocratic in sentimental novels) in an orchard; the end of the novel finds him a hard-working businessman and philanthropist.

15. I am indebted to Halttunen's analysis of sentimental conventions regarding dress in nineteenth-century America in *Confidence Men and Painted Women*.

16. I am picking up on just one strand of Hendler's complex and thought-provoking argument, which teases out the contradictions in the sentimental novel caused by its simultaneous commitment to the mass market and to normative ideas of womanhood.

17. Victoria Olwell identifies this trope of the overcome speaker and discusses how it was taken up by women both to gain political power and to excuse themselves for exercising it.

18. Lauren Berlant and Hortense Spillers have recognized this tendency, and it makes them dismiss the idea that sentimentality could model meaningful political action for its readers.

19. Hendler reads this line as suggesting, contrary to my reading, that all girls are naturally actors. This reading fits with his larger claim, with which I am mostly in agreement, that the novel associates acting and true womanhood.

20. This is also true of Alcott's books themselves. For example, Bessie Jones characterizes "Hospital Sketches" as "a mixture of humor, realism, and pathos" (qtd. in Showalter xxi).

21. As the director admonishes in Constantin Stanislavski's *An Actor Prepares*: "'Never lose yourself on the stage. Always act in your own person, as an artist. You can never get away from yourself. The moment you lose yourself on the stage marks the departure from truly living your part and the beginning of exaggerated false acting'" (192).

22. Here Christie echoes the ideal actor in Denis Diderot's "The Paradox of the Actor" (1772) (see chapter 4). Diderot's dialogue involves a debate between a proponent of natural actors, "who play from the heart" (8), and a proponent of actors who do not draw on their own emotions and experiences. Diderot favors the latter, and Christie resembles what we might call the "unnatural actor." Christie is unlike the natural actor in that she lacks any distinguishing characteristics. Diderot describes the natural actor's opposite, this "unnatural" actor, thus: "Anyone in society who wants to please everyone, and has the unfortunate talent to be able to, is nothing, possesses nothing which is proper to him or distinguishes him, nothing which might bring delight to some and tedium to others" (133). In Diderot's eyes, this person cannot escape the taint of duplicity. Diderot's speaker continues (and here he seems to predict Henry Ward Beecher more than Alcott):

"He talks all the time, and always talks well; he is a professional sycophant, a great courtier, and a great actor" (133).

23. The dance historian Nancy Lee Chalfa Ruyter "estimates that 85 percent of the Delsartists in American during its entire time span were women" (qtd. in Suter 99). As Suter's own article notes, Delsartism was instrumental in specifically female colleges of oratory and in starting a reform movement composed of women, whom Suter calls the "American Delsartists."

24. Although what is happening with the audience might be more complicated than what is happening with Christie. In this scene, are the audience members identifying with the playwright brought comfort by the "good angel" or are they identifying with the "good angel" herself or both? Or perhaps they are being overcome by emotion from the way the scene fulfills a fantasy that their culture has about how the world should work: the poor, deserving victim being succored by a true woman. Regardless of these different possibilities, the crying audience member seems at that moment to forget herself, to become suffused with another person's emotions, even in the last case, where the emotions she might be suffused with are those of a primal citizen in the act of being interpellated into her culture's dearest-held values.

25. Hendler and Olwell, who have both written on *Work*, can provide insight into how critics react to these contradictions. Hendler initially appears to have been willing to take this novel's word about Christie's artlessness but then to become disillusioned by the novel's slide into theatricality; he tends to be unsympathetic to the way this novel envisions political efficacy. Christie seems too much like a charlatan for Hendler. But Olwell begins by letting us know that the self-forgetful orator was a common trope of the time: Olwell from the start acknowledges the craftedness of Alcott's rhetoric and is thus not in a position to be disillusioned: she finds something of potential political value in the novel, a way of "mediat[ing] . . . the discursive and bodily differences that magnetizing women's genius is imagined to coordinate" (60). Both recognize contradictions in the way the novel represents Christie's eloquence, but Hendler sees them as undermining a coherent message and Olwell as enabling Alcott to escape the usual "antinomies between the particular and representative, personal and impersonal, interested and disinterested" that have ordinarily been used to confine women to the political margins (41).

26. This also comes up briefly in David's confession about his shabby treatment of his sister and his subsequent depression. David talks about how he first had to act as if he loved certain things before he actually did: "I did not love my work; but it was good for me, and helped cure my sick soul. I never guessed why I felt better, but dug on with indifference first, then felt pride in my garden, then

interest in the plants I tended, and by and by I saw what they had done for me, and loved them like true friends" (218).

27. According to Joseph Fahey, Delsartism came to America via the teaching and lectures of Delsarte's American protégé, Steele MacKaye; after MacKaye, the Delsartean system was promulgated by a plethora of women, including Eleanor Georgen, who taught at the American School of Dramatic Art, and the outspoken Geneviève Stebbins, who extended the system to apply not just to acting and elocution but to physical culture and self-improvement.

28. I refer both to the audience of working women that Christie addresses at the end and to many of the actual reviewers of the novel. The novel was generally well received. This remark from a Philadelphia paper is representative: "[Alcott's] writings have a purpose, and that always an elevating and refining one, and a tone as healthful and invigorating as the breezes from her New England hills" (qtd. in B. Clark 221). Critics also praise *Work* for its characteristic vivacity and "realism." The following patterns emerge in terms of the problems that some reviewers found with the novel: problems with the structure (e.g., too episodic); the wanness of Alcott's depiction of David; and, most interestingly to me, a critique of the book's intervention into the question of women's work. For example, the *Nation*'s review of 31 July 1873 faults Alcott for offering a story that is too idiosyncratic to illuminate the labor question and adds that "as a guide for poor girls, it is useless" (qtd. in B. Clark 206). Yet no reviewer doubts the sincerity of Christie or of Alcott; indeed, some of the more critical reviewers assume Alcott's sincerity and ingenuousness to be at the root of her problems as a novelist. For example, the *Springfield Daily Republican* of 12 June 1873 notes condescendingly that "[w]holesome and kindly as Miss Alcott is, and never more so than in this novel, she does not go deep enough" (qtd. B. Clark 192).

CHAPTER FOUR

1. In terms of Beecher's actual feelings about the theater, the actor and playwright Dion Boucicault writes in his memorial that three years before his death Beecher admitted to Boucicault that he had changed his mind regarding their debate in the *New York Tribune* over the morality of the stage. In 1857 Beecher had attacked it. Almost thirty years later they met again, and Boucicault records this exchange, where he plays the devil's advocate to Beecher's change of heart: "I remarked that many sincere and good people objected to the stage because its very soul was a fiction, and its art was a moral conveyed in a falsehood. After a reflection of a moment, [Beecher] remarked, almost to himself, 'And the parables of our Saviour?'" (40). Beecher was never a man to damn deceptive means if they

served a good end; Boucicault's description of the stage describes quite well Rose's deceptive conversion of Pete Sawmill.

2. Beecher was widely known in fact for conducting reverse slave auctions, in which he would display a runaway slave before his congregation and, acting like an auctioneer, raise money for her freedom. For a description of one such event that was widely noted at the time, see Wayne Shaw.

3. Herbert Ross Brown, for example, describes the sentimentalists in this way: "Imbued with a lyric faith in the perfectibility of man, they regarded the America of their own day as a mere vestibule to Utopia. They preferred to dwell in a cozy cloudland of sentiment, secure in a haven of dreams" (359). Henry Nash Smith characterizes their optimism similarly and also notes their commitment to social climbing and the derivative nature of their reliance on emotion: "The women novelists depicted this anxiety [of upward mobility] and allayed it by bringing together in a form the new audience [the middle class] could comprehend several major cultural forces: the cult of success, the emotional piety that had found expression in the revival movement, [and] the yearning of plain people with money for aristocratic elegance in manners" (58).

4. This claim inevitably associates Beecher with femininity (as the commentators who mentioned his ability to make his audience cry often did). But this association is disavowed in a collection of eulogies for Henry Ward Beecher given by famous men and women. Oliver Wendell Holmes, for example, seems rather to insist upon Beecher's masculinity, as in the following remark: "What a comfort it was . . . to hear a sound, strong-bodied, healthy minister of the Gospel speak with virile force and ringing accents, as a *living* man to *living* men" (2; emphases in the original). I suspect that, perhaps unconsciously for these eulogists, celebrating Henry Ward Beecher involved masculinizing him.

5. Libby Tilton would recant her damning letters and then recant her recantation. "In one twenty-four-hour period, she wrote a 'confession' of adultery that her husband showed to Beecher, a 'revocation' of those accusations when Beecher visited her where she lay in bed recovering from a miscarriage, and a 'retraction' of the revocation when her husband came home and found out about the letter she had given Beecher" (Korobkin 101).

6. Douglas believes that *Uncle Tom's Cabin*'s Little Eva does not ask of her readers anything but a self-indulgent response: "[Little Eva's] sainthood is there to precipitate our nostalgia and our narcissism. . . . [Little Eva's] only real demand on her readers is for self-indulgence" (4). Douglas further charges sentimentality (which she calls "sentimentalism") with deceptiveness, in a quotation that I will return to in the final chapter: "[Sentimentalism] asserts that the values a society's activity denies are precisely the ones it cherishes" (12).

7. Writers other than Beecher and Stowe praised silence; it is a theme in nineteenth-century rhetoric (see Baskerville 20–22). The critic David Simpson notes a tension in James Fenimore Cooper between his valorizing the polite, genteel language of his educated characters (which leads to the accusation of his being a snob) and his "positive coding" of Natty Bumppo's "silence, or minimal speech" (196):

> The orgy of naming that is transcribed in the later novels, the grandiloquence of the transplanted New England middle class, and the loud invocations of the authority of the people are all forms of *noise*. Cooper dislikes noise because it is a symptom of change and debate, and most of all of disturbance, whereby every fractious element in the social contract seeks to drown out its rivals. Cooper's thematic affinity is therefore with silence, broken only by the enunciation of a few well-chosen words. (196; emphasis in the original)

Cooper, as well as Thomas Carlyle in his 1850 pamphlet "The Stump Orator," illustrates that the sentimentalists were not alone in recognizing in silence a logical solution to the problem of disingenuous eloquence. And Cooper and Carlyle also illustrate the paradox that such a solution entails: as many have commented, Carlyle devotes an enormous number of words to the proposition of silence.

8. This difference, of course, seems gendered, but it also suggests the influence of transcendentalism and Romanticism on Beecher. In her biography of Beecher, Applegate briefly discusses his relationship with transcendentalism, but it seems a lacuna in the scholarship that no full-length article on this subject exists. As for Beecher's relationship with Romanticism, the German philosophy that served as a source for Transcendentalism, O. C. Edwards, Jr., has identified a kind of preaching that occurred in the mid- to late nineteenth-century America as Romantic. Edwards classifies Beecher as a Romantic preacher (along with Horace Bushnell and Phillips Brooks). In Edwards's taxonomical approach, some of the primary characteristics of this Romantic preaching were a commitment to nature, "an epistemological understanding of feeling" that "saw feeling as a path that ultimately gave greater access to knowledge than reason," and a "conviction . . . that behind the finite . . . there is always the infinite" (298). These elements can be found in Beecher's preaching and novel.

9. Barthes rejects the idea of an "author" of a text (by which he means not just the writer but ideological lenses like Marxism and psychoanalysis that promise definitive interpretations) because it cuts short the play of the text. Like reader-response critics, he finds the reader to be at the center of meaning-making activity.

10. Applegate notes Beecher's aversion to interpretation: "As a man of The Word, Beecher voices strong resistance to the practice of interpretation in any

form. In contesting the authority of form over content, interpretation clears the way for a dangerous promiscuity of meanings" ("Seductions" 84). She explains how Beecher invites interpretation in the very sermon in which he is condemning it.

11. This is not, however, an idea foreign to earlier twentieth-century literary criticism. William K. Wimsatt and Monroe C. Beardsley's "The Affective Fallacy" has as a ramification the idea that sufficiently informed readers, once they have excluded any idiosyncratic emotional responses, will produce near-identical interpretations of the same poem, at least in terms of the poem's "emotive value" (1260). They assert that "[p]oetry is a way of fixing emotions or making them more permanently perceptible when objects have undergone a functional change from culture to culture" (1260).

12. Sigmund Freud's "The Uncanny" acquainted me with this way of reading Gothic literature. According to Freud, "an uncanny experience occurs either when infantile complexes which have been repressed are once more revived by some impression, or when primitive beliefs which have been surmounted seem once more to be confirmed" (838–39).

13. Although Merish does not take a psychoanalytic approach in *Sentimental Materialism*, I think that this kind of analysis can co-exist with hers. For example, when Merish discusses the significance of window scenes in the sentimental novel, she uses an example from *The Lamplighter*, where Gerty spies inside an opulent home whose furnishings have lifelike qualities. Merish does point out the affect attaching to this scene, linking it to the character's desire to be middle class: "sentimentalism filled [domestic spaces] with *psychological* content, depicting it as site and constitutive sign of emotional 'refinement'" (142; emphasis in the original). Yet Gerty's window scene also seems, most basically, a case of projection: Gerty and Cummins project their unconscious desires onto rooms and their contents.

14. Douglas defines the "rigorous theology" (6) of the Calvinist ministers in opposition to the sloppy thinking by which she characterizes the sentimental authors: "They [the Calvinist ministers from 1740 to 1820] exhibited with some consistency the intellectual rigor and imaginative precision difficult to achieve without collective effort, and certainly rare in more recent American annals" (7).

15. Applegate writes that by 1882 "[Beecher] officially renounced all form of Calvinism and withdrew from the New York Congregational Association" (*The Most Famous Man* 462).

16. In an oration he gave in 1875, Beecher discusses sympathy in terms similar to the way it is depicted in *Work:* "sympathy . . . connects [the orator] with his fellow-men, and which so makes him a part of the audience which he moves as that his smile is their smile, that his tear is their tear, and that the throb of his heart becomes the throb of the hearts of the whole assembly" (*Oratory* 22).

17. Applegate finds this sermon deeply self-contradictory in the way that it actually uses some of the techniques it attacks, such as those attributed to the Strange Woman (and duplicitous speech): "[Beecher's] vivid personification of licentiousness in the Strange Woman, his use of euphemistic yet evocative 'mirror-words, which cast a sidelong glance image of an idea,' forces the audience to their imaginations, and echoes the Strange Woman's Wiles of Reason, in which she 'readeth the bible to him; she goeth back along the line of history'" ("Seductions" 84).

18. With these lines, Beecher summons up the shade of Benjamin Franklin, who describes his own efforts to stifle any rhetorical opposition thus: "I cannot boast of much Success in acquiring the *Reality* of this Virtue [humility]; but I had a good deal with regard to the *Appearance* of it. I made it a Rule to forbear all direct Contradiction to the Sentiments of others, and all positive Assertion of my own. . . . When another asserted something that I thought an Error, I denied myself the Pleasure of contradicting him abruptly" (75). Like Beecher, Franklin is "amorphous": at times seen as a paragon and at other times a scamp or much worse. His amorphousness has not a little to do with the way he seems both to reveal and to occlude his true character in his *Autobiography*.

19. Warhol's "As You Stand" first led me to Delsarte.

20. However, Warhol might not be historical enough in her account. She cites two sources for the model of emotion that she claims the sentimental authors follow: George Henry Lewes and François Delsarte. Lewes's theory about the continuum between the mind and body that Warhol cites was expounded in his *Problems of Life and Mind*, which was published between 1874 and 1879. Delsarte's work on acting and elocution was not promulgated in the United States until the 1870s. Their theories thus were available to be drawn on either directly or indirectly by Alcott and Beecher but not by Stowe.

21. But certain historical facts have helped me become a more sympathetic reader of Stowe. For example, I am able to feel the force of Stowe's enjoinder to "feel right" at the end of *Uncle Tom's Cabin* now that I know that she believed that a person's feelings had to be touched in order to act. It also helped me to feel the emotional force of Gustave Flaubert's *Madame Bovary* in high school when my teacher explained the scandalous nature of divorce in the nineteenth century. So I accept that learning certain things about the beliefs of the intended audience of a novel can make modern readers change their reaction to a novel (or, to be more technical, help them become part of the narrative audience). But I suspect that these two bits of historical context changed me because they did not change me that much: modern readers still believe that strong feelings can result in action and still feel echoes of the scandal that can be attached to divorce. The habit

of reading typologically seems much more foreign. See Winfried Flück for an extended discussion of how *Uncle Tom's Cabin* fails when it tries to represent a moral society through biblical metaphors that do not resonate for most modern critical readers.

CHAPTER FIVE

1. Jerome McGann et al. confirm these aversions as well as registering their worries about what I would describe as "reading to identify" in their description of University of Virginia's old "Introduction to Literary Studies" course: "So long as the fictions were not self-consciously reflexive and experimental, the undergraduates met the texts with pleasure and a certain kind of understanding. That pleasure and understanding, however, proved a serious obstacle to the students' ability to think critically about the works and their own thinking" (144). Their retooled course tried to break students of their habit of reading according to what they already knew—it taught them to focus on what did not initially make sense or was difficult.

2. There are exceptions to this rule. See, for example, the special 2000 issue of the Brazilian journal *Ilha Do Desterro: A Journal of Language and Literature*, which features articles on critical reading. In "Critical Reading and Critical Thinking," Loni Kreis Taglieber offers a range of definitions of "critical reading," including that it requires different thought processes like analysis, synthesis, and evaluation (16) and that it requires the students to bring their own values up against the values put forth in what they read (17) (what I would actually see more as "reading to identify"). Yet the very range of definitions offered gives the sense that critical reading's value might only be increased by our inability to define it precisely.

3. Salvatori's methods of teaching encourage her students to use their difficulties with a text as a way of catapulting themselves into a "transitive reading" that allows them to see reading as something that they perform on a text versus an understanding of reading as "'uncritically' accepted authority" ("Toward a Hermeneutic" 82). Salvatori encourages such reading through a series of recursive, self-reflexive writing assignments: students write a series of "position" or "difficulty" papers on the same difficult text. These papers allow the students to reflect in more and more sophisticated ways on the text and, relatedly, on their own (in most cases limited) model of reading ("Toward a Hermeneutic," "Reading Matters").

4. This might be a common, if mostly unarticulated, perception among professors, as can be seen by considering the politically resonant term "critical pedagogy."

5. See, for example, Marilyn Rye's "Using Composition Strategies," which describes how "naïve readers" (she uses Umberto Eco's term) are unable to resist the tyranny of the text in front of them. Rye wants her students to see how their

own interpretations are necessary in order to complete a text's meaning. I discuss her article more toward the end of the chapter.

6. Warner cites Mitchell Breitweiser's *American Puritanism and the Defense of Mourning: Religion, Grief, and Ethnology in Mary White Rowlandson's Captivity Narrative* (1990) as offering an "ingenious such reading" (38).

7. The origins of these simplifications grow out of Stowe's grounding in Scottish Common Sense Philosophy (and not her racism), as discussed by Gregg Camfield in "The Moral Aesthetics of Sentimentality."

8. For the sake of brevity, I have focused on Spillers in this chapter, but Lauren Berlant makes a similar argument in "Poor Eliza": sentimentality distorts both people and politics in certain devastating ways: "[S]entimental politics are being performed whenever putatively supra-political affects or affect-saturated institutions (like the nation and the family) are proposed as universalist solutions to structural racial, sexual, or intercultural antagonism" (638). With "putatively," Berlant asserts that there is not, in fact, a realm of feeling that transcends politics. Just because someone weeps does not mean that we know what she needs. As Baldwin does, Berlant believes that people and "slavery" are not self-evident despite the sentimentalists' ardent claims to the contrary.

9. We should recognize how Spillers justifies her claim that Stowe's notion that her view is not merely a view is a mistake. Spillers asks us to recognize how we know things really to be. Many people claim that the Bible offers a unified, internally consistent picture of the world. Yet we know that to be false: it is instead "an Ur-text of polyvalence." The example of the Bible is particularly useful here, because Stowe's representation of "slavery" does not just work as the Bible works (denying its own polyvalence) but in fact uses the Bible as its foundation for a denial of the polyvalence of its own biblically inspired text. Spillers assumes that both the Bible and *Uncle Tom's Cabin* are "polyvalent" (each has more than one possible meaning), an assumption with which few secular people, let alone most literary critics, would argue.

10. Critics have discussed how "Benito Cereno" is in specific dialogue with *Uncle Tom's Cabin* just as *Putnam's*, where "Benito Cereno" was first published, was in particular dialogue with the *National Era*, which first serialized Stowe's novel. For articles that put these two texts into dialogue with each other, see Sarah Robbins's excellent "Gendering the History of the Antislavery Narrative" (which discusses in detail how Melville's text self-consciously addressed Stowe's), Tony McGowan's "Suffering from Simultaneity in 'Benito Cereno,'" Teodor Mateoc's "Narrative Strategy and the Issue of Slavery in 'Benito Cereno,'" Peter Coviello's "The American in Charity," and Ezra Tawil's "Captain Babo's Cabin." I discuss the last two of these in more detail later in this chapter.

11. Yet this idea of a Melvillean-inspired self-critique is, interestingly, a fairly

recent phenomenon. As Carolyn Karcher points out, literary critics until the 1960s did not see the novella as having anything to do with racism: they could note what they took to be the symbolism of the book (white equals good/black equals evil) yet not think about whether their acceptance of that symbolism said anything about their own attitudes about race (ix). Yet in a more recent turnaround, John Haegert argues that our identification with Delano should not necessarily signal our racism but might, in fact, just be a result of the "formal patternings of the plot" (26).

12. For an even more extended discussion of the many candidates to whom this "leader" might refer, see Bruce Franklin's discussion of this line in *The Wake of the Gods*.

13. If it is a reader's second time through, not just particular lines but whole passages and scenes must be reconstructed. For example, we must reject the surface meaning of Delano's description of glorious mother-son slave bonding and reconstruct its meaning. On our first time through, we at least realize that Delano's description reveals his racism; the second time through, we realize that this scene of peaceful family love is actually a ruse to hide the intent of the mutinying blacks.

14. This distinction explains why Stowe's text can contain occasional examples of sarcastic lines yet still remain a completely unironic text.

15. As is the legal deposition that ends the story. Initially, it could seem that this reveals exactly what happened, but if readers look closely at the document, they notice that it is riddled with holes, "portions only are extracted" (93), and whole sections are "omitted" (97). In "The Gaze of History in 'Benito Cereno,'" Dennis Pahl makes a similar point based less on examining particular phrases in the deposition than on noting its ethos: "Displaying the same kind of racial and cultural bias that Delano clearly exhibits, Cereno's deposition invariably characterizes the Africans as heartless murderers and the Spanish slave-drivers as virtuous Christians (thus rendering a black-and-white version of a more contradictory historical truth)" (180). For another discussion of the inadequacies of the deposition, see Haegert.

16. Coviello makes a similar point.

17. For a recent author who shares my doubts as to "Benito Cereno"'s status as an antislavery novel, see Brook Thomas's "The Legal Fictions of Herman Melville and Lemuel Shaw." Thomas is also one of the few recent critics who does not identify with Melville (although Thomas would have had to begin by searching for his beliefs within the text in order to conclude that). For Thomas, Melville remains a cultural transcriber of the ideologies of his own time, not a subverter of them.

18. If the first part of the novella illuminates the workings of romantic racialism, as embodied by Amasa Delano, the second part (the excerpts from the court case)

brings to light what I am calling unromantic racialism: "That, had the Negroes not restrained [the Negresses], they would have tortured to death, instead of simply killing, the Spaniards slain by command of the Negro Babo; that the Negresses used their utmost influence to have the deponent [Delano] made away with; that, in the various acts of murder, they sang songs and danced" (99). The legal decision, lacking as it does any mitigating evidence, offers another version of racism, the mirror-image of the romantic racialism that Delano ascribed to these same "Negresses." Even if we, the readers, supply the mitigating circumstances that might justify these black women's actions (but does it justify torture?), we cannot deny the savagery with which they carried them out.

19. Coviello offers a very powerful reading of the way that Melville rebuts Stowe's insistence on transparency with "gothic occlusion and opacity" (157). So powerful is Coviello's demonstration of Melville's refusal to let the reader reach a definitive interpretation of "Benito Cereno" or of the text of American race relations that his conclusion that "a wise and healthy republic *demands* good readers, who can make truthful sense of the omens and portents, the mysterious characters and charismatic leaders which come before it" (175; emphasis in the original) seems unfounded. For where in the novella has Coviello identified Melville as giving us any clue about how a reading of the novella and, by extension, American race relations can ever get it right?

20. Even past critics, who could not recognize this novella's obvious referents to slavery and slave insurrection, could still identify what "Benito Cereno" means. For example, Harold Scudder's 1928 article, to which recent critics still refer because it reprints the original source for the novella (the real-life Amasa Delano's account of his voyage), ends with a claim that does not hesitate to tell us who Babo and Benito Cereno really are: "Melville with his ready apprehension of the allegorical or symbolical saw at once in Delano's story of the ill fated Spanish commander, a parallel with his own fate. . . . He came to realize that he was not only to be denied appreciation, but that he was even doomed never to be understood." Melville himself is Benito Cereno, and Babo is the personification of malicious criticism (531).

Scudder can confidently bring to light the meaning of "Benito Cereno" by assuming that he can locate Melville's voice in the story, though he does not tell us where he found it.

21. This pattern of first claiming that Melville's text undercuts definitive interpretation and then asserting a definitive interpretation seems to me to be the rule. Perhaps no article is more representative of this pattern than John Bryant's "Herman Melville," which discusses a range of Melville's works. Running through this article is an anecdote about having a student come up to Bryant and ask:

"Didn't [Melville] *hate* Indians?" (59; emphasis in the original). Bryant responded to the student by telling him: "No, quite the contrary" and then citing texts that he thought supported this view (59), but he regrets this definitive response. Bryant thinks that his reply went against the spirit of Melville, who "does not propose to tell us *what to think*, but to show us what it feels like *when we think*, and think deeply, passionately, creatively, daringly, even self-destructively" (61; emphases in the original). Yet he is still horrified at the idea that a person could question Melville's racial tolerance as manifested in his writings. Bryant wants the student to take up Melville's enjoinder to avoid definitive answers. Bryant seems convinced, however, that certain things will never actually be at issue in Melville's texts. He might have to reevaluate his unstinting praise of Melville's artistic methods if he acknowledged that Melville's works (as opposed to his life) might not allow us to decide that he did not hate the Indians (or blacks).

22. In fact, "identification" might explain our incredulousness that early critics of the novel, such as Harold Scudder, failed to see that this novella has everything to do with race and slavery. Our own critical context makes it impossible for us not to "recognize" that Melville wanted us to identify his own concern with these issues.

23. Of course, I do not actually know for sure that these political beliefs attributed to Melville are the authors' own; I make this inference based on what I think is plausible for a modern critic to believe and the rhetorical effect of these articles, which proffer these claims about Melville's novel as though they have independent truth-value in the world, even apart from whether they are true about Melville's novella.

24. Holdcroft prepares us for Melville's endless critique when he describes the radical ironist: "Given a choice between P and 'not-P' our ironist refuses to opt for either, but contents himself with pointing out the inadequacies of his opponent's arguments for P" (510).

25. As the quotation in note 8 above about "structural" antagonisms shows, Berlant believes that sentimentality tries to deny the *real* differences between different groups.

26. One notable exception is Amy Schrager Lang's "Slavery and Sentimentalism." She argues that St. Clare blurs the strict binary opposition between private and public, "risking the essential structure of [Stowe's] book" (48).

27. In fact, Stowe herself is not above occasional heavy-handed sarcasm, which is meant to reveal the true nature of those who misrepresent themselves. Low-class people with upper-class pretensions are sure to activate it. Describing Mr. Shelby and Haley as "gentlemen," Stowe then qualifies her characterization: "One of the parties, however, when critically examined, did not seem, strictly speaking,

to come under the species" (1). Later Haley and two of his disreputable companions are described as a "worthy trio" (65). Yet in contrast to St. Clare's irony, these utterances are completely unambiguous; the point is to register another problem with slavery: that it will elevate low-class people into the upper echelons of society.

28. St. Clare does promise to "make a provision" (283) for his slaves to be freed but, typically, puts it off for the "by and by" (283). He thus seals his own fate, of course, because Stowe wants to make the point that people must act immediately to rectify injustice. However, St. Clare's habitual indolence also seems symptomatic of his inability to close off any of his readings.

29. Richard Rorty might agree. In *Contingency, Irony, and Solidarity*, he launches a robust defense of irony, claiming that an attitude of "ironism," the rejection of any "final vocabulary" (for example, one that claims to be true rather than historically contingent), does not in fact prevent a person from being part of a community devoted to alleviating the suffering of others. For Rorty, ironism is exactly what allows people to be part of a community because it allows them to sympathize with those who share different beliefs (liberal ironists are not repulsed by people who hold radically different views because of their belief in the contingency of their own views). Rorty claims that ironism does not paralyze us because what we need in order to be part of a community is not truth about the world but an ability to make an "imaginative identification with the details of others' lives" (190). Thus we can see how much even a wholehearted embrace of irony requires a fundamental act of identification. As I hope I have shown with my reading of "Benito Cereno," it is precisely "identification" (in both senses: as recognition and as sympathy) that gets stymied.

30. I do not mean to imply that this recognition always has to be affirmative: for example, "*Uncle Tom's Cabin* espouses these values, which I also hold." The analysis could easily follow the pattern "*Uncle Tom's Cabin* espouses these values, which are foreign to me." The point is that the recognition of those foreign values can only come about through a process of looking for beliefs or values in the text, the process of trying to identify with the text.

CHAPTER SIX

1. I am combining two of Rabinowitz's works in this summary: "Truth in Fiction," which presents his taxonomy of the different kinds of audiences that fictional works call upon, and *Before Reading*, which builds on the work done in the article to consider the presuppositions or "rules of reading" that structure how we read a fictional work.

2. One way to extend Rabinowitz's work in *Before Reading* would be to attend

to how the different rules of reading that he delineates (rules of signification, etc.) work differently for different kinds of readers. I suspect that particularizing readers' ways of reading might be another way to provide a bridge between narrative theory and gender studies, which Rabinowitz attempts toward the end of his book. For examples of criticism that theorize about how to connect narrative theory with feminist and historicist concerns, see Susan Lanser's *Fictions of Authority* and works by Robyn Warhol, including "'Reader, Can You Imagine? No, You Cannot'" and *Having a Good Cry*.

3. In *The Minister's Wooing*, Stowe herself warns us against the morally dubious orator, the artful seducer, reminiscent of Giles's male sentimentalist, who, in a quotation used in chapter 2, "does not care a *sou* for truth on any subject not practically connected with his own schemes in life" (260; emphasis in the original). He is embodied in her rendering of Aaron Burr: "Burr was practised in every act of gallantry,—he had made womankind a study,—he never saw a beautiful face and form without a sort of restless desire to experiment upon it and try his power over the interior inhabitant" (217–18). Yet Burr, unlike Giles's male sentimentalist, is completely aware of what he is doing. For Stowe, this self-aware distance is one of the things that distinguishes the corrupt orator from the sentimental heroine.

4. For an interesting parallel discussion of the way sentimental literature has been devalued artistically, see Elizabeth Dillon's "Sentimental Aesthetics." She charts a similar process of sentimental unmasking via recourse to the category of "aesthetics." According to Dillon, critics tend to want art either to remain free from the taint of the marketplace or else, inversely, to be nothing but market-driven (or authority-driven). But the texts of sentimentalism disallow either extreme, causing both sides to turn against it: "Sentimentalism thus concerns both an affective immediacy (subjective autonomy) and a formal heteronomy—the connection of emotion to political and cultural ideals and aims" (515).

5. We can trace a clear line of descent from Baldwin's essay to Hortense Spillers's "Changing the Letter" and Lauren Berlant's "Poor Eliza." Many of the essays in Shirley Samuels's collection *The Culture of Sentiment* seem indebted to Douglas. See, for example, Amy Schrager Lang's "Class and the Strategies of Sympathy," which argues that in *The Lamplighter* Cummins tries to substitute the category of gender for the problems of class differences (an argument that follows Douglas's general claim about how these sentimental texts function not as critiques of their culture but as sops for it).

6. Although more theoretically dense, Christina Zwarg's essay on *Uncle Tom's Cabin* follows a pattern similar to that in Showalter's and Harris's works: the author plays bait-and-switch with the reader, who might fall for the ruse if not for the critic's intervention. Zwarg's description of the author's subversive

cleverness in *Uncle Tom's Cabin* involves Stowe's ability to offer obvious portraits that mutate into something else entirely, such as her portrayal of the "marginal" character Sam: "Yet the cunning nature of Stowe's portrait of him resides in the way that Sam does not stay firmly within this [Sambo] stereotype" (580). Stowe is not just a self-conscious artist in Zwarg's account but also a sophisticated theorist: "By exploring patriarchy in a variety of manifestations including capitalism, slavery, Christianity, and finally, literary history, Stowe inquires whether freedom, selfhood, paternity and maternity can be achieved without simply repeating the negative and consuming attributes of patriarchy" (569).

7. Marianne Noble and other recent New Historicist and cultural critics both follow and depart from this model of the sentimental unmasker. Noble's insightful and complex analysis of *Uncle Tom's Cabin* scrolls through a number of the false aspects of sentimentality; perhaps the most remarkable one is that sentimentality is asexual (instead sentimental rhetoric offers largely unremarked-upon masochistic pleasure to its women readers). This masochistic pleasure itself wears a false aspect (as, on one hand, merely masturbatory, self-directed, and on the other, allowing for multiple identifications, between white women and slaves, and so forth). Noble also becomes an unmasker par excellence by showing that a main ingredient in the popularity of *Uncle Tom's Cabin* was the way it enabled its female readers in particular to experience proscribed states of passion by providing a cover story for them. For example, Stowe's friend Georgiana May could give in to feelings of masochistic pleasure ("This storm of feeling has been raging, burning like a very fire in my bones" [qtd. in Noble 141; Gossett 167]) by supposing that *Uncle Tom's Cabin* was inspiring her only to help the slaves. In other words, *Uncle Tom's Cabin* provides a cover story for internal forms of gratification of dubious political value, by making it seem to the readers that they are actually engaged in altruistic acts. However, Noble's work (as well as works like Lora Romero's *Home Fronts* and Lori Merish's *Sentimental Materialism*) resists the urge to "celebrate or condemn" sentimental literature by doing both. These works' commitment to both celebrating and condemning sentimental literature in the same breath allows them a more balanced tone; they seem less suffused with emotion than many others. Moreover, these recent critics, unlike the older critics alluded to above, seem much less interested in addressing the question of how much Stowe herself was aware of her own "coverplotting." Yet their New Historical and cultural-critical orientations still allow for a kind of unmasking, if not of the author herself then of the culture that the text both reflects and produces, its hidden contradictions, and its impossible "logic."

8. As the actual audience members get further in time from the publication of the book, they often find it hard to make themselves into members of the

authorial audience. This intuition is the one that I think gives rise to the question about how to engage modern students with older books.

9. Rabinowitz suggests that readers are often members of the authorial and narrative audiences at the same time: this dynamic accounts for the sense that we have as readers of a fictional work that what is happening is both not true and true. This claim seems right to me: I remember when the stories that made up the long-running television medical drama *St. Elsewhere* were revealed in the final episode to be the product of an autistic child's fantasy life. I was crushed that these characters were never "real," although I knew quite well that the whole series was a fictional creation.

10. As I mentioned in note 21, chapter 4, Flück has suggested that *Uncle Tom's Cabin* falters in its persuasiveness when it depends on modern readers' finding a biblical understanding of the world credible. This suggestion seems to have legs, but then I consider whether it would be enough if we modern critics would acquaint ourselves with the beliefs that a nineteenth-century evangelical Christian like Stowe would have held, so that we can become part of the authorial audience. I do not think so. There is something else going on—another barrier to our becoming a member of the authorial and narrative audiences that has to do less with what we critics believe than with how we tend to read.

11. Robyn Warhol argues the opposite point in her excellent "As You Stand, So You Feel and Are." After outlining seven "mechanical techniques" that the sentimental novel uses to induce its readers to cry (115), Warhol says that she is not offering "this list . . . as a weapon against the sentimental effect. Like therapy, it does not work that way—even if you understand how the process is supposed to operate, that does not guarantee you will be impervious to its effects" (121). On one hand, I agree: for example, knowing why the real-life story of Scarlett the mother cat who rescued her kittens from a flaming building makes me cry does not prevent me from crying again upon reading about her rescuing said kittens. On the other hand, while I am reading the story, I think that this is "real": even though this story shares conventions with other sentimental stories, Scarlett is really experiencing this self-forgetting mother-love, not crafting her reactions (it helps that she is an animal) to make me feel a certain way. Thus I think that an awareness of the conventions of tear-generating sentimental scenes has to do with the timing: when the awareness of these conventions occurs. If it happens simultaneously when reading or seeing the sentimental scene, the reader's eyes will remain dry; but if it happens before or after, the reader can still experience the reaction.

12. For support of Sheridan's thesis, compare the amateur video-recording of New Yorkers responding to the collapse of one of the towers at the time it is

happening at http://www.youtube.com/watch?v=SEJbxyfrzUo&feature=channel to the "spontaneous" singing of "God Bless America" by members of Congress later that day (and notice the "coincidental" way in which the politicians have formed themselves into a map of the United States) at http://www.youtube.com/watch?v=IH_6EUCILew. The New Yorkers are infinitely more moving and persuasive about the depth of the tragedy than the representatives.

13. The idea of the formula is a complex one: when does something qualify as formulaic? Any author's body of work and any genre share certain habitual gestures and typical plot turns (what Rabinowitz calls "rules of configuration" in *Before Reading*). The issue is not that Hawthorne's works are not formulaic (here is yet another protagonist who looks too closely into the human heart) but rather that these works make no claim to be free from craft (as I explore later in this chapter). When a passage aims at the status of spontaneous outpouring of emotion and the reader consciously realizes that the scene is written exactly the same way as another "spontaneous" scene, the reader begins to doubt its authenticity.

14. To take two modern examples, both Lorrie Moore's story "People Like That Are the Only People Here" and Dave Eggers's memoir *A Heartbreaking Work of Staggering Genius* strike me as both very moving and very crafted. Moore highlights the craftedness of her story in the explicit and repeated musings of a mother on how to represent what strikes her as the unrepresentable illness of her son. Eggers's craftedness comes out in the very self-conscious and "postmodern" justifications that make up his "Introduction." Both these works would qualify as sentimental (Moore's story describes a mother's feelings while experiencing her toddler son's treatment for cancer, and the first part of Eggers's memoir recounts his parents' deaths in close succession) if the authors were not so deliberately thwarting many of the reader's presuppositions when it comes to sentimental fiction.

15. Yet I think that *Huck Finn* does not have nearly as adversarial a relationship to sentimental rhetoric as I imply here: I find it fascinating how this book elicits readings both of Huck as an unreliable narrator (whose utterances must be, as a result, highly crafted) and of Huck as possessing a kind of authentic, vernacular voice (which leads to quite sentimental readings of his character).

16. Elizabeth Fox-Genovese makes a similar point: she thinks Tompkins's "confessional criticism" (in *West of Everything*) is a direct result of her allegiance to reader-response criticism (69).

17. Warhol comes to a conclusion similar to mine in our desire for critics to stop being embarrassed about crying when reading sentimental fiction. But whereas she sees in this possibility a potentially terrific result ("its [the sentimental text's reading community's] potential for participating in the transformation of culture

and society will be considerable" ["As You Stand" 122]), I remain fixated on the damage that it can do to our literary criticism.

18. Alessandro Portelli notes the "intriguing modernity" of early American literature and attributes it to "the constant, problematic interaction with orality" that these written texts engage in (28).

Works Cited

Adams, John Quincy. *Lectures on Rhetoric and Oratory*. 1810. Ed. J. Jeffery Auer and Jerald L. Banninga. 2 vols. New York: Russell & Russell, 1962. Print.

Adams, Kimberly VanEsveld. "Family Influences on *The Minister's Wooing* and *Oldtown Folks*: Henry Ward Beecher and Calvin Stowe." *Religion & Literature* 38.4 (2006): 27–61. Print.

Adler, Joyce Sparer. "*Benito Cereno*: Slavery and Violence in the Americas." *Critical Essays on Herman Melville's "Benito Cereno."* 1981. Ed. Robert E. Burkholder. New York: G. K. Hall & Co., 1992. 76–93. Print.

Alcott, Louisa May. *Little Women*. Ed. Elaine Showalter. New York: Penguin, 1989. Print.

———. *Work: A Story of Experience*. Ed. Joy S. Kasson. New York: Penguin Books, 1994. Print.

Alexander, Lynn M. "Unsexed by Labor: Middle-Class Women and the Need to Work." *American Transcendental Quarterly* 22.4 (2008): 593–608. Print.

Ammons, Elizabeth. "Stowe's Dream of the Mother-Savior: *Uncle Tom's Cabin* and American Women Writers before the 1920s." *New Essays on Uncle Tom's Cabin*. Ed. Eric Sundquist. Cambridge: Cambridge UP, 1986. 155–95. Print.

Anderson, Dorothy. "Edward T. Channing's Teaching of Rhetoric." *Speech Monographs* 16 (1949): 69–81. Print.

Applegate, Debby. *The Most Famous Man in America: The Biography of Henry Ward Beecher*. New York: Three Leaves Press, 2006. Print.

———. "The Seductions of Strange and Painted Women." *Journal of American Studies* 27.1 (1993): 82–87. Print.

Austin, Gilbert. *Chironomia; or a Treatise on Rhetorical Delivery*. London: T. Cadell & W. Davies, 1806. Print.

Baker, Dorothy Z. "Harriet Beecher Stowe's Conversation with the *Atlantic Monthly*: The Construction of *The Minister's Wooing*." *Studies in American Fiction* 28.1 (2000): 27–38. Print.

Baker, Houston. "Autobiographical Acts and the Voice of the Southern Slave." *The Journey Back: Issues in Black Literature and Criticism*. Chicago: U of Chicago P, 1980. 27–52. Print.

Baldwin, James. "Everybody's Protest Novel." *Uncle Tom's Cabin*. 1955. Ed. Elizabeth Ammons. 2nd ed. New York: Norton, 2010. 532–39. Print.

Barthes, Roland. "The Death of the Author." *The Norton Anthology of Theory and Criticism*. 1968. Ed. Vincent B. Leitch. 2nd ed. New York: Norton, 2010. 1322–26. Print.

Bartholomae, David, and Anthony Petrosky. *Ways of Reading: An Anthology for Writers*. 8th ed. Boston: Bedford/St. Martin's, 2008. Print.

Baskerville, Barnet. "Principal Themes of Nineteenth-Century Critics of Oratory." *Speech Monographs* 19.1 (1952): 11–26. Print.

Baym, Nina. *Woman's Fiction: A Guide to Novels by and about Women in America, 1820–1870*. 1978. Urbana: U of Illinois P, 1993. Print.

Becker, Howard S. *Writing for Social Scientists: How to Start and Finish Your Thesis, Book, or Article*. Chicago: U of Chicago P, 1986. Print.

Beecher, Catharine E. *Treatise on Domestic Economy*. 1841. Boston: Thomas H. Webb & Co., 1843. Print.

Beecher, Catharine, and Harriet Beecher Stowe. *The American Woman's Home*. Ed. Nicole Tonkovich. New Brunswick: Rutgers UP, 2002. Print.

Beecher, Henry Ward. *Norwood: Or, Village Life in New England*. New York: Fords, Howard & Hulbert, 1887. Print.

———. *Oratory*. Philadelphia: Penn Publishing Company, 1899. Print.

———. "The Strange Woman." *Twelve Lectures to Young Men, on Various Important Subjects*. New York: D. Appleton & Co., 1879. 124–59. Print.

———. *Yale Lectures on Preaching*. New York: J. B. Ford and Company, 1872. Print.

Berlant, Lauren. "Poor Eliza." *American Literature* 70.3 (1998): 635–68. Print.

Bingham, Caleb, ed. *The Columbian Orator*. 1797. New ed. Washington: Caring Publishing, 2003. Print.

Booth, Wayne. *A Rhetoric of Irony*. Chicago: U of Chicago P, 1974. Print.

Boston Women's Health Book Collective. *Our Bodies, Ourselves*. 1973. New York: Touchstone, 2011. Print.

Boucicault, Dion. "Mr. Dion Boucicault." *Beecher Memorial: Contemporaneous Tributes to the Memory of Henry Ward Beecher*. Ed. Edward W. Bok. Brooklyn: Privately Printed, 1887. 39–40. Print.

Bourdieu, Pierre. *Distinction: A Social Critique of the Judgement of Taste*. Trans. Richard Nice. Cambridge: Harvard UP, 1984. Print.

Brodhead, Richard. *Cultures of Letters: Scenes of Reading and Writing in Nineteenth-Century America*. Chicago: U of Chicago P, 1993. Print.

Brown, Herbert Ross. *The Sentimental Novel in America, 1789–1860*. New York: Pageant Books, 1959. Print.

Bryant, John. "Herman Melville." *Prospects for the Study of American Literature*. Ed. Richard Kopley. New York: New York UP, 1997. 58–90. Print.

Buell, Lawrence. *New England Literary Culture: From Revolution through Renaissance*. Cambridge: Cambridge UP, 1986. Print.

———. "Rival Romantic Interpretations of New England Puritanism: Hawthorne versus Stowe." *Texas Studies in Literature and Language* 25.1 (1983): 77–99. Print.

Burkholder, Robert, ed. *Critical Essays on Herman Melville's "Benito Cereno."* New York: G. K. Hall, 1992. Print.

Burnham, Michelle. "Loopholes of Resistance: Harriet Jacobs' Slave Narrative and the Critique of Agency in Foucault." *Incidents in the Life of a Slave Girl*. Ed. Nellie Y. McKay and Frances Smith Foster. New York: W. W. Norton, 2001. 278–79. Print.

Camfield, Gregg. "The Moral Aesthetics of Sentimentality: A Missing Key to *Uncle Tom's Cabin*." *Nineteenth-Century Literature* 43.3 (1988): 319–45. Print.

Campbell, George. "The Philosophy of Rhetoric." *The Rhetoric of Blair, Campbell, and Whately*. Ed. James L. Golden and Edward P. J. Corbett. New York: Holt, Rinehart & Winston, 1968. 139–271. Print.

Carlyle, Thomas. "The Stump Orator." *The Works of Thomas Carlyle*. Ed. Henry Duff Traill. Vol. 20. New York: AMS Press, 1969. 172–213. Print.

Chamberlain, Lori. "Bombs and Other Exciting Devices, or the Problem of Teaching Irony." *Reclaiming Pedagogy*. Ed. Patricia Donahue and Ellen Quandahl. Carbondale: Southern Illinois UP, 1989. 97–111. Print.

"Change in the Employment of Women." 9 August 1896. *New York Times*. Web. 1 July 2010. http://query.nytimes.com/mem/archive-free/pdf?res=FA0713FF355E10738DDDA00894D0405B8685F0D3.

Channing, Edward Tyrrel. *Lectures Read to the Seniors in Harvard College*. 1856. Ed. Dorothy I. Anderson and Waldo W. Braden. Carbondale: Southern Illinois UP, 1968. Print.

———. *An Oration, Delivered July 4, 1817, at the Request of the Selectmen of the Town of Boston*. Boston: Buckingham, 1817. Print.

Chapman, Mary, and Glenn Hendler. *Sentimental Men: Masculinity and the Politics of Affect in American Culture*. Berkeley: U of California P, 1999. Print.

"The Christian Slave." *Uncle Tom's Cabin & American Culture*. Stephen Railton and the University of Virginia. Web. 24 July 2012. http://utc.iath.virginia.edu/uncletom/xianslav/xshp.html.

Clark, Beverly Lyon, ed. *Louisa May Alcott: The Contemporary Reviews.* Cambridge: Cambridge UP, 2004. Print.

Clark, Clifford E. *Henry Ward Beecher: Spokesman for a Middle-Class America.* Urbana: U of Illinois P, 1978. Print.

Clark, Gregory, and S. Michael Halloran, eds. *Oratorical Culture in Nineteenth-Century America: Transformations in the Theory and Practice of Rhetoric.* Carbondale: Southern Illinois UP, 1993. Print.

Coviello, Peter. "The American in Charity: 'Benito Cereno' and Gothic Anti-Sentimentality." *Studies in American Fiction* (Autumn 2002): 155–80. Print.

Cox, James M. "Harriet Beecher Stowe: From Sectionalism to Regionalism." *Nineteenth-Century Fiction* 38.4 (1984): 444–66. Print.

Crane, Stephen. *Maggie: A Girl of the Streets.* 1893. New York: Modern Library, 2001. Print.

Culler, Jonathan D. *The Pursuit of Signs: Semiotics, Literature, Deconstruction.* Ithaca: Cornell UP, 1981. Print.

Cummins, Maria Susanna. *The Lamplighter.* American Women Writers Series. Ed. Joanne Dobson, Judith Fetterley, and Elaine Showalter. New Brunswick: Rutgers UP, 1988. Print.

Dana, Richard H. "Biographical Notice." *Lectures Read to the Seniors in Harvard College.* 1856. Ed. Charlotte Downey. Delmar: Scholars' Facsimiles & Reprints, 1997. vii–xx. Print.

Davidson, Cathy. "Preface: No More Separate Spheres!" *American Literature* 70.3 (1998): 443–63. Print.

Delsarte System of Oratory. New York: Edgar S. Werner, 1893. *The Gutenberg Project.* Web. 21 August 2012. http://www.gutenberg.org/ebooks/12200.

Diderot, Denis. *Selected Writings on Art and Literature.* 1772. London: Penguin Books, 1994. Print.

Dillon, Elizabeth Maddock. "Sentimental Aesthetics." *American Literature* 76.3 (2004): 495–523. Print.

Dobson, Joanne. "Reclaiming Sentimental Literature." *American Literature* 69.2 (1997): 263–88. Print.

Douglas, Ann. *The Feminization of American Culture.* New York: Anchor Books, 1977. Print.

Douglass, Frederick. *Narrative of the Life of Frederick Douglass.* 1845. Norton Critical Edition. Ed. William L. Andrews and William S. McFeely. New York: W. W. Norton, 1997. Print.

Duguid, Sandra. "Introduction." *The Minister's Wooing.* Ed. Sandra Duguid. Hartford: Stowe-Day Foundation, 1978. No pag. Print.

Durivage, F. A. "Delsarte." *Atlantic Monthly* 27.163 (1871): 613–21. Cornell University Library: http://ebooks.library.cornell.edu/cgi/t/text/pageviewer-idx?c=atla;cc=atla;rgn=full%20text;idno=atla0027-5;didno=atla0027-5;view=image;-seq=0619;node=atla0027-5%3A10.

Edwards, O. C. "The Preaching of Romanticism in America." *American Transcendental Quarterly* 14.4 (2000): 297–312. Print.

Eggers, David. *A Heartbreaking Work of Staggering Genius.* New York: Vintage, 2000. Print.

Eliot, George. *Daniel Deronda.* Ed. Terence Cave. New York: Penguin, 1995. Print.

Emery, Allan Moore. "'Benito Cereno' and Manifest Destiny." *Critical Essays on Herman Melville's "Benito Cereno."* 1984. Ed. Robert E. Burkholder. New York: G. K. Hall & Co., 1992. 99–115. Print.

Fahey, Joseph. "Quiet Victory: The Professional Identity American Women Forged through Delsartism." *Mime Journal* 23 (2004/2005): 43–83. Print.

Flück, Winfried. "The Power and Failure of Representation in Harriet Beecher Stowe's *Uncle Tom's Cabin.*" *New Literary History* 23.2 (1992): 319–38. Print.

Foster, Hannah W. *The Coquette.* 1797. Early American Women Writers Series. Ed. Cathy N. Davidson. New York: Oxford UP, 1986. Print.

Fox-Genovese, Elizabeth. "Confession Versus Criticism, or What's the Critic Got to Do with It?" *Confessions of the Critics.* Ed. H. Aram Veeser. New York: Routledge, 1996. 68–75. Print.

Franchot, Jenny. "Unseemly Commemoration: Religion, Fragments, and the Icon." *American Literary History* 9.3 (1997): 502–21. Print.

Franklin, Benjamin. *Benjamin Franklin's Autobiography.* Ed. J. A. Leo Lemay and P. M. Zall. New York: Norton, 1986. Print.

Franklin, Bruce. *In the Wake of the Gods: Melville's Mythology.* Stanford: Stanford UP, 1963. Print.

Frederick, John T. "Hawthorne's 'Scribbling Women.'" *New England Quarterly* 48.2 (1975): 231–40. Print.

Freedman, Dianc P., Olivia Frey, and Frances Murphy Zauhar, eds. *The Intimate Critique: Autobiographical Literary Criticism.* Durham: Duke UP, 1993. Print.

Freud, Sigmund, "The 'Uncanny.'" *Norton Anthology of Theory and Criticism.* 1949. Ed. Vincent B. Leitch. New York: Norton, 2010. 824–41. Print.

Gabler-Hover, Janet. *Truth in American Fiction: The Legacy of Rhetorical Idealism.* Athens: U of Georgia P, 1990. Print.

Giles, Henry. "Sentimentalism." *Harper's New Monthly Magazine* 21.122 (1860): 203–11. Print.

Gilligan, Carol. *In a Different Voice: Psychological Theory and Women's Development.* Cambridge: Harvard UP, 1982. Print.

Godkin, E. L. "Chromo-Civilization." *Reflections and Comments 1865–1895*. 1874. Teddington: Echo Library, 2007. 85–90. Print.

———. "Rhetorical Training." *Nation* 20 (4 March 1875): 145–46. Print.

Golden, James L., and Edward P. J. Corbett. "Introduction." *The Rhetoric of Blair, Campbell, and Whately*. New York: Holt, Rinehart and Winston, 1968. 1–21. Print.

Gossett, Thomas F. *Uncle Tom's Cabin and American Culture*. Dallas: Southern Methodist UP, 1985. Print.

Graff, Gerald. *Clueless in Academe: How Schooling Obscures the Life of the Mind*. New Haven: Yale UP, 2003. Print.

Gustafson, Sandra M. *Eloquence Is Power: Oratory & Performance in Early America*. Chapel Hill: U of North Carolina P, 2000. Print.

Haegert, John. "Voicing Slavery through Silence: Narrative Mutiny in Melville's 'Benito Cereno.'" *Mosaic* 26.2 (1993): 21–39. Print.

Halttunen, Karen. *Confidence Men and Painted Women: A Study in Middle-Class Culture in America, 1830–1870*. New Haven: Yale UP, 1982. Print.

Hapgood, Norman. "Diderot's Paradox of Acting." *Harvard Monthly* 9.1 (1889): 7–13. Print.

Harris, Susan K. "The Female Imaginary in Harriet Beecher Stowe's *The Minister's Wooing*." *New England Quarterly* 66.2 (1993): 179–98. Print.

———. *Nineteenth-Century American Women's Novels: Interpretive Strategies*. Cambridge Studies in American Literature and Culture. Ed. Albert Gelpi. New York: Cambridge UP, 1990. Print.

Hatlen, Theodore W. *Orientation to the Theater*. 4th ed. Englewood Cliffs: Prentice-Hall, 1987. Print.

Hawthorne, Nathaniel. *The Scarlet Letter*. Ed. Seymour Gross et al. New York: Norton, 1988. Print.

Hedrick, Joan. *Harriet Beecher Stowe: A Life*. New York: Oxford UP, 1994. Print.

———. "'Peaceable Fruits': The Ministry of Harriet Beecher Stowe." *American Quarterly* 40.3 (1988): 307–32. Print.

———. "Stowe's Life and *Uncle Tom's Cabin*." 2007. *Uncle Tom's Cabin & American Culture*. Stephen Railton and the University of Virginia. http://utc.iath.virginia.edu/interpret/exhibits/hedrick/hedrick.html.

Hendler, Glenn. "The Limits of Sympathy: Louisa May Alcott and the Sentimental Novel." *American Literary History* 3.4 (1991): 685–706. Print.

———. *Public Sentiments: Structures of Feeling in Nineteenth-Century American Literature*. Chapel Hill: U of North Carolina P, 2001. Print.

Hibben, Paxton. *Henry Ward Beecher: An American Portrait*. New York: George H. Doran Co., 1927. Print.

Holdcroft, David. "Irony as a Trope, and Irony as a Discourse." *Poetics Today* 4.3 (1983): 493–511. Print.

Holmes, Oliver Wendell. "Dr. Oliver Wendell Holmes." *Beecher Memorial: Contemporaneous Tributes to the Memory of Henry Ward Beecher.* Ed. Edward W. Bok. Brooklyn: Privately Printed, 1887. 1–3. Print.

Howard, June. "What Is Sentimentality?" *American Literary History* 11.1 (1999): 63–81. Print.

Hutcheon, Linda. *Irony's Edge: The Theory and Politics of Irony.* London: Routledge, 1994. Print.

Iser, Wolfgang. "Interaction between Text and Reader." *The Norton Anthology of Theory and Criticism.* 1980. Ed. Vincent B. Leitch. New York: Norton, 2001. 1673–82. Print.

Jacobs, Harriet. *Incidents in the Life of a Slave Girl: Written by Herself.* Ed. Jean Fagan Yellin. Cambridge: Harvard UP, 1987. Print.

James, Henry. *The Bostonians.* Oxford: Oxford UP, 1998. Print.

Johnson, Nan. *Nineteenth-Century Rhetoric in North America.* Carbondale: Southern Illinois UP, 1991. Print.

Karcher, Carolyn. *Shadow over the Promised Land: Slavery, Race, and Violence in Melville's America.* Baton Rouge: Louisiana State UP, 1980. Print.

Kavanaugh, James. "That Hive of Subtlety: 'Benito Cereno' and the Liberal Hero." *Ideology and Classic American Literature.* Ed. Sacvan Bercovitch and Myra Jehlen. Cambridge: Cambridge UP, 1986. 352–83. Print.

Knapp, Steven. *Literary Interest: The Limits of Anti-Formalism.* Cambridge: Harvard UP, 1993. Print.

Kolodny, Annette. "A Map for Rereading: Or, Gender and the Interpretation of Literary Texts." *New Literary History* 11.3 (1980): 451–67. Print.

Korobkin, Laura Hanft. *Criminal Conversations: Sentimentality and Nineteenth-Century Legal Stories of Adultery.* Ed. Jonathan Arac. New York: Columbia UP, 1998. Print.

Lang, Amy Schrager. "Class and the Strategies of Sympathy." *The Culture of Sentiment: Race, Gender, and Sentimentality in Nineteenth-Century America.* Ed. Shirley Samuels. New York: Oxford UP, 1992. 128–42. Print.

———. "Slavery and Sentimentalism: The Strange Career of Augustine St. Clare." *Women's Studies* 12.1 (1986): 31–54. Print.

Lanser, Susan Sniader. *Fictions of Authority: Women Writers and Narrative Voice.* Ithaca: Cornell UP, 1992. Print.

Larsen, Elizabeth. "The Progress of Literacy: Edward Tyrrel Channing and the Separation of the Student Writer from the World." *Rhetoric Review* 11.1 (1992): 159–71. Print.

Laurent, Henri. *Personality: How to Build It.* Trans. Richard Duffy. New York: Funk & Wagnalls Co., 1915. Print.

Lawson, Andrew. "Class Mimicry in Stephen Crane's City." *American Literary History* 16.4 (2004): 596–618. Print.

Levine, Robert. "*Uncle Tom's Cabin* in *Frederick Douglass' Paper*: An Analysis of Reception." *Uncle Tom's Cabin.* Ed. Elizabeth Ammons. 2nd ed. New York: W. W. Norton, 2010. 562–82. Print.

Lewes, George Henry. *Problems of Life and Mind.* Vol. 1. Boston: James R. Osgood and Co., 1874. Print.

Little Women. Dir. Gillian Armstrong. Perf. Susan Sarandon, Winona Ryder, and Gabriel Byrne. Columbia Pictures, 1994. Film.

Locke, John. *An Essay Concerning Human Understanding*. Amherst: Prometheus Books, 1995. Print.

Looby, Christopher. *Voicing America: Language, Literary Form, and the Origins of the United States*. Chicago: U of Chicago P, 1996. Print.

Lowell, James Russell. "A Plea for Freedom from Speech and Figures of Speech-Makers." *Atlantic Monthly* 6.38 (1860): 740–45. Print.

Luciano, Dana. "Melville's Untimely History: 'Benito Cereno' as Counter-Monumental Narrative." *Arizona Quarterly* 60.3 (2004): 33–61. Print.

Mateoc, Teodor. "Narrative Strategy and the Issue of Slavery in 'Benito Cereno.'" *British and American Studies* (1998): 135–41. Print.

Matthiessen, F. O. *American Renaissance: Art and Expression in the Age of Emerson and Whitman*. London: Oxford UP, 1941. Print.

McCall, Laura. "'The Reign of Brute Force Is Now Over': A Content Analysis of 'Godey's Lady's Book,' 1830–1860." *Journal of the Early Republic* 9.2 (1989): 217–36. Print.

McGann, Jerome, and John Griffith et al. "'Reading Fiction/Teaching Fiction': A Pedagogical Experiment." *Pedagogy* 1.1 (2001): 143–65. Print.

McGowan, Tony. "Suffering from Simultaneity in 'Benito Cereno.'" *Q/W/E/R/T/Y* 11 (2001): 109–21. Print.

Melville, Herman. "Benito Cereno." *Bartleby and Benito Cereno*. 1855. New York: Dover, 1990. 37–104. Print.

Merish, Lori. *Sentimental Materialism: Gender, Commodity Culture, and Nineteenth-Century American Literature*. Durham: Duke UP, 2000. Print.

Michaels, Walter Benn. "Romance and Real Estate." *American Renaissance Reconsidered.* Ed. Donald Pease and Walter Benn Michaels. Baltimore: Johns Hopkins UP, 1985. 156–82. Print.

Miller, Joshua. "The Discovery of What It Means to Be a Witness: James Baldwin's Dialectics of Difference." *James Baldwin Now*. Ed. Dwight A. MacBride. New York: New York UP, 1999. 331–59. Print.

Moore, Lorrie. "People Like That Are the Only People Here: Canonical Babbling in Peed Onk." *Birds of America*. New York: Picador, 1999. 212–50. Print.

Mukherjee, Bharati. *The Holder of the World*. New York: Knopf, 1993. Print.

Newbury, Michael. *Figuring Authorship in Antebellum America*. Stanford: Stanford UP, 1997. Print.

Noble, Marianne. *The Masochistic Pleasures of Sentimental Literature*. Princeton: Princeton UP, 2000. Print.

Olwell, Victoria. "'It Spoke Itself': Women's Genius and Eccentric Politics." *American Literature* 77.1 (2005): 33–63. Print.

Ong, Walter. "The Writer's Audience Is Always a Fiction." *Cross-Talk in Comp Theory*. Ed. Victor Villanueva. 2nd ed. Urbana: NCTE, 2003. 55–76. Print.

"Our Whispering Gallery, V." *Atlantic Monthly* 27.163 (1871): 639–53. *Cornell University Library*. http://ebooks.library.cornell.edu/cgi/t/text/pageviewer-idx?c=atla;cc=atla;rgn=full%20text;idno=atla0027-5;didno=atla0027-5;view=image;seq=0645;node=atla0027-5%3A14.

Pahl, Dennis. "The Gaze of History in 'Benito Cereno.'" *Studies in Short Fiction* 32.2 (1995): 171–83. Print.

Peabody, Andrew P. *Harvard Reminiscences*. Boston: Ticknor and Co., 1888. Print.

Pearson, Roberta. *Eloquent Gestures: The Transformation of Performance Style in the Griffith Biograph Films*. Berkeley: U of California P, 1992. Print.

Perkins, Joseph. "Extract from an Oration on Eloquence, Pronounced at Harvard University, on Commencement Day, 1794." *The Columbian Orator*. 1794. Ed. Caleb Bingham. Washington, DC: Caring Publishing, 1997. 21–24. Print.

Plato. *The Collected Dialogues of Plato Including the Letters*. Bollingen Series. Ed. Edith Hamilton and Huntington Cairns. New York: Pantheon Books, 1966. Print.

Poe, Edgar Allan. "Berenice." *Complete Tales and Poems of Edgar Allan Poe*. New York: Vintage, 1975. 642–48. Print.

———. "The Black Cat." *Complete Tales and Poems of Edgar Allan Poe*. New York: Vintage, 1975. 223–30. Print.

Portelli, Alessandro. *The Text and the Voice: Writing, Speaking, and Democracy in American Literature*. New York: Columbia UP, 1994. Print.

Porter, David D. "Admiral David D. Porter." *Beecher Memorial: Contemporaneous Tributes to the Memory of Henry Ward Beecher*. Ed. Edward William Bok et al. Brooklyn: Privately Printed, 1887. 5–6. Print.

Potkay, Adam S. "Theorizing Civic Eloquence in the Early Republic: The Road from David Hume to John Quincy Adams." *Early American Literature* 34.2 (1999): 147–70. Print.

Pratt, Mary Louise. *Toward a Speech Act Theory of Literary Discourse*. Bloomington: Indiana UP, 1977. Print.

Quintilian. *Quintilian on the Teaching of Speaking and Writing*. Ed. James J. Murphy. Carbondale: Southern Illinois UP, 1987. Print.

Rabinowitz, Peter J. *Before Reading: Narrative Conventions and the Politics of Interpretation*. Ithaca: Cornell UP, 1987. Print.

———. "Truth in Fiction: A Re-Examination of Audiences." *Critical Inquiry* 4.1 (1977): 121–41. Print.

Radway, Janice A. *Reading the Romance: Women, Patriarchy, and Popular Literature*. Chapel Hill: U of North Carolina P, 1991. Print.

Reed, Ishmael. *Flight to Canada*. 1976. New York: Scribner, 1998. Print.

Reid, Ronald F. "The Boylston Professorship of Rhetoric and Oratory, 1806–1904: A Case Study in Changing Concepts of Rhetoric and Pedagogy." *Quarterly Journal of Speech* 45.3 (1959): 239–57. Print.

Reid, Thomas. "Of Judgment." *Essays on the Intellectual Powers of Man*. Ed. A. D. Woozley. Charlottesville: Ibis Publishing, 1941. 313–419. Print.

Rigsby, Mary. "'So Like Women!': Louisa May Alcott's Work and the Ideology of Relations." *Redefining the Political Novel: American Women Writers, 1797–1901*. Ed. Sharon M. Harris. Knoxville: U of Tennessee P, 1995. Print.

Robbins, Sarah. "Gendering the History of the Antislavery Narrative: Juxtaposing *Uncle Tom's Cabin* and *Benito Cereno, Beloved* and *Middle Passage*." *American Quarterly* 49.3 (1997): 531–73. Print.

Romero, Lora. *Home Fronts: Domesticity and Its Critics in the Antebellum United States*. Ed. Donald Pease. Durham: Duke UP, 1997. Print.

Rorty, Richard. *Contingency, Irony, and Solidarity*. Cambridge: Cambridge UP, 1989. Print.

Rowlandson, Mary. "The Sovereignty and Goodness of God (1682)." *Puritans among the Indians: Accounts of Captivity and Redemption 1676–1724*. 1682. Ed. Alden T. Vaughan and Edward W. Clark. Cambridge: Belknap P, 1981. Print.

Rowson, Susanna. *Charlotte Temple*. 1794. Early American Women Writers Series. Ed. Cathy N. Davidson. New York: Oxford UP, 1986. Print.

Russett, Cynthia Eagle. *Sexual Science: The Victorian Construction of Womanhood*. Cambridge: Harvard UP, 1989. Print.

Rye, Marilyn. "Using Composition Strategies in the Literature Classroom to Develop 'Critical' Readers and 'Critical Relativism.'" *Teaching Composition/Teaching Literature: Crossing Great Divides*. Ed. Michelle M. Tokarczyk and Irene Papoulis. Vol. 4. New York: Peter Lang, 2003. 13–25. Print.

Salvatori, Mariolina. "Reading and Writing a Text: Correlations between Reading and Writing Patterns." *College English* 45.7 (1983): 657–66. Print.

———. "Reading Matters for Writing." *Intertexts: Reading Pedagogy in College Writing Classrooms*. Ed. Marguerite Helmers. Mahwah: Lawrence Erlbaum Associates, 2003. 195–217. Print.

———. "Toward a Hermeneutic of Difficulty." *Audits of Meaning: A Festscrift in Honor of Anne E. Berthoff.* Ed. Louise Z. Smith. Portsmouth: Boynton/Cook, 1988. 81–95. Print.

Samuels, Shirley. *The Culture of Sentiment: Race, Gender, and Sentimentality in Nineteenth-Century America.* New York: Oxford UP, 1992. Print.

Saxton, Martha. *Louisa May Alcott: A Modern Biography.* New York: Noonday P, 1995. Print.

Scudder, Harold. "Melville's *Benito Cereno* and Captain Delano's Voyages." *PMLA* 43 (1928): 502–32. Print.

Shamir, Millette, and Jennifer Travis. *Boys Don't Cry?: Rethinking Narratives of Masculinity and Emotion in the U.S.* New York: Columbia UP, 2002. Print.

Shaw, Wayne. "The Plymouth Pulpit: Henry Ward Beecher's Slave Auction Block." *American Transcendental Quarterly* 14.4 (2000): 335–43. Print.

Sheridan, Thomas. *A Course of Lectures on Elocution.* 1768. Ed. R. C. Alston. Menston: Scholar Press Limited, 1968. Print.

———. *A Course of Lectures on Elocution: Together with Two Dissertations on Language.* London: W. Strahan, 1762. Print.

Showalter, Elaine. "Introduction." *Alternative Alcott.* Ed. Elaine Showalter. New Brunswick: Rutgers UP, 1988. ix–xliii. Print.

Simpson, David. *The Politics of American English, 1776–1850.* New York: Oxford UP, 1986. Print.

Smiley, Jane. "'Say It Ain't So, Huck': Second Thoughts on Mark Twain's Masterpiece." *Harper's* 292.1748 (1996): 61–67. Print.

Smith, Henry Nash. "The Scribbling Women and the Cosmic Success Story." *Critical Inquiry* 1.1 (1974): 47–70. Print.

Spillers, Hortense. "Changing the Letter: The Yokes, the Jokes of Discourse, or, Mrs. Stowe, Mr. Reed." *Uncle Tom's Cabin.* Ed. Elizabeth Ammons. 1st ed. New York: Norton, 1994. 542–68. Print.

Stadler, Gustavus. "Louisa May Alcott's Queer Genius." *American Literature* 71.4 (1999): 657–77. Print.

Stanislavski, Constantin. *An Actor Prepares.* 1936. New York: Routledge, 1964. Print.

Stowe, Harriet Beecher. "Letter to Gamaliel Bailey." *Uncle Tom's Cabin & American Culture.* Stephen Railton and the University of Virginia. http://utc.iath.virginia.edu/uncletom/utlthbsht.html

———. *The Minister's Wooing.* 1859. Ed. Sandra R. Duguid. Hartford: Stowe-Day Foundation, 1978. Print.

———. *Uncle Tom's Cabin.* 1852. Norton Critical Edition. Ed. Elizabeth Ammons. 2nd ed. New York: Norton, 2010. Print.

Sundquist, Eric. "'Benito Cereno' and New World Slavery." *Herman Melville: A Collection of Critical Essays*. Ed. Myra Jehlen. Englewood Cliffs: Prentice Hall, 1994. 174–86. Print.

Susman, Warren I. *Culture as History: The Transformation of American Society in the Twentieth Century*. New York: Pantheon Books, 1984. Print.

Suter, Lisa. "'Living Pictures, Living Memory': Women's Rhetorical Silence within the American Delsarte Movement." *Silence and Listening as Rhetorical Arts*. Ed. Cheryl Glenn and Krista Ratcliffe. Carbondale: Southern Illinois UP, 2011. 94–110. Print.

Taglieber, Loni Kreis. "Critical Reading and Critical Thinking: The State of the Art." *Ilha Do Desterro: A Journal of Language and Literature* 38 (2000): 15–37. Print.

Tawil, Ezra. "Captain Babo's Cabin: Stowe, Race and Misreading in 'Benito Cereno.'" *Leviathan* 8.2 (2006): 37–51. Print.

Thomas, Brook. "The Legal Fictions of Herman Melville and Lemuel Shaw." *Critical Essays on Herman Melville's "Benito Cereno."* 1984. Ed. Robert E. Burkholder. New York: G. K. Hall, 1992. 116–26. Print.

Tompkins, Jane. "Let's Get Lost." *Confessions of the Critics*. Ed. H. Aram Veeser. New York: Routledge, 1996. 268–81. Print.

———. "Me and My Shadow." *New Literary History* 19.1 (1987): 169–78. Print.

———. *Sensational Designs: The Cultural Work of American Fiction, 1790–1860*. New York: Oxford UP, 1985. Print.

———. "Sentimental Power: *Uncle Tom's Cabin* and the Politics of Literary History." *Sensational Designs: The Cultural Work of American Fiction, 1790–1860*. New York: Oxford UP, 1985. 122–46. Print.

———. *West of Everything: The Inner Life of Westerns*. New York: Oxford UP, 1992. Print.

Tonkovich, Nicole. "Rhetorical Power in the Victorian Parlor: Godey's Lady's Book and the Gendering of Nineteenth-Century Rhetoric." *Oratorical Culture in Nineteenth-Century America: Transformations in the Theory and Practice of Rhetoric*. Ed. Gregory Clark and S. Michael Halloran. Carbondale: Southern Illinois UP, 1993. Print.

Twain, Mark. *Adventures of Huckleberry Finn*. Ed. Gerald Graff and James Phelan. Boston: Bedford Books, 1995. Print.

Underwood, June O. "Western Women and True Womanhood: Culture and Symbol in History and Literature." *Great Plains Quarterly* 5 (1985): 93–106. Print.

Valkeakari, Tuire. "The Politics of Perception in Herman Melville's 'Benito Cereno' and Charles Johnson's *Middle Passage*." *Studies in American Fiction* 33.2 (2005): 229–51. Print.

Villanueva, Victor, ed. *Cross-Talk in Comp Theory: A Reader*. 2nd ed. Urbana: NCTE, 2003. Print.

Vlastos, Gregory. "Socratic Irony." *Socrates, Ironist and Moral Philosopher*. Ithaca: Cornell UP, 1991. 21–44. Print.

Wallace, James D. "Where the Absent Father Went: Alcott's *Work*." *Refiguring the Father: New Feminist Readings of Patriarchy*. Ed. Patricia Yaeger and Beth Kowalsky. Carbondale: Southern Illinois UP, 1989. 259–74. Print.

Ward, John William. *Red, White, and Blue: Men, Books, and Ideas in American Culture*. New York: Oxford UP, 1969. Print.

Warhol, Robyn. "As You Stand, So You Feel and Are: The Crying Body and the Nineteenth-Century Text." *Tattoo, Torture, Mutilation, and the Denaturalization of the Body in Culture*. Ed. Frances E. Mascia-Lees and Patricia Sharpe. Albany: State U of New York P, 1992. 100–25. Print.

———. *Having a Good Cry: Effeminate Feelings and Pop-Culture Forms*. Columbus: Ohio State UP, 2003. Print.

———. "Reader, Can You Imagine? No, You Cannot: The Narratee as Other in Harriet Jacobs's Text." *Narrative* 3.1 (1995): 57–72. Print.

Warner, Michael. "Uncritical Reading." *Polemic: Critical or Uncritical*. Ed. Jane Gallop. New York: Routledge, 2004. 13–38. Print.

Warren, James Perrin. *Culture of Eloquence: Oratory and Reform in Antebellum America*. University Park: Pennsylvania State UP, 1999. Print.

Welter, Barbara. "The Cult of True Womanhood." *American Quarterly* 17 (1966): 151–74. Print.

Whately, Richard. "Elements of Rhetoric." *The Rhetoric of Blair, Campbell, and Whately*. Ed. James L. Golden and Edward P. J. Corbett. New York: Holt, Rinehart, and Winston, 1968. 279–399. Print.

Wilson, Christopher P. "Tempests and Teapots: Harriet Beecher Stowe's *The Minister's Wooing*." *New England Quarterly* 58.4 (1985): 554–77. Print.

Wimsatt, William K., and Monroe C. Beardsley. "The Affective Fallacy." *Norton Anthology of Theory and Criticism*. 1949. Ed. Vincent B. Leitch. New York: Norton, 2010. 1246–61. Print.

Zaeske, Susan. "The 'Promiscuous Audience' Controversy and the Emergence of the Early Woman's Rights Movement." *Quarterly Journal of Speech* 81 (1995): 191–207. Print.

Zagarell, Sandra. "Reenvisioning America: Melville's 'Benito Cereno.'" *Critical Essays on Herman Melville's "Benito Cereno."* 1984. Ed. Robert E. Burkholder. New York: G. K. Hall & Co., 1992. 127–45. Print.

Zwarg, Christina. "Fathering and Blackface in *Uncle Tom's Cabin*." *Uncle Tom's Cabin*. 1989. Ed. Elizabeth Ammons. New York: Norton, 1994. 568–84. Print.

Index